Judging Justice

Some injustices are so massive, so heinous, and so extraordinary that the justice of ordinary courts is no longer adequate. The shift to the creation of international courts and tribunals to confront major violations of human rights sought to bring justice to the affected communities as well as the entire world, whose international laws had been violated. Yet, if justice is a righting of the imbalance between what has happened and what is reflected in the law, no amount of punishment imposed and no judgment conceived could compensate for the suffering and loss.

To understand the meaning of justice, Meernik and King look to the perspective of witnesses who have testified before a particular international tribunal, the International Criminal Tribunal for the Former Yugoslavia (ICTY). Using a unique survey of witnesses who appeared before the ICTY, Meernik and King look at the identity of the victims and their perception of the fairness of the ICTY. They find that because of the need to testify effectively in order to justify the substantial practical and emotional difficulties involved in testifying before an international tribunal, witnesses will judge effectiveness by looking not just at the institution, but also at their own contribution. The central elements of the theory developed here —identity, fairness, and experience— transcend specific conflicts and countries providing insight for practitioners and scholars alike interested in better understanding the most critical stakeholder in the search for justice—the witnesses.

James David Meernik is Regents Professor of Political Science and Director of the Castleberry Peace Institute at the University of North Texas.

Kimi Lynn King is Distinguished Teaching Professor of Political Science at the University of North Texas.

JUDGING JUSTICE

How Victim Witnesses Evaluate International Courts

James David Meernik and Kimi Lynn King

University of Michigan Press
Ann Arbor

Published in the United States of America by the
University of Michigan Press
Manufactured in the United States of America
Printed on acid-free paper
A CIP catalog record for this book is available from the British Library.
Library of Congress Cataloging-in-Publication data has been applied for.

ISBN: 978-0-472-13126-6 (hardcover : alk. paper)
ISBN: 978-0-472-12485-5 (ebook)

Acknowledgments

Professors Kimi Lynn King and James David Meernik wish to thank many individuals at the International Criminal Tribunal for the Former Yugoslavia, including: President, Judge Carmel Agius; Registrar John Hocking; Deputy Registrar Kate Macintosh; Chief of Court Support Services Gregory Townsend; Victims and Witnesses Sections (VWS) staff and invaluable interviewers Adisa Agić and Marija Marković; interns Amela Jakubović, Jasenko Jašarević, and Rafaela Tripalo; finally last, but most definitely not least Jan Kralt in Outreach. We also owe gratitude to the Norwegian Ministry of Foreign Affairs who provided partial funding to the Tribunal allowing us to complete the survey.

We are indebted to the following individuals at the University of North Texas for their work and assistance on this project: Melissa McKay, Sabra Messer, Taylor Ledford, Savannah Leigh Shuffield, Kara Hoffpauir, Ayal Feinberg, Roman Krastev, Rachel Ferris, Eliza Kelly, and Dr. Mark Vosvick, and Eliot Lopez in the Department of Psychology and the Center for Psychosocial Health Research.

We are especially appreciative to three extraordinary women who took on an impossible mission to make this project a reality—Helena Vranov Schoorl, Sara Rubert, and Tiago de Smit of the Victims and Witnesses Section.

Finally, we dedicate this work to all of the witnesses and their families whose collective voices have endeavored to see justice done.

Contents

ONE

Introduction

> I won't praise the Hague Tribunal much, but this should perhaps be recorded, maybe someone will listen to this in a hundred years from now. . . . I am grateful to the Tribunal after all. We have reached a part of the truth and justice. My soul hurts and we victims, as long as we are alive . . . especially me . . . what happened in this part of the world will always hurt me. It should never have happened.[1]
>
> —ICTY witness

Courts are created to provide justice when there have been acts of injustice. Whether a lawbreaker has committed a minor indiscretion, major offense or even a civil dispute between individuals, societies expect courts to right the imbalance between what is and what ought to be. The institutions of justice—particularly the police and the courts—develop procedures and routinize their practices so that even if they are not always successful at righting these imbalances, they follow expected norms and processes in an effort to provide justice. What happens when the injustices are so massive, so heinous, and so extraordinary that the normal justice of ordinary courts is no longer adequate? How do courts manage conflicts that involve one group of individuals committing crimes against another group? Most troubling of all, how do courts confront situations in which government itself is the perpetrator of massive injustice against people in acts of mass violence? In such situations, the "normal" justice of domestic courts falls drastically short, and thus into this breach step the international courts, to confront major violations of human rights.

We are interested in how people evaluate international justice that must address these horrific crimes committed in the midst of societal upheaval. We know a great deal regarding how individuals view justice at home (especially the judicial systems in the United States), such as the importance of fairness (Levanthal 1980; Thibaut and Walker 1975; Tyler 1988, 1990), race (Hurwitz and Peffley 2005; Peffley and Hurwitz 2010; Sears et al. 2000; Unnever 2014), legitimacy (Gibson 1989, 2007; Gibson, Lodge, and Woodson 2014; Ivković and Hagan 2016a; Salzman and Ramsey 2013), and other types of psychological factors (Ask and Granhag 2005; Garland and Newport 1991; Kunda 1987, 1990; Taber and Lodge 2006). Yet knowledge about how individuals evaluate justice in these interpersonal interactions is considerably greater than knowledge of how individuals develop views on justice in the interstate context. Public opinion surveys regarding the International Criminal Tribunal for the Former Yugoslavia (Arzt 2006; Clark 2009a; Ford 2012; Hagan and Ivković 2006a; Klarin 2009; Meernik 2015a; Nettelfield 2010; Orentlicher 2008; Subotić 2009), the International Criminal Court, the International Criminal Tribunal for Rwanda, and the Special Court for Sierra Leone (Brounéus 2010; Stepakoff et al. 2014, 2015; Cody et al. 2014) have shed considerable light on the views of those who have participated in international justice. Our goal in the present study is more expressly focused around the development of a general theoretical framework for understanding the most critical factors that explain how individuals, the witnesses who testify, develop opinions in this institutional context.

To understand just how individuals form opinions about the justice delivered by international courts, we look, in this study, to those who have appeared as witnesses before one particular tribunal, the International Criminal Tribunal for the Former Yugoslavia. We develop a model of individual evaluations of international justice that incorporates the unique natures of international courts and of the deadly conflicts over which they exercise jurisdiction, as well as the insights gained from research on public opinion regarding domestic justice. This model of individual evaluations of international justice is premised on the critical roles that identity, fairness, and experience play for the individual, and it is tested using data from a unique survey of three hundred individuals who have testified before the ICTY. This survey, which was several years in the making, provides us with the first comprehensive and systematic data on all aspects of the witness experience regarding the testimonial process. The insights from this analysis are as rich as they are revealing. To set the stage before proceeding, however, we begin this introduction by telling the story of the burgeoning development of and interest in international justice.

International Justice

International justice is, in historical terms, a fairly new phenomenon. Crimes against humanity are as old as humanity (Graven 1950, 423, as quoted in Cryer et al. 2007, 230), and with a few historical exceptions, violations of law were considered to be within the sovereign rights of states to address. The shift to the creation of international courts and tribunals[2] was a recognition that national courts were either incapable of providing justice for the most severe crimes or untrustworthy because they were associated with regimes that had committed such crimes. It was also a recognition that the international laws on crimes committed during the course of warfare (*jus in bello*), which had been evolving since the mid-nineteenth century, were not being adequately applied when these violations were driven by state military and political leaders rather than committed ad hoc by ordinary soldiers. Military courts might address the latter, but were ill-equipped to deal with the former. International justice was thus borne out of the desire to recognize and punish those major violations of human rights that were so severe and systematic that national legal systems were incapable of providing justice to the victims and to the international community whose international laws were violated. In the words of Robert Jackson, the chief US prosecutor in the post–World War II Nuremberg Tribunal,

> The wrongs which we seek to condemn and punish have been so calculated, so malignant, and so devastating, that civilization cannot tolerate their being ignored, because it cannot survive their being repeated. That four great nations, flushed with victory and stung with injury stay the hand of vengeance and voluntarily submit their captive enemies to the judgment of the law is one of the most significant tributes that Power has ever paid to Reason.[3]

The International Military Tribunal at Nuremberg and the International Military Tribunal for the Far East in Tokyo, which respectively prosecuted top Nazi officials and Japanese war criminals, were the first such courts established to provide international justice. While undoubtedly, these courts were a form of victor's justice imposed on Germany and

Japan by their victorious adversaries, they represented a significant step forward in confronting massive and state-sponsored violations of human rights. Sovereignty concerns, which had, for years, allowed political and military leaders to hide behind the artifice of "the state" to excuse or justify their actions and to evade any kind of reckoning for their misdeeds, were finally abrogated. International law was applied, albeit unevenly and sometimes stretched beyond the written word. Regime leaders were punished for their horrific crimes, and the cry of "never again" seemed to presage a new era in international relations, where international laws and courts would be woven more deliberately and closely into the fabric of interstate relations. Indeed, after the World War II tribunals concluded their business and after other military and domestic courts took up the task of prosecuting the lesser lights of the Axis powers, new international laws like the Geneva Conventions on War Crimes and the Genocide Convention were created and adopted. For a time in the late 1940s, international justice was ascendant.

Subsequently, these efforts stalled and, in some sense, were forgotten, as the more pressing matters of rebuilding war-torn economies and the battles of the Cold War took precedence. While the victorious powers of the world could all agree that the fascist regimes were evil and had to be confronted, the grave stakes of the struggle between the forces of communism and democracy ensured that realism would triumph over idealism and that violations of international law would be countenanced as the price to be paid for winning this long, twilight struggle. Whether violations were committed by the major powers or their proxies through which they contested for dominance, each side might rail against the abuses perpetrated by the other, but the application of international law became impossible as each side protected its own.

Two things that happened when the Cold War ended affected international justice. First, reflexive rejection of any effort to confront major human rights abuses, whether committed by a repressive regime or in the course of war, was eroded. The zero-sum competition of the Cold War had melted, and new forms of cooperation evolved. Communist regimes were replaced by governments that accepted the need to employ international justice. Second, conflicts that formerly would have been managed and tamped down by the superpowers broke out, such as the conflicts in Yugoslavia. The resulting wars and conflicts became unhinged from Cold War politics and followed their own violent logic, often rooted in identity and extremist ideologies. This created a demand for international justice to confront the massive human rights violations of the now former Yugoslavia, Rwanda, and eventually other states as well. The establishment of the ICTY in 1993 and the International Criminal Tribunal for Rwanda (ICTR) in 1994 began a new era of international law and the search for justice (see Rudolph 2017 for an analysis of the role of power and principle in the development of international legal institutions). That search for justice and its meaning as perceived by those who come to testify before these courts, particularly the ICTY, is the subject of this book.

The international criminal tribunals—both the ad hoc variety, such as the ICTY and the ICTR, and the permanent International Criminal Court—were created to bring justice to the affected communities as well as the entire world, whose international laws had been violated. The United Nations established the ICTY through a UN Security Council resolution and declared that it was "determined to put an end to such crimes and to take effective measures to bring to justice the persons who are responsible for them." Furthermore, UN Security Council Resolution 827 asserted that the ICTY would also contribute to peace and the deterrence of future violations of international law.[4] Given the frequency with which war crimes, crimes against humanity, and genocide—the jurisdictional subject matter of this and the other international courts—had been committed for centuries, there was hope that the establishment of the ICTY would send a powerful signal to would-be war criminals that their days of impunity were over. Nonetheless, for some of these aspirational goals, such as regional peace, the ICTY, like other international courts, would have relatively little direct influence. Swift and certain justice might cause some rebel and regime leaders to adjust their decision calculus of violence, but few beyond the most ardent supporters of these courts believed that the courts' establishment and functioning would end violations of international law. Their principal mission is the provision of justice.

International justice, like its domestic variant, involves the indictment and prosecution of those suspected of violating the law and the punishment of those found or pleading guilty. Hence, in one sense, it is similar to domestic justice but scaled up to adjudicate larger, more systematic, and more severe crimes. There are not just differences in degree, however, but differences in kind between domestic and international justice. First, unlike domestic law, international law is mostly but not entirely codified. There are international agreements prohibiting war crimes and genocide, but not crimes against humanity. Second, over decades or, in many cases, centuries, domestic laws and domestic judicial systems have developed to address behaviors that societies seek to curtail based on their individual customs and norms. The *application* of international laws by courts are a fairly recent phenomenon, and it has not evolved organically (as have domestic courts), but has been constructed in a more top-down fashion. This means that it is a diverse blend of international and national legal principles and practices representing a confluence of common-law and civil legal systems. Finally, international courts have no enforcement mechanisms but mostly rely on the goodwill and cooperation of states' parties and supporters to secure the apprehension of those suspected of violating international law. The crimes that international courts adjudicate are larger, more horrific, and typically involve greater levels of planning and action by state or non-state actors. In a word, they are too "big" for domestic courts.

How can an international court provide justice when the crimes committed are so massive and so heinous as to defy imagination? More pointedly, how can these tribunals provide *any* meaningful justice to the victims of these conflicts? When we conceive of justice as a righting of the imbalance between what has happened and what is desired as reflected in the law, it is obvious that no amount of punishment and no judgment could ever be invented to compensate for the suffering and loss.

Yet the international community persists in the creation and use of these courts to provide redress. Retribution for such crimes, however, is a necessary but not a sufficient condition for justice. The symbolism inherent in the creation of these international tribunals—which affirms the magnitude of the crimes committed and recognizes the right of the victims for redress—is a powerful and necessary component of international justice as well. The tribunals can also help satisfy the demand of the international community to see that its laws are upheld. What kind of justice do these international courts provide to their most important constituents? Does this justice resonate with the victims or provide some measure of relief and recognition for their suffering? In short, can international justice rise to the occasion and provide what is possible in righting the scales of injustice?

One could approach such questions philosophically and debate the meaning of justice in the realm of ideas (e.g., Nussbaum 2015; Rawls 1971; Sen 2011). One could address the nature and consequences of justice by examining what happens to societies after the violence and the trials are over (Akhavan 2009; Barria and Roper 2005; Clark 2014; Gilligan 2006; Greig and Meernik 2014; Jo and Simmons 2012; Kim and Sikkink 2010; McAllister 2014; Meernik 2005; Olson, Payne, and Reiter 2010; Simmons and Danner 2010). We are acutely aware that this approach fails to appreciate the perspective of those who experience the violence and experience justice. The divorce between the world of ideas and the world of the suffering of victims is too great to focus only on scholarly inquiry. If we are to develop a deeper understanding of the meaning of justice both in general terms and in regard to international laws and tribunals, we believe that a rigorous examination of this subject should concentrate on those who have the most direct stake in its outcomes. The present study's focus instead is in understanding the meaning of justice for those who were affected by the violence.

In this book, therefore, we look to understand international justice from the perspective of those who have testified before an international tribunal, the ICTY. The witnesses possess two characteristics that are vital to our efforts to understand the impact of international justice. First, these are witnesses to the violence and violations of international law, but they are also typically victims too. Most of the witnesses who have appeared before the ICTY were personally affected by the Balkan wars. And while not all were direct victims, all of them did live in a society torn apart by war for which they were called so the ICTY could "do justice."Substantial majorities lived through shelling and other wartime violence, experienced deprivation, or suffered some type of personal loss as their region underwent brutal upheaval. It is for these individuals that international justice is most obviously directed. Second, these individuals are witnesses who have appeared before the ICTY and thus have firsthand knowledge of the machinery of international justice. Hence, they are stakeholders of international justice, and indeed, one could argue that no other people, except perhaps the defendants, have a greater personal stake in the outcome. We contend that studying the opinions of the witnesses regarding international justice provides us with a "hard" and very powerful test for assessing our explanations of the meaning of international justice.

The central purposes of this book are to develop a theory of individual evaluations of international justice and to test this theory against the witnesses' opinions of this judicial enterprise. In this introduction, we next discuss general knowledge regarding public opinion and international justice, as well as why theoretical development in this area is critical for scholarly purposes and for understanding the value and legitimacy of international justice. Subsequently, we describe a unique survey of ICTY witnesses that we developed with the Victims and Witnesses Section of the ICTY and that gives us the necessary leverage to investigate these questions.

Explaining Individual Attitudes Toward International Justice

Previous and Ongoing Research

The inquiry into public attitudes toward international courts is a relatively new one. As Voeten writes (2013, 412), "We know surprisingly little about public support for international courts. After a series of groundbreaking studies about the Court of Justice of the European Union (CJEU), the topic has been virtually ignored by social scientists. Indeed, questions about international courts are rarely asked in comparative surveys." To be sure, some studies regard public opinion and international justice more generally (Caldeira and Gibson 1995; Gibson and Caldeira 1995; Hagan and Ivković 2006b; Ivković and Hagan 2016b; Meernik 2015a; Meernik and King 2013; Voeten 2013), and there has been significant research on the attitudes toward specific international tribunals (Brounéus 2010; Clark 2014; Doak 2011; Findlay and Ngane 2012; Ford 2012; Horn Charters, and Vahidy 2009; Stepakoff et al. 2014; Stover 2005).

From this research, we know that, in general, public knowledge about international justice lags. Though knowledge and opinions on international courts tend to be rather scant (Caldeira and Gibson 1995; Gibson and Caldeira 1995; Meernik 2015; Meernik and King 2013; Voeten 2013), individuals will use more readily accessible decision cues to offer opinions on these courts. For example, Gibson and Caldeira (1995) find that many people base their views of the CJEU on their own values regarding law and liberty and that people extrapolate from their opinions on their own national legal institutions to supranational institutions like the CJEU. Gibson and Caldeira also argue that because these international courts are so new, they have not had sufficient time to develop deep or wide legitimacy. Their legitimacy tends to depend more on the extent to which individuals identify with the larger international entity to which a court is attached—in the case of the CJEU, the European Union. Unlike Tyler (1990), who has consistently argued and found that views of the fairness of the people and procedures involved in domestic justice systems are critical in helping these institutions earn legitimacy, Caldeira and Gibson (1995; Gibson and Caldeira 1995) find that perceptions of the quality of procedural justice are not important in individual evaluations: outcomes matter more than fairness per se.

Voeten (2013) describes a similar sort of process at work in governing individual evaluations of international justice and suggests three key relationships.

> First, perceptions about international courts are correlated with perceptions about the international organizations with which these courts are associated. Second, individuals who trust national courts are also more likely to trust international courts. Third, support for international courts drops precipitously in the face of public controversy over unpopular decisions. (416)

There is general agreement that individual opinions about international courts are not informed by a great deal of knowledge and that individuals structure their opinions by using decision cues regarding other, similar institutions and situational cues. Much of the research has been focused on determining whether such institutions gain support or legitimacy despite the unpopular decisions they must make (Benesh 2006; Caldeira and Gibson 1995; Gibson and Caldeira 1995; Ura 2014). Scholars interested in the extent to which courts retain residual levels of support based on long-standing public acceptance of the courts' right to rule—their legitimacy—have found that such bedrock support does not seem to exist to a great extent in attitudes toward international courts. Rather, the lack of experience and knowledge by the various peoples surveyed seems to have prevented such underlying attitudes from fully forming and taking root. We cannot always expect that knowledge regarding international courts, like the ICTY, will be available in sufficient depth to structure and influence opinions to any significant degree. Hence, we share the skepticism that many have about the clarity and objectivity with which individuals view international justice. Our theory of individual attitudes does not make any strenuous assumptions regarding individuals' level of knowledge about international justice but, rather, focuses on factors that we hypothesize are most important to *individuals*—their identity, their experiences, and their sense of fairness—and on how those factors help us understand their attitudes. We do, however, specifically examine how the verdicts and punishments handed down by the ICTY influence individual opinions about the quality of justice.

Other explanations of opinions about international courts emphasize the importance of individual-level and community-level effects (Elcheroth 2006; Elcheroth and Spini 2009; Spini, Elcheroth, and Fasel 2008). Elcheroth and Spini (2009, 190) argue that when a community undergoes the type of trauma that the people of the former Yugoslavia experienced, its members "become more critical toward local authorities and more supportive of international institutions that prosecute human rights violations." Research supports the proposition that as the level of violence in a society increases, individuals develop a common perception of threat, which then leads to increased support for human rights and humanitarian norms (Spini, Elcheroth, and Fasel 2008). We also know that individuals who have experienced trauma are less likely to desire retribution as a solution to the violence (Elcheroth 2006) and that support for international justice depends on individual views of the morality and legitimacy of the law and on the victim experience.(Meernik and King 2013)

Whereas much of the research cited above looks to understand individual attitudes toward regional human rights courts that rule on a variety of nationally important issues, our focus is on the opinions of those who have been affected by the human rights issues over which the ICTY exercises jurisdiction. Similarities and analogies do exist between our study and earlier studies of institutions like the CJEU (Caldeira and Gibson 1995) and other research on public opinion toward the ICTY finding that ethnicity matters a great deal (Clark 2014; Ford 2012; Ivković and Hagan 2016a; Meernik 2015). The most fascinating and directly relevant research on opinions regarding international justice concerns the impact of testifying on witnesses, particularly whether it does more harm than good to the witnesses who testify. Some have found more positive findings that testifying may provide some sort of closure or catharsis for those who have undergone traumatic experiences (Moghalu 2004, 216; Stover 2005). Others are skeptical (Bandes 2009, 16), especially regarding the ICTY witnesses (Clark 2009a–d, 2014). As Mendeloff (2009, 596) writes, we are only now starting to understand "the individual psychological and emotional effects of national truth-telling and accountability mechanisms" or "about victims' experiences with criminal justice more broadly."

Research shows that witnesses experience a diversity of positive and negative emotional reactions to testifying, depending on whether the venue is a truth and reconciliation commission (Byrne 2004; Hamber, Nageng and O'Malley 2000), community justice court (Brounéus 2010), or war crimes tribunal (Stepakoff et al., 2014, 2015; Stover 2014). While opinions about international justice may also change with the passage of time (Backer 2010), research is inconclusive about whether individuals are permanently affected over time by their experiences in testifying before a transitional justice institution (Stepakoff et al. 2015). Neither does it demonstrate which of the experiences individuals undergo on the witness stand will subsequently affect their opinions and attitudes or how such processes work. Thus, the research on which we build the foundation for our theory of individual attitudes toward international justice is suggestive of several potentially viable relationships by stressing the critical role of individual values and experiences, rather than institutional attributes.

A Theory of Individual Opinions regarding International Justice

Chapter 2 provides the full, detailed theory of individual support for international justice generally and for the International Criminal Tribunal for the Former Yugoslavia more specifically. Here, we outline the theory and address the importance of developing such models as ours premised on three critical assumptions. First, we believe that the individual is the proper locus of our theory. The institution that is our focus—the ICTY—is critical, but our goal is not to develop a model of institutional legitimacy per se; such efforts have often focused on the political context in which these institutions operate, to determine how their age, outcomes, and other characteristics influence legitimacy (Hayashi and Bailliet 2017). We contend that individual identity and experiences during wartime form the foundation from which opinions about the ICTY develop. In particular, we focus on individual ethnic identity as a key indicator of the social and political milieu in which these attitudes are formed. We hypothesize that these individual-level factors exercise prominent direct and indirect effects on attitudes regarding ICTY support.

A second critical assumption guiding our work is that individual attitudes regarding international justice are premised on individuals' perceptions of the fairness with which the ICTY operates. Long-standing research by Tyler (1990) and his coauthors has consistently found that "the fairness of the manner in which the police and the courts are believed to treat citizens when exercising their authority" (Tyler 2003, 318) is key to understanding opinions about justice systems. Our previous research on witnesses and the ICTY (King and Meernik 2017) finds that fairness matters significantly for individuals when asked to evaluate the ICTY and given the opportunity to specifically comment on the work of the judges and attorneys, witnesses are candid about their treatment by these actors. The witnesses are especially concerned with whether they were able to tell the story they had traveled so far (in both physical and emotional distance) to tell. Therefore, we contend that individual perceptions of fairness are critical in determining attitudes toward international justice generally and the ICTY specifically.

The third assumption guiding our theory is that individual perceptions of their own experience on the witness stand provide a critical decision cue. Witnesses may not possess a great deal of substantive information about the ICTY to grade the institution's success in discovering the truth and providing justice, but like all of us, they care about their own performance and the contributions they hope to make. We suggest that because of these concerns and because of a need to testify effectively given the substantial commitment of time and emotion involved in testifying, witnesses make their judgements not just by looking at the institution, but also by perceptions about their own contributions to the institution and its mission. We suggest that the cognitive processes at work in evaluating the ICTY's effectiveness for uncovering the truth and dispensing justice are based partly on how witnesses grade their own performance. Those who believe they have performed well, we hypothesize, will be more likely to extend similar positive evaluations of the ICTY.

Our theory of individual evaluations of international justice is one of the first and more comprehensive explanations on public opinion and international justice—though we note the aforementioned research of Gibson and Caldeira (1995) and Voeten (2013). Indeed, as recently as 2013, Voeten (2013, 412) argued that the topic has been "virtually ignored" by social science researchers. Gibson and Caldeira (1995) speculate that the lack of scholarship and the underlying lack of interest in these transnational and international courts may result from a substantial lack of public interest in the work of the courts. Most people do not care about them. We cannot say for certain whether such ignorance (and we do not dispute this basic characterization) leads to ill-defined opinions that, in turn, hinder interest in this research topic. We argue, however, that international courts adjudicating international law are extremely relevant to the people over whom they exercise jurisdiction. Thus, even if individual attitudes may not always be as structured or well-formed on the subject of international courts as on domestic political matters, we contend that there are important, accessible, and useful decision cues that individuals utilize to judge whether these institutions have provided justice.

Explanations for judging justice tend to focus on specific factors, such as ethnicity (Arzt 2006; Ford 2012; Meernik 2015) or to assume international courts can be perceived and evaluated in the same way as national institutions of justice (Calderia and Gibson 1995; Gibson and Caldeira 1995; Voeten 2013). We do not take issue with the importance of identity politics, nor doubt that individual evaluations of transnational courts like the CJEU are similar to the ways in which people judge their own domestic courts. Rather, we argue that the subject matter of these tribunals is qualitatively and quantitatively different than those issues adjudicated by national courts. Where national courts deal with disputes between and among small numbers of individuals, the international tribunals confront violence between groups of people, one of which is usually represented by the state itself. This calls for the development of a theory about individual evaluations of justice that recognizes critical differences between domestic and international courts, such as the nature, magnitude, and scope of the conflict at issue, as well as key similarities, such as the desire for fairness, which transcends jurisdiction. We suggest that our theory regarding individual evaluations of international justice provides a more comprehensive model for understanding internal and international conflicts adjudicated by transitional justice mechanisms.

Our focus in this particular research is on the opinions of witnesses who have testified before the International Criminal Tribunal for the Former Yugoslavia, but the theory is generalizable to other forums. The central elements of the theory—identity, fairness, and experience—transcend specific conflicts and specific countries and, we believe, will be of importance to people everywhere if and when their conflict situation comes under the jurisdiction of an international court. We suggest that identity and fair treatment, along with individual experiences during the conflict and during the time of testimony affect perceptions of justice. We look at the impact of ethnicity on individual support for the ICTY, and we argue that identity in general—whether measured by ethnicity, religion, race, or political party—is a critical factor in the instigation of conflict and the use of violence as a political means to an end. This function that identity fulfills does not end just because the active fighting has ceased. While the degree of influence that identity exercises on opinions of justice will likely vary across conflicts (some leaders are more skillful at manipulating fears about identity, and some people are more susceptible than others to such mobilization), the importance of identity remains. Therefore, we believe that our theory can be used to help explain individual attitudes toward international justice in other countries whose conflicts have come under the jurisdiction of one of the ad hoc tribunals or the permanent International Criminal Court.

Our focus on the ICTY witnesses has theoretical limits in one sense, but it provides us with a more rigorous test of our theory for allowing us to control for the underlying conflict and institution with data rarely found in this kind of research. With the exception of some of the early surveys of public opinion among witnesses from the former Yugoslavia (Stover 2005) and the path-breaking work by Sanja Kutnjak Ivkovich and John Hagan (2016), much of the research on public opinion and justice has focused on the general public. Such research is necessary for understanding the general popular support for these international courts, but our focus on the witnesses is critical for other reasons. First, the witnesses are arguably among the most important (if not the most affected) groups of individuals for whom these international courts provide justice. Their firsthand knowledge of the horrors of war and the act of testifying give the witnesses a dual perspective that no others have. Understanding how the witnesses perceive justice yields deeper insights into the meaning of international justice and what the affected people desire than we are likely to find in the more general population of individuals because the opinions of the general public are not nearly so informed by personal experience and are often simply premised on attitudes toward local courts.

Second, testing our theory of public opinion on the witness data is also a hard test. If we can explain how individuals who have experienced the greatest injustices feel about justice and how they evaluate it, we will emerge with a deeper understanding of what justice means at its very core. For those of us fortunate enough to have lived in countries that have not been ripped apart by violence, it is easy to speculate, from the comfort and security of our privileged surroundings, about the nature and meaning of justice. As one witness put it in regard to the ICTY,

> All future witnesses, and I believe that all of us who survived the misfortune of war, survived camps, hardship, beatings, suffering, the taking of blood and everything else that goes with days spent living in camps, have just one duty and that is to speak the truth and only the truth before God, before men, before witnesses, before the investigators of the Hague Tribunal. That is perhaps what can help younger generations to forget more easily the loss of their closest family members, friends, acquaintances, comrades, you have children victims and everything else. All this to a certain extent, if it is based on the truth, can contribute to reconciliation in these areas, which, in my personal opinion, we will wait for still for a long time to come.

In the present study, we demonstrate that it is possible to develop a general theory of public opinion toward international justice and that this model can be tested on the most engaged and affected individuals, whose opinions have been formed through hard experience rather than armchair speculation. If we can understand what justice means when it is stripped of all pretense and theoretical artifice, we have made a major contribution for all those interested in the meaning of justice.

The ICTY Witness Survey

The ICTY was established by UN Security Council Resolution 827 in 1993 and was intended to "bring justice" to those responsible for serious violations of international humanitarian law which occurred during the conflicts in the former Yugoslavia. To that end, the ICTY depends on the testimony of both fact and expert witnesses (over 4,700 called to date)[5] demonstrating "the crucial nature of witness testimony" (Wald 2002, 219). The Office of the Prosecutor, the Defence, and even the Trial Chamber judges have called these individuals to testify at the ICTY headquarters in The Hague, Netherlands, to tell their story, to establish the historical record, and to speak for others who could not so that justice may be done. As part of this process, the ICTY Victims and Witnesses Section (VWS) housed officially in the Office of the Registry, is responsible for witness well-being during the testimonial process. As part of its mission and to better understand the impact and legacy of the ICTY before shuttering its doors, the unit reached out to witnesses one last time to gauge their perceptions about testifying and to see how the witnesses were doing, what challenges they faced, and how they viewed their experience of testifying in general and the Tribunal in particular.

Partnering with the University of North Texas, the VWS worked to reach out to a representative sample of witnesses selected via a stratified and quota process from a VWS database of all individuals who had testified by the date of the study (their case had to have completed the trial phase), and it includes witnesses who still had their cases pending on appeal.. Persons were selected if they 1) testified in person as "fact witnesses" in one or more trials; 2) were called by the OTP, the Defence, and/or the Trial Chamber; 3) currently reside in one of four countries in the former Yugoslavia (Bosnia and Herzegovina, Croatia, Serbia, or Kosovo); and 4) were eligible for recruitment.

There were several types of witnesses who were not eligible for recruitment and whom we did not survey. First, expert witnesses (e.g., those with knowledge of military operations or forensic science, some high-ranking political leaders, and witnesses expert in other specialized areas) were not included, because of our focus on witnesses with direct knowledge of the events over which they testified. Second, we did not include those living outside of the former Yugoslavia, due to logistical limitations. Third, witnesses testifying or listed as prospective witnesses in the last four trials being held at the ICTY at the time of survey administration were not included, to avoid any perceived prejudicial effect on the trial proceedings. Among these were witnesses from arguably the most important trials of Ratko Mladić, Radovan Karadžić, Vojislav Šešelj, and Goran Hadžić. Finally, those who testified from 1994 to 1998 were excluded, as their contact details were unknown to the VWS (contacts were through local authorities and not kept by the ICTY during that time). If a witness from this earlier period also testified after 1998, contact information was available, and these witnesses were contacted.

UNT researchers worked with the VWS to ensure that the types of witness we sought to survey (a representative sample of fact witnesses who lived in the region and who were not involved in current trials) were represented in the lists of random witnesses we developed. UNT provided the VWS with lists of witness identification numbers that would yield a survey population resembling the characteristics of the target population of witnesses from the former Yugoslavia. We supplemented that process to include adequate numbers of individuals from each of the principal ethnic groups, as well as defense, prosecution, and chamber witnesses and women—to ensure sufficient sample size for more in-depth analyses.

Because the recalling of traumatic events can trigger emotional and physical reactions, only VWS staff with a relevant professional background, training, and experience were allowed to conduct the in-person interviews. This ensured that trained personnel would be available to assist a witness who became emotionally and/or physically distressed or had some other type of reaction. VWS staff received training on presenting information about the study in a secure and sensitive way to victim witnesses, who may not have heard from the ICTY for years. At no time, however, did any survey personnel from outside the ICTY ever know the identities of these individuals or have contact information. In all, 302 witnesses were surveyed from 2013 to 2015, although two witness surveys had to be dropped because the individuals surveyed were subsequently called to testify in the Mladic trial.[6]

One of the most important considerations in developing a representative sample was ensuring adequate gender representation. Percentages of eligible female witnesses from the region were needed to ensure sufficient sample size for generalizable conclusions. Women's involvement in testifying was limited at the Tribunal in general (ranging from less than 9 percent from Serbia to over 16 percent from Bosnia and Herzegovina with 13 percent of *all* witnesses being female). Given that focus groups indicated there was reason to believe women would be less likely to participate in the survey, we developed an 80/20 quota sample male/female to have sufficient numbers of women to analyze as a separate group. This necessitated reaching out to additional women to participate in the survey because of the low numbers of female witnesses.[7]

To recruit individuals to take the survey, VWS personnel attempted initial contact with a phone call, to explain the purposes of the survey and to stress the witness's choice in deciding whether to participate. A second phone call was *always* made so the witness had time to think about participation and to consult with other persons. If witnesses confirmed their participation, the VWS arranged for a meeting at a location selected by the witnesses, where they felt comfortable and secure. Witnesses *could refuse to do the survey at any point in the process, including after arrival at the location for the interview and even if the survey had been started.* To develop our sample pool of three hundred eligible witnesses, VWS staff contacted or sought to contact approximately twelve hundred individuals. We found that 38.4 percent of witnesses had outdated contact details, while another 4.7 percent did not answer the phone calls, despite multiple attempts. Approximately 4 percent of the witnesses (forty-three) had passed away in the intervening years (over fifteen years for some witnesses).

Overall, the researchers and VWS personnel were very pleased with the high response rates. Table 1.1 records the outcomes of VWS efforts at survey recruitment of those individuals who were part of the random samples generated by the UNT researchers. When considering the responses of individuals with whom VWS personnel were able to speak (excluding those who were deceased, those whose contact information was incorrect, and those who were excluded for other reasons), the cooperation rate was approximately 56.8 percent (the rate is based on the total number of individuals who responded in some manner to attempts to contact). Of the 1116 in the sample, 206 former witnesses refused to participate. Among those who declined to participate in the survey (results not shown), health (26.6 percent), stress (21.4 percent), and a busy schedule (20.9 percent) were among the top reasons for refusal. Approximately 19.7 percent gave no reason for declining. A number of interviewees (17.7 percent) expressed dissatisfaction with some aspect of the tribunal, did not wish to associate with or trust the ICTY, or were unhappy with a particular office at the ICTY. In addition, 5 percent of those contacted raised some type of security concern and declined to participate.

TABLE 1.1. Outcomes of VWS Survey Calls

Outcome	Number	Frequency (%)
Interview Not Completed	5	0
Agreed, but Not Interviewed	19	2
Deceased	43	4
Not Available	52	5
Excluded	61	6
Not Willing to Participate	206	19
Interviewed	302	27
Outdated Contact Details	428	38

Note: $N = 1{,}116$.

Regarding the survey population, one important issue that warrants discussion is the generalizability of the survey sample. We found that among the top reasons for refusing to take the survey were health and emotional distress, while a number of individuals also did not wish to have any further contact with the ICTY. Therefore, it is possible that there may be some type of selection bias if our sample tends to consist more of healthy witnesses or witnesses who are more likely to be satisfied with the ICTY. Our sample may include an emotionally and physically healthy population of individuals who are more likely to have positive views of the ICTY than the actual witness population. We are fortunate, however, in that since 2009, the VWS has been using an anonymous survey of all witnesses after they have testified and before they leave The Hague. That survey is mostly concerned with feedback from the witnesses regarding their experiences with the logistical and psychosocial support provided by the VWS. Some of the survey's questions regarding witnesses' emotions before and after testimony are relevant to the present study. In fact, we found that witnesses who have testified since 2009 were somewhat more likely than the witnesses in our sample to report positive impressions of their experience with the ICTY. Therefore, we believe that our sample data are mostly reflective of the overall witness population and are not necessarily biased toward a positive view of the ICTY.

We must also acknowledge that while this survey is very comprehensive and in-depth, the witnesses are being asked to recall events and emotions from the more recent past to many years ago. Witnesses may have faulty memories or recall events that have subtly changed over time and have been shaped by their post-war experiences. We must accept the witnesses' memories as they are—imperfect and incomplete, but with a powerful influence on their mental and decision-making processes. Despite these caveats, we believe that the survey data provide us with the best accounting of the experiences, attitudes, and opinions of the witnesses.

The thirty-two-page survey instrument includes 149 multiple-choice questions, along with 37 follow-up questions and 31 opportunities for witnesses to write in their own short answers to questions throughout the questionnaire. In five sections, the survey evaluates (1) witness background and reasons for testifying (28 questions with 2 follow-ups), (2) socioeconomic impact on witnesses (8 questions with 7 follow-ups), (3) security concerns for witnesses (10 questions with 21 follow-ups), (4) physical and psychological health and well-being of witnesses (82 questions with 3 follow-ups), and (5) witness perceptions about justice and the ICTY's legacy (21 questions with 4 follow-ups). A sixth section asks three open-ended questions that were audiotaped at the conclusion of the written survey. This section provided witnesses with an opportunity to elaborate more freely on concerns or issues about the testimonial process, their advice for future witnesses in trials on war crimes, and their feedback to the ICTY regarding what they would change about the proceedings or the process of testifying. Below, we briefly describe the distribution of witnesses across several of the more important characteristics, such as gender, ethnicity, and similar factors.

Overview of the ICTY Survey Data

The Victims and Witnesses Section and our team of scholars at the University of North Texas, relying on VWS statistics, established a set of target numbers for the sampling process to ensure that adequate numbers of persons from different parts of the former Yugoslavia would be included in the study in numbers approximating their actual distribution in the witness population. In recognition that ethnic identity is a fraught concept and that some individuals might not wish to disclose their ethnic identity, survey respondents were provided with the option to write down their ethnic identity on the survey instrument or choose not to provide any ethnicity information (table 1.2). The responses indicate that 81 individuals (27 percent) called themselves Croat; 78 (26 percent), Bosniak; 95 (32 percent), Serb; 25 (8 percent), Albanian; 2 (n = 2) Macedonian; and 1 (n = 1), Croat-Bosniak. A number of people did not list an ethnicity.

Table 1.3 provides data on ethnicity and the witnesses' country of origin. For example, while Croats identify ethnically as "Croat," but if their national origin is in Bosnia-Hercegovina, then their ethnic identity is really Bosnian Croat. This distinction is important because it encompasses a broader view of ethnic identification. Table 1.3 shows that Bos-

TABLE 1.2. Ethnic Self-Identification

Ethnicity	Number	Frequency (%)
Croat Bosniak	1	0
Macedonian	2	1
Did Not Identify	18	7
Albanian	25	8
Bosniak	78	26
Croat	81	27
Serb	95	32

niaks (Bosnian Muslims from Bosnia-Herzegovina) are the largest single group. However, as we saw in table 1.2, there are more total Croatians and more total Serbians when we consider the number of those individuals from across the regions of the former Yugoslavia.[8] Similarly, there are more Croats from Croatia and Serbs from Serbia than their counterparts within Bosnia-Hercegovina.

Completing the administration of the survey is especially important given the aging population of witnesses, especially the elderly male population.[9] The average age of the interviewees is 59.3 years old—with ages ranging from 28 to 94 years. There are significant differences with gender, as women are, on average, seven years younger than men who testify. Figure 1.1 clearly shows that women are younger in every age category, save for the two youngest, and on the average age for men was 60.2 and women 53.6 years of age.

Among other relevant characteristics of the sample, we note that approximately 23 percent (71) of respondents have a high school diploma, 100 individuals have a college degree, and 41 individuals indicated that they have some form of advanced college degree. On the whole, the male witnesses in our sample had higher levels of education than female witnesses. Figure 1.2 shows that women were more likely to have a secondary degree, but men were more likely to have a university degree.

Interviewees and ICTY Trials

To ensure validity we included representative numbers of witnesses from the various trials and for the various sides—the Office of the Prosecution (OTP), the defense, and the Trial Chamber judges. Witnesses can testify more than once in any given trial or multiple times in multiple trials and may also appear for one or more of the calling parties (OTP, defense, or Trial Chamber) in the same or different trials. The 300 respondents have

TABLE 1.3. Ethnic Identification among Key ICTY Nationalities

Ethnicity/Nationality	Frequency	Percentage
Bosnian Serb	42	14
Croat	51	17
Bosnian Croat	30	10
Serb	46	15
Bosniak	78	26
No Response / Other	30	10
Kosovar Albanian	23	8

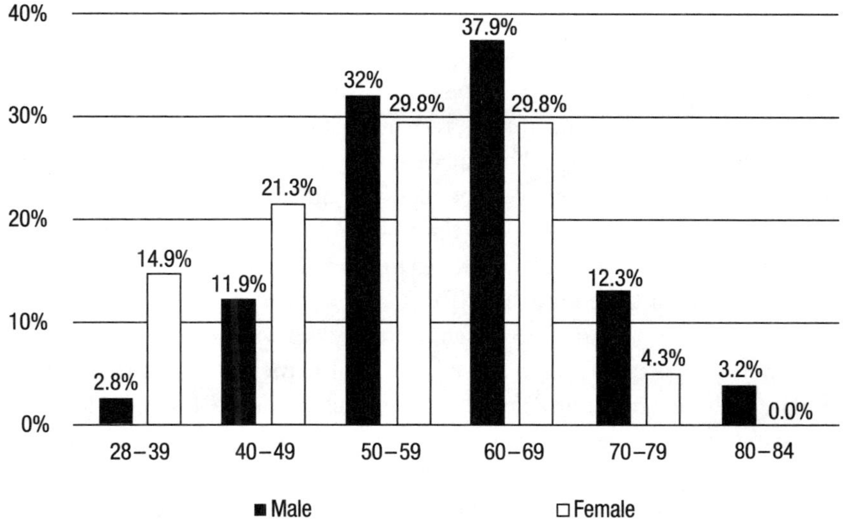

Figure 1.1. Witness age distribution by gender

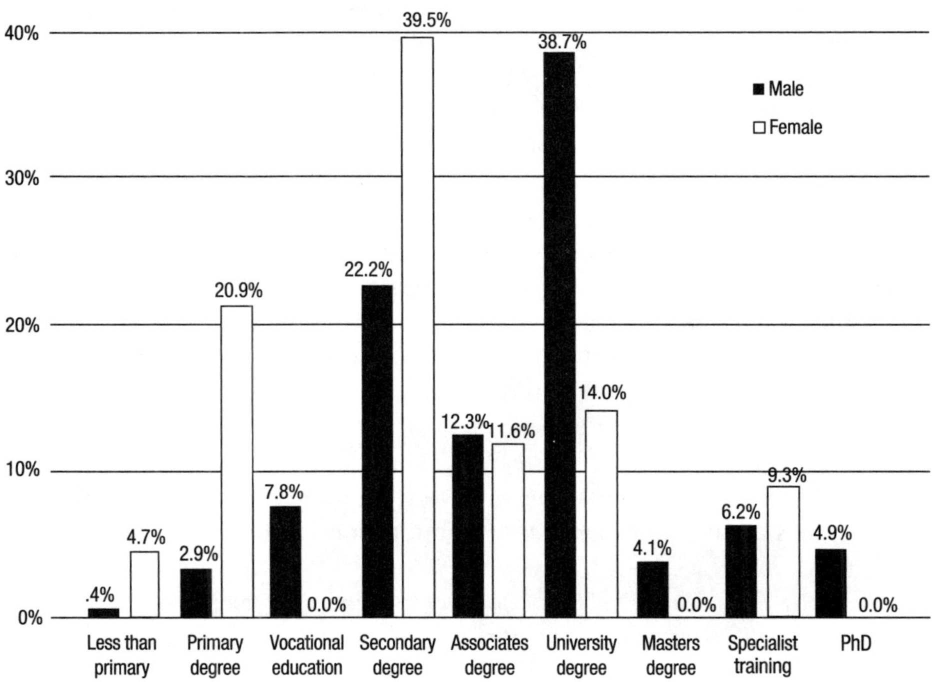

Figure 1.2. Witness education level by gender

appeared to provide testimony in trials 448 times (twenty of those respondents appeared twice in the same trial).[10] Most witnesses testified in only one trial (65 percent) or two (24 percent), while the highest number of trials in which individuals have appeared in court is five (two individuals testified in five trials). Among all of our witnesses, two-thirds have appeared on behalf of the OTP, and approximately one-third testified for the defense. In addition, seventeen witnesses have appeared in The Hague forty-five total times while testifying for the OTP and the defense. Four chamber witnesses also appeared for the OTP.

The ICTY has conducted dozens of trials, and we endeavored to ensure that there was a roughly even distribution of witnesses across the eligible trials (to guard against any potential for or accusations of witness tampering, we were not able to survey witnesses from trials that were ongoing at the time of the survey). Table 1.4 provides data on which trials the sample witnesses appeared in and on which side they testified. Larger, more complex trials with a higher volume of witnesses contributed a greater number of witnesses to the sample: for example, the trials of Kordić and Čerkez, Milutinović et al., Popović et al., Prlić et al., and Slobodan Milošević—had approximately 240–350 witnesses each, and thus they have higher numbers reflected. Other trials made far less use of witness testimony: for example, the trials of Dokmanović, Aleksovski, Jelisić, Sikirica et al., and Kunarac et al. had approximately 40–70 witnesses each).

The witnesses who comprise our sample constitute approximately 6.6 percent (300 witnesses out of an approximate total of 4,650)[11] of all those called to testify before the ICTY. These individuals have undergone untold suffering and have devoted days, if not weeks, to testifying before the ICTY. Their experiences give them a distinctive window into the functioning of an international tribunal. Only the witnesses can directly compare the injustices they suffered with the justice provided by the tribunal.

To provide a more full picture of the witness experience of justice, in addition to the statistical evidence that we marshal in this book, we also provide context for the witnesses' evaluations of international justice. As part of the survey process, the witnesses were asked three, open-ended questions about their experience with international justice:

1. *Could you describe what the experience of testifying for you personally, in your life, means or has meant to you? Please indicate any positive and negative aspects that have left an impact on you.*
2. *What advice would you give to help future witnesses at war crimes trials prepare for and cope with the process of testifying?*

TABLE 1.4. Trials and Side for Which Witnesses Testified

Defendants	Prosecution Witnesses	Defense Witnesses	Chamber Witnesses
Milutinovic et al.	18	17	1
Milosevic, Slobodan	28	3	
Kordic and Cerkez	6	24	
Prlić et al.	18	10	
Gotovina et al.	14	12	
Dordevic	18	6	
Popovic et al.	11	8	
Hadzihasanovic and Kubura	12	6	1
Galic	16	3	
Stanisic and Zupljanin	13	3	
Naletelic and Martinovic	9	4	
Martic	12	1	
Brrdanin	12		
Tolimir	10		
Kvocia et al.		8	
Blaskic	3	5	
Vasiljevic	4	3	
Strugar	7		
Simic, Tadic, and Zaric	4	3	
Stanisic and Simatovic	4	3	
Mrksic et al.	4	3	
Krnojelac	3	4	
Perisic	4	2	
Oric	2	4	
Krstic	6		
Krajisnik	5	1	
Haradinaj	6		
Delic, Rasim	3	2	1
Milosevic, Dragomir	1	4	
Lukic and Lukic	3	1	1
Limaj, Musliu, and Bala	1	3	
Halilovic	4		
Stakic	2	1	
Kunarac et al.		3	
Kupreskic et al.	2		
Dokmanovic	2		
Blagojevic and Jokic	2		
Sikirica et al.	1		
Jelisic	1		
Alexsovski	1		
Total	**272**	**147**	**4**

3. *What would you change about the proceedings or the process of testifying?*

We quote from the responses to these questions throughout this book, as they help elucidate and provide context for the statistical findings. The responses did not always remain confined to the questions asked but addressed various topics the witnesses desired to discuss. As one witness describes, the act of testifying was a watershed event in witnesses' lives.

> Coming to The Hague and being chosen by the people who select witnesses meant a lot to me psychologically, it stabilised me somehow, although I had gotten all that out of my system. I believe my coming to The Hague in a way closed the circle of emotional and physical decompression in which I was ensnared just because I belonged to a different faith or, I don't know, a different nation, regardless of whether I had done something wrong or not.

As one witness explains, some witnesses testified reluctantly but out of a deep sense of obligation to their country and to future generations.

> That is the reason why I agreed to testify and to speak because of this. I do not wish anything bad to happen to my child and therefore I don't wish it on the child of another, you know. A child is a child to me. And I wouldn't want anybody's children to experience again what we experienced, but the way it is going I am not sure that the future generations will not experience this.

One witness explained how the power of the witness experience remains for some to this day: "I feel fulfilled even after so many years, when it happened, perhaps nearly twenty years ago, and that feeling of satisfaction and pride because I was a part of this has not, has not diminished at all." There is much they have to tell and much we can learn about the meaning of justice through the witness' eyes.

Outline of Book Chapters

In this book, we develop our theory of individual evaluations of international justice and test the hypotheses derived from that theory. Chapter 2 develops the theory. We describe in depth the unique and critical features of international justice as provided by the ad hoc tribunals and by courts such as the permanent International Criminal Court, distinguishing international justice from the justice meted out in domestic courts. These distinctions guide us in establishing what features of international justice should be incorporated into our theory.

We especially discuss how international crimes generally involve the targeting of groups of people and thus constitute violations of international law. As the focus of the violence and the work of the tribunals centers on these identity crimes, we describe how the international trials engage the group identities of all those in the affected nations, such as the former Yugoslavia. Hence, the first component of our theory is the key role ethnic identity plays in how individuals interpret international justice, as they look to tribunals like the ICTY to affirm their group's narrative of why and how the violence unfolded and who did what to whom. Ethnic identity serves as a prism through which individuals, including the witnesses in our sample, view the conflict and the work of international justice.

The second component of our theory is witnesses' views of the fairness with which they and others have been treated. As research has shown (Tyler 1990; Tyler and Huo 2002), individuals accord much greater weight to the fairness with which they are treated by the criminal justice system than to the outcomes of cases. People who believe they have been treated fairly by the police and the courts tend to grant them greater legitimacy and deference.

The third component to our model is the individual experience in war and on the witness stand. Recent research has found that individuals who have suffered greatly during war and other periods of violence are surprisingly resilient and display a range of socially positive behaviors (Bauer et al. 2016). We take these findings as a starting point to develop our argument regarding why those individuals who have suffered the most during the wars of the former Yugoslavia are more apt to support the work of international justice. We also discuss why an individual's experience on the witness stand and belief about his or her contribution to the discovery of truth and delivery of justice influence perceptions of the justice provided by the ICTY.

In chapter 3, we derive a series of hypotheses regarding the impact of ethnic identity on individual views of the ICTY. First, we discuss and describe the direct impact of ethnicity on our measures of support for the ICTY—for its performance in establishing the truth regarding what happened during the Balkan wars, delivering justice, providing punishment for those convicted of crimes, and helping to prevent such wars from happening again. Second, we analyze the extent to which individuals link specific outcomes of ICTY trials to their evaluations of the tribunal's work. Thus, in contrast somewhat to the aforementioned research suggesting that fairness matters more than outcomes (Tyler 1990; Tyler and Huo 2002), we examine the possibility that individuals evaluate the ICTY's work based on the frequency and severity of the punishment meted out to the guilty from other ethnic groups, as well as on the extent to which their own group members are not targeted for prosecution or punished severely when found guilty.

Chapter 4 is concerned with whether the fairness issues that have been highlighted by Tyler and his various coauthors can help us understand how individuals evaluate international justice. That research suggests that process matters more than outcome and that people want their voices to be heard and want their input into their criminal justice situation to be understood. They want authorities to treat them with respect, politeness, and dignity and are willing to accept outcomes antithetical to their interests if they believe decisions were appropriately made. We describe in general the witnesses' views of the fairness with which they and witnesses and defendants from their ethnic group and from other ethnic groups were treated. We assess the utility of the fairness explanation, especially in light of the power of ethnic identity to shape people's views of international justice. The results demonstrate that fairness is assessed in a more complex manner than previous research might suggest.

In chapter 5, we delve more deeply into the experiences of witnesses during war and while at the ICTY. First, we review the data on the wartime traumas that the witnesses in our sample experienced and the extent to which suffering a greater range of traumatic experiences influences their evaluations of the ICTY. Then, we analyze how witnesses felt about their own performance on the witness stand and the extent to which they believe their testimony contributed to the discovery of truth and delivery of justice. The final portion of chapter 5 is devoted to assessing the significance of all hypotheses derived from our model of individual evaluations of international justice. The full model is tested, and the final set of findings are analyzed.

We conclude this study, in chapter 6, by assessing the evidence supporting our theoretical model, critiquing where the theory and its statistical tests do not provide an accurate or comprehensive accounting for individual evaluations of international justice, and offering suggestions regarding where future research should focus. We believe this is a particularly consequential moment for judging justice in international relations in general and for expanding our understanding of the meaning of justice for its stakeholders and the impact of the international courts in particular. Given the burgeoning interest in the field of transitional justice, there are extraordinary opportunities for scholars and practitioners to learn more about these institutions and their constituents. We regret only that the need and demand for these international courts and other forms of transitional justice is still so great.

TWO

A Theory of Individual Evaluations of International Justice

We often think of justice in terms of a *just* society or a *fair and unbiased* court system designed to confront those who violate societal norms. Both conceptions represent generalized, aspirational goals for a society and are intended to apply to all citizens of a polity, but justice is also defined from the life-altering experiences of those who are the victims of injustice. The real world of justice in our domestic courts and the institutions we establish to protect and order our lives does not always point toward a more enlightened place of the good life. The real world of justice can be a personal, social, and political battle in which justice is shaped by looking backward at the crimes of the past rather than forward to the hopes of the future. In this chapter, we delve deeply into the more complex and messy world of justice as it is delivered rather than promised, examining justice from the perspective of those who have lived through the worst of injustices. We do this to develop a theory and a model of the determinants of justice, based on the most difficult of circumstances in which people seek redress and a rebalancing of the scales. We examine how justice is defined by those who lived through the violence of the breakup of the former Yugoslavia as experienced by victims of the worst crimes against humanity. We subject the definition of justice to that difficult test so that we might better understand and appreciate justice's most essential features.

What does justice mean to a person whose village and its inhabitants were forcibly removed, its women raped, homes burned to the ground, and whose family was slaughtered in front of his or her eyes? That moral, theoretical, and legal conundrum lies at the heart of the opinions of individuals who have come to bear witness before war crimes tribunals. Our "normal" systems of justice, not generally structured to adjudicate such extraordinary events, strain to the breaking point when confronted with massive and horrific violations of human rights, such as the 1994 genocide in Rwanda, the civil war of Sierra Leone, or the ethnic cleansing in the former Yugoslavia. The various justice systems of the world spring from cultural traditions, values, and aspirations from which we derive our rights and responsibilities as citizens in a regularized pattern of dispute resolution. Justice in the aftermath of atrocity is anything but regular or normal. How can we begin to understand what justice means in contexts where the most basic purposes of laws and the courts—to provide security and predictability—have been subverted and even turned on their head to justify massive violence? Who or what is responsible for adjudicating such crimes? When these crimes are so severe as to constitute a violation of international law, how do judicial institutions address both acts of violence perpetrated by individuals and government policies devised by state leaders carried out by a militarized population? Which of the diverse components of justice, such as fairness, closure, and retribution, resonate with those who survive and must live again in the post-war society?

From these fundamental questions, this chapter builds our theory of justice in the international setting. Our model of justice is premised on the assumption that individuals view justice from both personal and sociopolitical perspectives. Individuals who interact with a system of international justice, such as the witnesses in our surveys, perceive and evaluate that system in terms of how it treats them personally and how it judges the individual's identity group (e.g., nation, ethnic group, religion). We argue that in the context of international crimes, justice is individual, collective, and ultimately contingent. It is based not necessarily on fixed assumptions about higher values and principles or on particular processes and rules for delivering a "just" outcome. Instead it is based on the powerful personal experiences and equally powerful, collective narratives of those who survive in the aftermath. These are the meaningful forces in their lives that, we contend, the witnesses utilize to make sense of something that is wholly outside their personal and social experience, an international tribunal seeking to deliver justice. While those who have lived through these conflicts to tell their stories are a small and unique group whose views cannot always be generalized to wider populations, they have much to teach us about justice. When we subject our notions and theories of justice by looking at it through the lens for whom it has the deepest meaning, we are given a window into the most fundamental meaning of justice challenging universalist and abstract values about justice on which the great thinkers have focused.

We begin this chapter on our theory of individualized justice by delving into how the subject matter of international laws at issue in international tribunals—war crimes, crimes against humanity, and genocide—can help us understand how individuals perceive and evaluate justice. The laws at issue focus not on the more routine and "lesser" types of crimes and disputes that occur among individuals and are addressed by domestic criminal justice systems, but instead focus on extraordinary and large-scale crimes perpetrated by organizations, militias, militaries, and governments. Not only is the magnitude of the injustice in these cases exponentially greater in comparison to domestic crimes, but the rationales behind the crimes are social and political and implicate people at the highest rungs of power. The size of these crimes and the implications for societies that must be repaired in the aftermath of atrocities and wars are enormous.

Perhaps the most consequential aspect of international adjudication of these crimes is that the verdicts judges render are ultimately not just legal, but also historical. These tribunals must confront the diverse and divisive social, political, and historical narratives that are often at the root causes of international crimes. Whether a group's narrative stresses its people's fate as victims or as saviors, accepts responsibility or directs blame to others, or is deeply entrenched in history or part of instrumentalist propaganda of state officials, international justice must deliver a verdict which necessarily means taking sides. Thus, we begin the development of our theory in this chapter by examining how the crimes at issue in international law set up a battle over identity and history and help shape individual views of justice. We focus on justice as a social and political construct where individuals link their belief in and support for justice based on support for their narratives and argue that international justice is often framed as resolving this contest of battling, historical narratives.

After this, we address the bilateral interaction between the witness and the ICTY to better understand how individuals perceive justice as a function of fairness. Research on public opinion, justice, and the legitimacy of courts (e.g., Tyler 1990) has identified several criteria in public evaluations. Individuals, especially in the United States, are thought to base their support for domestic justice on the perceived fairness of the justice system, the respect given to individuals by judicial institutions, and the individual's sense of efficacy regarding the judicial system (Tyler 1990; Tyler and Darley 2000). Individuals are interested in both how international tribunals treat them in particular and how "fairly" their group's sociopolitical narrative is judged by international courts. Witnesses' personal interactions with the ICTY and its staff are especially important given that witnesses generally will have had no prior court experience to influence their behavior and will probably know very little about the workings of international tribunals. Witnesses enter into the courtroom *tabula rasa* with little prior knowledge about the court and how fairly they will be treated, and their views may be more pliable compared to the views of those who interact with established and familiar courts in their societies. The second component of our model of individual evaluations of justice thus stems from individual witnesses' perceptions of not only the tribunal's fairness toward them as individuals but also its treatment of other witnesses and defendants, including those who share the same identity group as the perceivers and those who do not.

We conclude the development of our model by incorporating the witness's own personal experiences with testifying, focusing on the individual's opinions about his or her performance in court. Individuals who testify before international tribunals, like the ICTY, recognize the historical and legal enormity of their testimony having survived the horrors of war and are (mostly, although with some exceptions) highly motivated to tell their stories. There is much riding on their appearances on the witness stand, which makes testifying such a powerful experience. We argue that because individuals have been through so much that has warranted their testimony and have invested so much personally and socially into appearing before the ICTY, their own sense of efficacy and accomplishment and their own personal war experiences that helped lead to their testimony play a critical role in how they assess international justice. Such powerful personal narratives may lead to a sort of motivated bias in evaluations of international justice, as individuals seek to psychologically justify their sunk costs. A greater sense of personal efficacy in testifying might, we suggest, lead individuals to have a more positive view of international justice in general. We explore the importance of the individual's own story and emotions in constructing our model of evaluations of international justice in this chapter, to complete our theory and launch the statistical models we employ in subsequent chapters to test it. Before describing our model of justice from the perspective of the ICTY witnesses, we first comment on the meaning of justice.

Justice and Its International Forms

Philosophical treatises on the nature and meaning of justice tend to point toward the ultimate good of a just society in which citizens are treated fairly and given the opportunity to reach their fullest potential. Scholars have characterized justice as originating in abstract and aspirational values like morality (Kant 1795), fairness (Rawls 1971), the greatest good for the greatest number (Bentham 1780), or as part of perceptual experiences (Locke 1997). These conceptions of justice focus on the creation of an idealized society whose governing principles must be elucidated in order to develop the best possible approximation of this goal. They reach far beyond the meaning of justice in the courtroom, to consider justice more existentially, in terms of the nature and purposes of governance. These are larger and more fundamental questions about humanity and society, while international justice is subsequent to the development of the state and its national conceptions of justice. International justice, even though it confronts larger and messier problems, must also address normative questions about what sort of just world we seek and how the world should approach dealing with nations that reject a just future for their own peoples. The ambitions of international justice, no less than those of domestic justice, are expansive and universal in their aspiration. Below, we review the nature of these aspirations for international justice, as well as how such ambitions have collided with the necessities and practicalities of running a trial and dealing with an international community still hesitant about the implications of these universalist aspirations.

In the period of heady optimism that followed the establishment of the ICTY and ICTR, there was no shortage of claims that these tribunals could help deliver not only justice, but also deterrence (of future violations of international law), peace, and reconciliation. As Mendeloff (2004, 358) points out in his excellent analysis of the hyperbole surrounding the creation of international courts, scholars and practitioners have asserted that the truth telling of international justice can contribute to social healing, establish an accurate historical record, help promote democracy, and deter future atrocities. Mendeloff quotes former ICTY chief Prosecutor Richard Goldstone, who crystallizes this perspective: "The work of truth commissions or judicial inquiries share with criminal prosecution the ability to bring significant satisfaction to victims. If that satisfaction is sufficiently widespread within a community, it can have a soothing effect upon a whole society." As we have learned, since scholars have begun testing these assumptions and predictions about the purported benefits of international justice, our expectations regarding these courts have grown more realistic and more grounded in practice rather than hope.

Part of this debate over the meaning of international justice and its purported benefits for nations resulted from a political need to justify the creation of the first two tribunals after a lengthy hiatus in world affairs with no such courts. Thus, part of these justifications can be treated as rhetoric in defense of a lofty and presumably worthwhile goal of bringing international justice to victims of national conflicts for whom there would be no redress in domestic courts. We should not, then, attach excessive weight to some of the more far-reaching claims. Nonetheless, the political debate and the scholarly analysis over what to expect from international justice have helped inject a needed dose of realism into these discussions. There is a growing recognition that while international courts might contribute indirectly in the pursuit of these idealistic goals (Meernik 2016), their impact is limited and contingent, especially given the tenuous nature of national and international support for this project (Clark 2014; Meernik 2016; Mendeloff 2004, 2009). Unlike domestic courts that can rely on the assistance of the state to apprehend suspects, fund their operations, and support their mission (even when some judicial decisions may be greeted with deep or wide opposition), international courts must rely on states' willingness (rather than obligation) to provide this support. Thus, our understanding of the meaning and reach of justice at the international level has become more circumscribed as we have gained greater appreciation for the limitations these courts face in attaining more far-reaching objectives, such as peace and reconciliation. We do not wish to downplay the roles that can be played by international courts in contributing to reconciliation, deterrence, and peace, but our exploration into the meaning of international justice should focus on its core mission, redress, over which these courts do retain significant power and discretion.

In creating the ICTY, the UN Security Council proclaimed belief that "the establishment of an international tribunal and the prosecution of persons responsible for the above-mentioned violations of international humanitarian law will contribute to ensuring that such violations are halted and effectively redressed." The ICTY's most elemental purposes have been to deter further human rights violations and bring to justice people found responsible for the atrocities that have occurred. One of the most fundamental questions regarding the meaning and purpose of international justice is whether the international tribunals are the most appropriate venues from which to dispense this justice and whether the basically retributive justice handed down by these courts represents the best possible form of justice for local communities (Drumbl 2007; Findlay and Henham 2005, 2010; Henham 2003, 2007c; Kelsall 2009; Sloane 2007). Are there alternative forms of justice that are not focused on retribution? There has been no shortage of critics who have argued that international justice falls short of the justice they see as crucial for affected communities. As Henham (2003, 68) argues, "Retribution in international criminal justice has been more readily equated with the concept of victor's justice, vindication and western exculpation."

A number of scholars and practitioners advocate a restorative justice model in which the needs of the victims, defendants, and local communities are accorded greater weight (Drumbl 2007; Findlay and Henham 2005, 2010; Henham 2003, 2007c; Kelsall 2009; Sloane 2007). Restorative justice looks to repair the ruptures in social relations that are both causes and consequences of political violence, by attending to the needs of local communities and individuals for repair and reconciliation. According to its critics, retributive justice, with its focus on removing dispute resolution from those most directly affected and on incarceration (rather than reintegration) of those responsible, does not allow for social healing and privileges the interests of institutions rather than people. For example, in the Rwanda government's local justice remedy, the gacaca courts, those found guilty by the community often performed some type of penance work for the victims, such as giving them livestock or working on their plots of land. Proponents believe that such strategies will help bring healing at the microlevel, between individuals, which may make these strategies better than retributive justice at guaranteeing long-term stability and peace. One sees these debates flourishing recently as the permanent International Criminal Court (ICC) weighs its involvement in a number of situations where there are actors arguing for more localized and restorative justice (e.g., Uganda). One also finds arguments advancing the need for rehabilitation and reintegration of wrongdoers into society, as well as social defense theories, which look at how society can best protect itself from future human rights violations. These conceptions of justice point toward an idealized society and share traits in common with many of the idealized conceptions of justice we mentioned at the outset of this discussion. Can we learn from the messy realities of international politics? Are such restorative justice schemes guilty of the same sort of aspirational thinking and overreach that characterized many of the arguments that initially supported the need for international justice? Most especially, what does it mean for international justice if it is in competition with this local and restorative model of justice and its divergent goals?

As we look to understand the meaning of international justice, it is essential to bear in mind that it is international in nature and orientation. Restorative justice and its variants are a form of local justice that may or may not be available or appropriate for affected nations. Local, restorative justice may be helpful and what is needed for a nation, but the state retains a powerful (if not dominant) role in it, with all of the necessary costs and benefits this involvement entails (e.g., the possibility of state involvement in the very crimes being adjudicated). Local and restorative remedies also may not consider the international community as victim, even though its laws are violated and its norms offended. To be sure, the goal of restorative justice is not to entirely supplant international justice; rather, proponents of restorative justice who critique international justice question the latter's retributive premises. An emphasis on local remedies may coexist with international justice (e.g., the ICC's emphasis on complementarity with national governments, but not necessarily the judicial supremacy of the ICTY and ICTR over local courts). If we take the arguments of restorative justice to their logical conclusion, however, they tend toward a diminished role for international justice.

To be clear, our purpose is not to disparage local and restorative judicial remedies, for they certainly can and do work. Rather, in our quest to understand the meaning of international justice, we must recognize that while restorative justice can provide a very different mechanism for the resolution of disputes, its principles are quite different from the retributive justice authorized and practiced by the international tribunals. What we share in common with those who study and advocate for restorative justice is a focus on those affected by violence and on how the justice they receive affects their values and well-being. The purpose of our research is to determine how individuals evaluate the international justice that is delivered. To answer these questions, we concentrate on three central factors that we contend witnesses utilize in assessing institutions of international justice: identity, fairness, and experience. By subjecting this model to a series of tests using data from our survey of ICTY witnesses, we can assess which factors are most critical in shaping individual evaluations of international justice. This assessment can tell us a great deal about what international justice means to the individual.

Because justice at the international level is a multifaceted yet somewhat nebulous concept, we do not seek to provide one definition; indeed, justice may have very different meanings for the victims, society, defendants, and the international community, all of whom have a stake in the work of international tribunals. Instead, we measure justice along four dimensions. The witnesses were asked if they "believe that *in general* the ICTY has done a good job" in (1) "***establishing the truth*** about what happened in the former Yugoslavia," (2) "***determining*** who was responsible for the grave crimes committed in the former Yugoslavia," and (3) "***punishing*** those responsible for the grave crimes committed in the former Yugoslavia," as well as whether they believe that "*in general* the ICTY will help" in" (4) "***preventing*** grave crimes from occurring again in the former Yugoslavia." We see these four concepts not only as critical dimensions of a complex concept but as integral to the ICTY's mandate to provide redress for violations of international law (establishing truth, determining responsibility, and allocating punishment) and to help prevent future violations (deterrence).

International Law, Identity, and the Meaning of Justice

The international laws that comprise the substantive jurisdiction of the ICTY and of other such tribunals regard grave crimes that generally affect large numbers of people and that are the product of governments and other organizations in societies, such as the armed forces or rebel militaries. There is rarely anything simple or straightforward in the application of these laws to modern conflicts. Rather, because these crimes arise from the policies of political actors, they implicate critical state and leadership interests, especially the quest for and maintenance of power. Because they typically affect large numbers of people (e.g., crimes against humanity must be widespread or systematic, and genocide involves the attempted extermination of a group of people), they affect people both as individuals and as members of a community. Families are targeted, villages are destroyed, or large swaths of land are emptied in the name of military necessity or because of uncertainty over the loyalty of the inhabitants. In addition, the violence afflicted on people is as cruel as it is pervasive, as even a brief reading of the transcripts or judgments of most any trial will reveal. In essence, the enormity of these international crimes means that very few people are left unscathed. International law involves crimes with many, many stakeholders.

The convergence of these elements of international law in the targeting of certain groups of people for violence or extermination for political purposes is the key feature of most (albeit not all) violations of international law. These violations typically involve violence that is planned and executed by organized actors, such as states and rebel movements, and inflicted on people because of their membership in a suspect group or class. At the heart of this violence are the clashing ambitions and fears of two or more groups who can no longer exist peacefully within a society or polity. Members of one group or perhaps members of both groups perceive their security and their identity as a group as existentially threatened by the other group. Hence, when one group of people seeks the removal or the destruction of another group of people, issues of identity are paramount. Those directing the violence often believe their efforts are preserving their culture or their way of life from those who are different in some manner or who subscribe to a different political ideology. Some leaders will believe their conquests are necessary, if not preordained. Those peoples targeted because of their ethnic, political, or religious affiliation have no choice, then, but to perceive the conflict in terms of identity; their adversaries have defined it as such. Survival of the group is at stake.

In fact, if such conflicts and their attendant crimes were not so prevalent and so severe, we would not find international laws focusing on genocide and crimes against humanity. To be sure, not all conflicts involve such crimes or identity issues. Some scholars argue that identity issues, particularly ethnicity, are not so powerful in explaining conflict (Seymour and Cunningham 2016). Some find such an explanation too simplistic for understanding complex conflicts that often concern more localized factors and shifting alliances that transcend identity, as we often see in the violence in eastern Congo (Kalyvas 2003a). Greed and grievances are also powerful motivators of civil war and violence (Collier et al. 2003). Other findings have shown that leaders can use ethnicity not so much to mobilize an entire population (to recognize a threat or commit acts of violence), but to sideline those who oppose an extremist political agenda because they are considered insufficiently loyal (Gagnon 2004). Nonetheless, research indicates that almost two-thirds of all civil wars stem from ethnicity and identity issues (Denny and Walter 2014; Seymour and Cunningham 2016; Themner and Wallensteen 2012).

Unfortunately, there are ample instrumentalist motivations for regimes and rebels to target members of other ethnic groups. Some groups may view the very existence of other peoples as a threat to their dominance, such as the Nazis in Germany or the Interahamwe in Rwanda. Some states or non-state actors who do not perceive other identity groups in such apocalyptic terms may still consider those groups a threat to their dominance (e.g., Afrikaners in South Africa during apartheid). The rationale for such beliefs may rest on suspect evidence or irrational beliefs, but the fear of the "other" is certainly prevalent in today's world, as it has been throughout history. Rarely do massive ethnic crimes occur, but there are other, more instrumentalist rationales that make targeting groups based on their identity militarily advantageous. When regimes or rebels lack information on the loyalties of groups during the course of their military operations, especially in areas where their group is the minority, targeted killings can eliminate potential opposition and cow the survivors into submission. Furthermore, Fjelde and Hultman (2014) argue that "warring actors have incentives to strategically target civilian co-ethnics of the enemy as a means to deny the enemy a civilian support base." Targeted or random violence can be used to create conditions of insecurity and terror to dissuade an adversary's co-ethnics from cooperating with or joining enemy forces. Governments, their militias, and the rebel armies they fight against may also use violence to eliminate dissent. As Valentino, Huth, and Croco (2006) argue, indiscriminate killings of innocent civilians are a "calculated military strategy designed to achieve victory by coercing the adversary or by undermining the war-related productive capacity of his civilian population." The benefits to be gained from attacking people on the basis of their ethnicity, religion, or political beliefs are powerful and numerous for leaders and rebels seeking to foment conflict. Much of international law stems from a recognition that there are such instrumentalist motivations inspiring violence, and thus the normative goal is put in place mechanisms and doctrine to ameliorate it.

Identity conflicts are prevalent, and their violence is substantial, creating the rationale and the focus of international laws that seek to protect the innocent and punish the guilty. The regimes and rebels that perpetrate such violence comprehend the nature of this violence, who is being targeted, and why. The victims recognize that they are being targeted as members of the "other," even if they find no basis for the fears and violence of their adversaries. In such divided societies, this kind of violence is pervasive, deeply felt, and, most important, understood in the context of historically rooted social and political narratives (Clark 2014; Ford 2012). Those perpetrating the violence perceive their group as under threat (e.g., the extremist Hutu government in power before and during the Rwanda genocide), as fulfilling a historical mission (e.g., the Serbs who see themselves as a Christian bulwark against the spread of Islam in Europe), or as responsible for eliminating a perceived political-economic threat (e.g., the Nazis). The victims may view the violence as part of a history of discrimination and oppression practiced on them (e.g., the Jewish population in Europe during Hitler's reign). They may perceive their adversaries as implacable foes long bent on appropriating their wealth or capturing their lands. The victims may simply see themselves as victims because of their identity, whether such beliefs are long-standing or arise in the present conflict.

In the Balkan conflicts, each of the warring factions had its dominant narrative. For the Serbs, the narrative strands begin hundreds of years ago, with their defeat by the Ottoman Empire at the 1389 Battle of Kosovo, which began an enduring view of their people as the last line of defense of European Christianity, a responsibility for which they estimate that they have never received proper credit. Nationalist politicians like Slobodan Milosevic in Serbia and Radovan Karadzic in Bosnia played on, rose to power on, and exploited these views. They cast themselves as the saviors of their peoples, especially against their enemies in Bosnia-Herzegovina and Kosovo. Even when the Bosnian Serbs and the nation of Serbia were clearly the dominant powers in their respective regions and when their political/military leadership embarked on ethnic cleansing campaigns in Bosnia and Kosovo (as well as against Roman Catholics in Croatia), their leadership, whether truly or disingenuously, saw these wars as defensive. Even today, as we read through the transcripts of audio interviews with trial witnesses, it is striking how many Serb witnesses argue strenuously that perhaps *some* people died during the Srebrenica massacre, for example, but there was *no* genocide, and besides according to those who deny the violence, those who died were combatants anyway. Lest we single out the Serb leadership for such views, the Croatian government under Franjo Tudjman engaged in its own ethno-nationalist propaganda and ethnic cleansing designed to unite the Croatian people under one central state. Croatians in Bosnia committed horrific atrocities in their war against the Muslims, and several of their generals were indicted for crimes committed during their Homeland War of 1995, when the Croatian army drove out the Croatian Serbs from their self-proclaimed autonomous republics. The Bosnian Muslim army and the Kosovar Liberation Army did not always have clean hands either, and a number of their leaders have stood trial at the ICTY. Their dominant narratives, however, tend to emphasize the role of their peoples as victims of a powerful campaign of ethnic cleansing and violence. Bosniaks are also without a neighboring and co-ethnic partner state that they look to for leadership and support. This helps to create more division over the interpretation of recent history and the purpose of the entire international justice enterprise. Members of each group, especially their political/military leadership, understand the conflict and perceive the violence in social terms, as identity struggles.

The dominant narratives of each of these groups are on display not only in the policies and propaganda of the respective governments and their supporters but in their perceptions of international justice. The ICTY was created to provide justice and help deter future violations of international law, but for the peoples of the former Yugoslavia, it exercises a far more important role: it is the arbiter of the accuracy and honesty of these narratives. As Ford (2012, 433) writes, "Perceptions of the ICTY in the former Yugoslavia are driven to a large degree by whom the court indicts and whether these indictments contradict the dominant internal narratives within the various affected populations." Ethnic identity provides a powerful lens through which all consequential decisions made by the ICTY and the United Nations are assessed. Many Serbs, especially regime leaders, have argued that if the ICTY indicts Serbs or sentences them to lengthier terms of incarceration than other ethnic groups, the Tribunal is biased. A Bosniak might assert that ICTY prosecution of Bosnian Muslims would be a misguided attempt to more equally allocate blame among the Balkan ethnic groups and to deflect Serb charges of bias. Croatians might argue that if the tribunal convicts their people, the judges have failed to properly understand the defensive nature of Croatia's battles against the Serbs. Ford (2012, 410–11) explains,

> The fundamental problem facing international criminal courts (and other transitional justice mechanisms) is a mismatch between dominant internal narratives within a group and what actually happened in the conflict. Most groups are predisposed to see themselves as victims in the conflict, whether or not this is historically accurate.

Thus, we find that these identity narratives play out in the courtrooms of the ICTY as a continuation of the political and military battles that produced the very need for the tribunal. We must expect that as these groups present their version of the "truth" of the Balkan wars, which are grounded in their intensely held social and political narratives, the adversarial nature of these proceedings takes on new meanings. For the victims, defendants, and, most importantly, their supporters back home, these are not just exercises in the law and the adversarial trial system. Their very identities, their histories, and their integrity are on trial. The prosecutions are not merely about the guilt or acquittal of individuals; they are the world's judgment on each group's emotionally laden, historical narratives and personal war experiences. The impact of these judgments that play out on the world stage for all to see is tremendous. Hence, for many of those living in the former Yugoslavia, even those who might not have given much consideration to the wars or the deliberations of the ICTY, their assessments of international justice are heavily influenced by whether they believe the judges have vindicated their truth or, instead, undermined the cultural and historical narratives that help constitute their very identity.

As we have asserted, the international laws over which the ICTY and other international tribunals exercise jurisdiction concern crimes that involve violence directed against civilians and military personnel who are *hors de combat*—that is, not involved in war fighting because of injury, capture, or incapacitation. One can view the Balkan wars as well as other conflicts as characterized by two types of violence: that which is typical of military campaigns and is driven by military rationales (such violence does affect civilians, but if it is governed by military necessity, it does not run afoul of international law) and violence that purposefully targets civilians and those who are *hors de combat*. The targeting of such individuals is at the heart of international humanitarian and human rights law. A subset of this type of violence targets individuals specifically because of their identity and has featured most prominently in the caseloads of international tribunals. This type of discriminatory violence, often the most horrific and widespread, engages the historical and cultural narratives of the perpetrators and the victims.

As defined in the Genocide Convention—as well as the statutes of the ICTY, ICTR, and ICC—genocide is a crime characterized by the "intent to destroy, in whole or in part, a national, ethnical, racial or religious group, as such." The charge of genocide is exceptionally serious, and genocide is often viewed as the most severe of all the crimes under the jurisdiction of the international tribunals, as it involves the attempted elimination of a particular group. Those charged with genocide contest these allegations vigorously, because convictions on these charges carry the lengthiest sentences (Meernik 2011) and because the charges run directly counter to the narratives told by their identity group. When such charges are proven, they undermine the entire logic of the identity narratives in which each group perceives itself as the victim fighting a defensive struggle. Indeed, still to this day, many Serb leaders in Bosnia and Serbia deny that a genocide took place in Srebrenica. One finds hints of these views in the words of a survey witness who stated,

> Srebrenica. I am not saying that a crime didn't take place. A crime did take place. But, how, for instance, were Serbs from Sarajevo in Srebrenica? That one. So they were placed there by a decision. How come there were so many victims? How many, I don't know how many thousands. I think it's absurd and the Hague Tribunal accepted it. I think, and I may be wrong, and God forbid, it would be a sin. You understand? But it's impossible. I was in the war. I know what war is. I fired shots. I did all sorts of things.

To accept that one's people perpetrated a genocide is to call into question the very nature and content of one's group narrative. No defendant has ever pled guilty to a charge of genocide at the ICTY. Naturally, other witnesses take issue with the genocide deniers. One witness claimed,

> That is, when they start to deny the genocide . . . well, those people should—it is ugly to say—they should be grabbed by the ears and taken to Srebrenica and say here, sir, this is it, you see, do you see what happened here.

Given the legal, political, and social implications of international trials featuring allegations of genocide, these cases thoroughly and deeply engage the narratives of identity groups.

Crimes against humanity concern actions that target civilians, whether or not there is an armed conflict around which violence and coercion revolve. Of the various types of crimes against humanity, the crime of persecution has featured most prominently at the ICTY. That crime involves at least one of the enumerated actions forbidden under international law (e.g., torture, murder, sexual assault, and deportation) and targets individuals on racial, religious, or political grounds.[1] While a number of individuals at the ICTY have been convicted of genocide, charges of crimes against humanity, particularly persecution, have been especially prevalent. We find that crimes targeting individuals for their membership in identity groups are preeminent at the ICTY and, indeed, all of the international courts. The dominant purpose of these institutions is to adjudicate disputes that involve discriminatory, identity crimes. It is to be expected that the criminalization of this conduct arouses great passions among the affected groups. Not just persons, but peoples, are on trial.

We contend that membership in these identity groups is critical in shaping how individuals perceive international justice. We do not argue that these identities are determinative of the opinions of the witnesses in our sample or, for that matter, all the peoples of the former Yugoslavia. For many individuals, identity is fundamental in producing their perceptions of conflict and their attitudes toward international justice; for some individuals, their social identity may be merely influential in shaping their opinions; for others, it may only be a minor factor. Nonetheless, issues of identity were central to the very nature of the Balkan wars, they are at the heart of the international laws over which the ICTY exercises jurisdiction, and they are important to the peoples of the former Yugoslavia. As Ford

(2012, 423) argues, "People's views of themselves are intricately bound up with their social identities. Thus attacks on social or group identities can be treated as attacks on the self."

In chapter 3, we explore in depth just how we expect identity issues to influence witnesses' perceptions of international justice. Our reasoning is fairly straightforward and can be summarized here. Essentially, we argue that identity *per se* will influence individual attitudes. As other researchers have found, identity is key to predicting opinions of the ICTY (Arzt 2006; Clark 2009c; Ford 2012; Hagan and Ivković 2006b; Klarin 2009; Meernik 2015a; Nettelfield 2010; Orentlicher 2008; Subotić 2009; UNDP 2005). For example, Bosniaks and Albanians in Kosovo are most supportive of the ICTY, Croats are less positively inclined, and Serbs are most critical (Arzt 2006; Hatay 2005; Meernik 2015a; Nettelfield 2010; Peskin 2005, 2008; UNDP 2005). Ethnicity thus plays a direct role in influencing evaluations, but as we argue, it will also exercise an indirect impact, by shaping attitudes on other issues, such as the perceived fairness of the ICTY. As one of the witnesses in our study argued (in a statement that stands out as an eloquent exception to the tendencies we have discussed thus far), "It is unrealistic to speak about the justice when someone, let's say, is sentenced to 40 year imprisonment, and one group is applauding the verdict, the second group has no opinion, while the third group completely condemns the verdict."

More specifically, we argue that ethnicity will shape witnesses' expectations regarding the outcomes of the ICTY trials. We contend that those individuals who believe their group fought a defensive struggle to preserve their identity against adversaries who fought an offensive war of conquest will evaluate the work of the ICTY in light of the severity of treatment accorded to the enemy and the leniency with which their own co-ethnics were treated. In this sense, many individuals view international justice as a distributive enterprise. The ICTY allocates indictments, convictions, and sentences. To the extent that these "goods" are perceived to fall disproportionately on one's group, we expect individuals to lower their opinions of international justice and the work of the ICTY. The perception that the ICTY has targeted one's identity group is, in effect, a rebuke to that group's historical and cultural narratives and will meet with disapproval, if not condemnation, from many. As individuals perceive the ICTY as "properly" allocating blame and punishment to their adversaries and thus as legitimating their group narrative, we would expect support for the ICTY to increase. Therefore, we assess the impact of ethnic identity as a characteristic of the individual and via the goods distributed by the tribunal—namely, the convictions and punishments meted out to the individual's ethnic adversaries.

Fairness and Perceptions of Justice

Ethnicity creates a foundation and provides a lens through which the past and present are understood, but witnesses' attitudes regarding international justice are profoundly influenced by another socially constructed value, fairness. As scholars have shown in the domestic context, people have a strong sense of the extent to which authorities, such as the police and the court system, follow proper procedures (Benesh 2006; Moorhead, Sefton, and Scanlan 2007, Tyler 1990, 2001; Voeten 2013; Wood et al. 2015). Tyler focuses on perceived fairness in his work on why people obey the law and which factors lead them to grant legitimacy to the judicial system and its laws consistently (Tyler 1990; Tyler and Darley 2000). He explains (1990, 7),

> The normative perspective on procedural justice views people as being concerned with aspects of their experience not linked only to outcomes. Normative aspects of experience include neutrality, lack of bias, honesty, efforts to be fair, politeness and respect for citizens' rights.

As Tyler (1990) further argues, individuals from diverse backgrounds rely on evaluations of fairness in their understanding of both the process of justice and its outcomes. This reliance is especially striking and important to understand in light of the dominance of rational actor models of political behavior, which stress the all-encompassing importance of the costs and benefits of outcomes as the driver of human decision-making.

Fairness is critical to individuals because it is something they understand and experience personally. Given the wide range of outcomes that result from complex and lengthy judicial processes, of which individuals have only a limited understanding, a reliance on perceptions of fairness, especially those based on individual experience, provides a better metric of evaluation. Tyler observes (1990, 109, citing Bellah et al. 1985 and Schwartz 1978),

> Because there is no single, commonly accepted set of moral values against which to judge the fairness of outcomes or policies, such evaluations are difficult to make. People can however agree on the fairness of procedures for decision making. Evaluations of authorities, institutions and policies therefore focus on the procedures by which they function, rather than on evaluations of their decisions or policies.

Tyler's work and research from other scholars have focused on evaluations of the American criminal justice system. To what extent can these findings be generalized to an international tribunal?

The International Criminal Tribunal for the Former Yugoslavia is a *sui generis* institution, although it does have antecedents in the Nuremberg and Tokyo tribunals. Shortly after its establishment by the UN Security Council in 1993, that body created a sister institution, the International Criminal Tribunal for Rwanda, in 1994. These institutions were later followed by ad hoc tribunals for Sierra Leone, Cambodia, Lebanon, and East Timor and, ultimately, by the International Criminal Court. For the peoples of the former Yugoslavia, this was an institution wholly unlike anything found in their domestic criminal justice system. The ICTY combined the principles and practices of common-law systems and civil law to create an entirely new type of judicial system, with which most individuals were unfamiliar, even after the ICTY had been operating for many years (Cibelli and Guberek 2000; Clark 2009c; Orentlicher 2008). One survey witness recounted,

> The thing about The Hague Tribunal that I've objected to from day one is this: in Bosnia, many people do not understand the way the trials are continental system to a different, Anglo-Saxon system, is very, very difficult, [*sic*] and some legal concepts that exist in that system and do not exist in our own seem strange, incomprehensible, people find it hard to understand.

Other reports indicate that people from the former Yugoslavia focus on more personal and less institutional factors. One scholar reported that while most of the population surveyed knew that former Bosnian Serb leader Biljana Plavsic was serving her sentence in a Swedish prison that had a sauna, 93 percent of the population surveyed were unaware to what exactly Plavsic had confessed (Mladjenovic 2004, 63). Furthermore, their understanding may also be biased by the propaganda of state institutions and by misinformation from local media (Klarin 2009).

We do not wish to belabor the point regarding either the lack of familiarity that most individuals in the former Yugoslavia have with international justice or tribunals or, for that matter, the knowledge of any peoples regarding courts in general. Our argument is that while many people may lack knowledge of the workings of these complex institutions, this problem does not necessarily inhibit individual evaluations of the justice delivered by these courts. At issue is how individuals make decisions and which factors they utilize in their evaluations of justice in an environment in which their knowledge may be limited. We suggest that individuals in this type of environment utilize decision-making heuristics based on their perceptions of key attributes of these institutions and that the concept of fairness provides individuals with a key method by which to evaluate the ICTY. As individuals—in our case, the witnesses—interact with the tribunal, they assess their treatment, as well as the treatment of others, with reference to the multifaceted value of fairness.

Exactly what does fairness entail in regard to procedural justice in the international context? We suggest that it encompasses individuals' perceptions of both how they have been treated by authorities and how these authorities have treated others. Fair treatment toward the individual personally (microlevel fairness) and an institution's fair treatment toward others generally (macrolevel fairness) should shape individual evaluations of international justice. To best understand the meaning of fairness, one must also keep in mind the context within which such judgments are made and, in particular, the extent to which individuals accept judicial outcomes rather than view those outcomes in terms of the advantages they gain. Research has shown that people will accept an outcome that does not redound to their advantage so long as they believe that both the process by which the conclusions were derived and the individuals who made the decisions were fair (Tyler 1990). The experiences individuals have in dealing with justice systems are then utilized to draw more general conclusions about the fairness and legitimacy of these institutions (Casper, Tyler, and Fisher 1988; Tyler 1984, 1990). In particular, as Tyler (1990) argues, people place more emphasis on whether they are allowed to explain their situation to those who make a decision than on their own degree of influence over the decision. For example, when someone reports a robbery and is visited by police who take the person's evidence, that individual's concern in evaluating the justice system is more whether the victim believes he or she been given proper treatment by the police in this encounter than whether the police are able to locate and return the missing items. Understanding that the authorities cannot always resolve cases as victims would prefer, victims tend to judge the work of the authorities based on the interactions that they feel competent to evaluate (Tyler 1990; Tyler and Huo 2002). People have a better understanding of how others treat them than of the workings of the criminal justice system, and they adjust their evaluations accordingly.

We would expect to find a similar logic operating in our model of witness evaluations of the ICTY's justice: perceptions of fair treatment should matter more than outcomes. To be sure, the deep influence of identity should predispose many individuals to feel very strongly about the verdicts and sentences issued by the ICTY. For some individuals who see the ICTY as founded on and permeated by bias, perceptions of the degree to which they were accorded fair treatment may not matter as much. Interestingly, however, Tyler (2001, 416) notes that strong identity attachments can heighten the importance attached to fairness concerns.

> People value fair treatment by others because fair treatment communicates to them that the group to which they belong is a valuable, high status group. As members, therefore, they also have high status, which leads to favorable feelings of self-worth and self-esteem.

Individuals' ability to express their views matters greatly and would seem to be equally important, if not even more so, in the context of judicial decision-making regarding identity conflicts, where the passions of individual opinions on the subject are likely to be quite powerful (Moorhead, Sefton, and Scanlan 2007). Indeed, when witnesses were prompted to reflect on what they liked and disliked about their treatment by the ICTY, a principal concern they often referred to related to their ability to state their case while on the witness stand. The most frequently occurring criticism that witnesses made of their experience while testifying concerned whether they were denied the opportunity to describe their experiences. Often, these witnesses felt they were disrespected in their efforts to articulate their story and suffering, by defense attorneys who questioned their veracity, by prosecutors who cut their answers short, or by judges who did not intervene to limit such treatment. As one witness describes the range and depth of feeling that many of those surveyed had about the testimonial process,

> It is difficult to control it . . . because you know, while you are testifying and while the Defence and the Prosecution are asking you a string of questions, very precise, very detailed with many drawings and details, then the pictures do come back to you . . . and now I have the picture of the little girl I carried in front of me, you know. . . . My general attitude in life and not only on that question, but on all other questions is: "confront the problem," I mean. So the same goes for these tyrants: in spite of the powers they might have at that moment.

Conversely, among the most recurrent favorable comments made, especially regarding the judges, was that they allowed witnesses to state their case and protected them from attorneys who sought to curtail their testimony. After waiting years to give evidence regarding perhaps the most important and deeply felt events of their lives, the witnesses wanted, more than anything, to tell their stories. As Moorhead, Sefton, and Scanlan (2007, 90) write,

> A related issue is the quality of treatment and, in particular, respect shown to the participant during their involvement in the justice process. This relates to concerns about evidence giving, and the courtesy of both prosecution and defence lawyers in particular; but also to the behaviour of judges and court staff and the extent to which participants' concerns about court dates are met or managed. Protection of participants from intimidation is also important.

Witnesses' personal experience with international justice and their views regarding its fairness are viewed in the context of this courtroom encounter. In chapter 4, we describe in more detail just how we measure and test for the influence of factors involving the witnesses' views about the fairness with which they were personally treated by the ICTY.

The witnesses are also aware of how others were treated by the tribunal. Whether these others are fellow witnesses or defendants, witnesses are attuned to such macrolevel fairness issues, particularly given that identity issues are central to the mission of the tribunal. Witnesses are part of an ethnic community with which they share membership with co-ethnic witnesses and defendants. As such, they have strongly felt opinions regarding what kind of treatment they might expect from the ICTY toward their group and toward other groups who do not share the same identity. While opinions about the fairness with which others are treated are likely not as personally felt as those based on one's own interactions, the witnesses and even the defendants constitute a literal and figurative community who have had shared experiences during the conflict and at the ICTY. Additionally, many of the witnesses come from small, rural communities where everyone knows each other and knows who did what to whom. Witnesses may be part of support groups who share stories about their opinions of the ICTY and their own encounters with the tribunal. Some witnesses even interact with other witnesses while in The Hague. These interactions and communities of interest can serve to heighten awareness of how the ICTY has treated others and can make such knowledge more salient in the witnesses' evaluation of the tribunal. Therefore, we expect that the witnesses in our sample will consider the degree to which both they and others have been treated fairly by the tribunal.

We began the development of our theory of witness evaluations of the justice rendered by the ICTY by focusing on the centrality of identity in witness perceptions and assessments. Identity, as a theoretical construct, we argued, tended to divide the witnesses, as well as the peoples of the former Yugoslavia, and inclined them to evaluate the tribunal on the basis of outcome and whether those outcomes served to uphold their identity narratives. Here, echoing the work of Tyler (1990), we stress that there are also constructs that highlight the similarities in the manner in which individuals, regardless of identity, view the ICTY. Fairness, we argued, is a universally valued construct that witnesses, as well as other individuals, regard positively. "People think about procedural justice in a similar way, even if characteristics of their background differ" (Tyler 1990, 157) argues, Identity serves to divide, structure, and direct opinions regarding international justice, while fairness can serve as a more general concept that permeates how individuals regard the quality of their interactions with and the processes of international justice, regardless of outcome. To complete our theory of witness evaluations of the ICTY, we look to how witnesses view their own role in international justice. We stress the degree to which witnesses perceive the tribunal through the prism of their own experiences and background, as well as their contributions toward the discovery of truth and the delivery of justice. These factors, which we argue tend to be universally important, are ultimately unique to each individual.

The Individual Experience and Perceptions of Justice

Every witness that comes before an international tribunal brings a unique perspective to international justice, shaped both by their individual circumstances that led to their appearance before the tribunal and by their sense of how well they were able to convey these experiences to the tribunal. Like fairness, we contend that these factors are universally influential and important to all witnesses, regardless of their identity. All those living in the former Yugoslavia experienced the wars that tore apart the region in the 1990s, even if some felt the impact more directly than others. Regardless of identity, each witness comes before the ICTY to convey his or her wartime experiences. Each witness, we contend, also seeks to convey these experiences in a meaningful way that judges will consider and value as a contribution to the decision-making processes. In the following section we develop our theory of justice from the perspective of the witnesses focusing on these individual experiences and cognitive processes to demonstrate why they exercise such a powerful influence on opinions of international justice.

Witness Experiences during the Wars of the Former Yugoslavia

Most individuals who bear witness before an international tribunal testify to their knowledge of the crimes perpetrated by the accused. While expert witnesses and insider witnesses may have escaped the wars of the former Yugoslavia without personally experiencing its consequences, that cannot be said of most of the fact witnesses who took part in our survey. Nearly all of them experienced, in some manner, the cost of war. In fact, the three hundred interviewees in our survey reported that they directly experienced a total of 2,876 events, ranging from shelling, to food deprivation, to torture and kidnapping, to rape and sexual assault. Female witnesses reported experiencing an average of 11.8 wartime traumas, while male witnesses reported undergoing approximately 9.5 experiences on average (King and Meernik 2017). When these individuals testify before the ICTY, they bring tremendous first hand knowledge of the crimes at issue, which is, of course, why they are called to testify and why the tribunal was established. In this study, we are most interested in the impact of these experiences on shaping the witnesses' attitudes toward the tribunal.

We contend that the wartime trauma suffered by the witnesses not only provides the witnesses a compelling rationale to testify but also gives them a tremendous stake in the success of the ICTY. We should expect to find that many of the witnesses are highly motivated to testify and that this may incline them to perceive the tribunal in a more positive light. Why would wartime trauma inspire more favorable attitudes toward the ICTY? An emerging body of research finds that many individuals who have undergone some type of severe trauma, especially during wars, emerge from these experiences with more positive social attitudes. In a survey of research across several fields, particularly in economics, Bauer et al (2016) find that people who are exposed to violence are more likely to become cooperative, participate in social activities, take leadership roles, and give altruistically. Such effects hold for men and women, young and old, and victims and perpetrators and do not diminish, with many people actually becoming more socially cooperative over time.

Bauer and his co-authors discuss several potential reasons for these findings. Individuals emerging from the demands of surviving a long and harsh war during which strong ties are vital for protection and the necessities of life might develop a greater appreciation for the benefits of community and cooperation. Identity conflicts may lead individuals to become more integrated into their particular group as it experiences threats from others, which might suggest that pro-social attitudes tend to be directed primarily to those within one's group. Bauer et al. (2016, 27) also suggest that wartime traumas may produce life reorientations among victims:

> After war violence, it is possible to imagine victims changing their priorities in life and placing renewed value on relationships with family and community, and even changing other-regarding preferences. Such changes need not be parochial in nature; the existing literature in this area is silent on this point.

Bauer et al. (2016, 22) conclude, however, that research has done a better job at finding evidence of these effects than at explaining why they occur.

Similar research in the area of victim resilience has sought to understand why some individuals become stronger over time because of or despite the traumas they experienced. Scholars across a variety of fields, including psychology, sociology, and political science, have studied the notion of "resilience." The concept has been defined as a "process of patterned adjustments adopted by a society or an individual in the face of endogenous or exogenous shocks." This definition recognizes that resilience is not a "quality, a paradigm, or a theory" but, rather, an "inherently dynamic and complex process" (Bourbeau 2015, 376). The notion of resilience has been used to understand the ability of societies and individuals to adapt and potentially grow stronger after having experienced personally or socially destructive events. Resilience has proven useful in studying everything from the aftermath of a natural disaster (Cassar, Healy, and Von Kessler 2017; Goldstein 2012) to urban violence (Davies 2012; Muggah 2013), postelection violence (Becchetti, Conzo, and Romeo 2014), and political and ethnic violence (McAdam 2013; Hobfall et al. 2011). Among individuals, it has been found that resilience is more likely to be associated with higher education, younger age, and social support networks (Hobfall et al. 2011).

Given the substantial number of traumatic experiences suffered by the witnesses in our survey, we assume that many of them have a strong need to testify—to tell their stories, to confront a defendant in court, or as some sort of psycho-social obligation to the community. In other research, we have found that the greater the number and range of traumatic experiences witnesses have lived through are, the stronger their motivation to testify is (King and Meernik 2017). We find that those witnesses who have experienced the most traumatic events are more likely to indicate that they are strongly compelled to testify, for a variety of reasons, such as to "speak for the dead," "tell my story," or "confront the defendant" or to "put the past behind" them (King and Meernik 2017). Indeed, among those who study transitional justice, the phenomenon of "testimony as catharsis" has received a great deal of attention. A number of scholars have found that for many individuals who testify before tribunals and truth commissions, the opportunity to tell their stories can provide them with a feeling of vindication, a sense of satisfaction from seeing the defendant in a submissive role and facing justice, and most fundamentally, a sense of closure (Brounéus 2010; Stepakoff et al. 2014, 2015; Cody et al. 2014). Nonetheless, critics find much of the research anecdotal and reflective of the wishful thinking of the proponents of transitional justice (Mendeloff 2009).

In our model of individuals' evaluations of international justice, we suggest that there is sufficient evidence from prior research to indicate: (1) that the witnesses will be strongly influenced in their perceptions of the ICTY by the traumatic experiences they suffered that ultimately lead to their appearance(s) before the tribunal; and (2) that the depth of the experiences of many of these individuals will lead them to develop positive attitudes toward the ICTY. Based on the findings of Bauer et al. (2016) and others who find that many individuals, although certainly not all, can become more resilient in the face of trauma, we suggest that the greater the degree of trauma witnesses experienced during the wars is, the more likely they are to hold favorable attitudes toward that institution. We suggest that one particularly powerful explanation for these positive opinions is the tendency among many to develop more pro-social attitudes, including toward international institutions that play such a prominent role in their lives. We also suggest, however, that there is another important reason why these individuals may be psychologically predisposed to develop positive evaluations. Given the long, painful journeys witnesses endure through war and its aftermath, as well as the more practical, personal and logistical issues involved in testifying before an international tribunal, not only do these individuals want to see the ICTY succeed, but many may also actually need the justice mechanism to be successful.

We hypothesize that the greater the personal cost the witness has undergone during the wars of the former Yugoslavia is, the more motivated he or she will be to have a favorable view of the international institution that is central to the witness's quest for affirmation and closure. One witness stated,

> [A]s for my testimony, especially in The Hague, I felt a strong need, just as if it had been my mother who gave birth to me. I went there with this great sense of injustice, great pain and sadness, with the loss of my family members, neighbours, family.

We are suggesting, in effect, that something akin to motivated reason or confirmation bias is operating among many of these individuals (Ask and Granhag 2005; Garland and Newport 1991; Kunda 1987, 1990; Nickerson 1998; Taber and Lodge 2006), although we hasten to add that there are key differences between how we and other scholars conceive of this cognitive phenomenon. In the context of the relationship between individuals' wartime experiences and their beliefs about the ICTY, we are not suggesting that individuals necessarily seek out confirmatory information or reject disconfirming evidence regarding the merits of the work of the ICTY. Rather, we are hypothesizing that in view of the life-altering events that individuals experienced during the Balkan wars, coupled with the difficulties and anxieties associated with testifying in the fraught environment of international justice, the witnesses have developed attitudes and perceptions that have come at a high cost. Given this, we suggest that witnesses are likely to hold strongly to these attitudes, which may then influence their beliefs about the quality of the justice provided by the tribunal (Taber and Lodge 2006). Hence, one might also consider this cognitive mechanism a form of wishful thinking, or of the strong influence of the desire to believe those things that are preferable (Nickerson 1998, 197). Like those who need to believe there is reason behind tragedy and that their sacrifices and loss have meaning, we suggest that the witnesses who have experienced traumatic events will be strongly motivated to seek closure for their experiences and to justify the personal and other costs associated with appearing in this alien international court located hundreds of miles from home. Indeed, as Taber and Lodge write (2005, 756), the "tension between the drives for accuracy and belief perseverance underlies all human reasoning." In effect, we are suggesting that these psychological mechanisms shape witnesses' cognitive processing of their experiences in and opinions of the ICTY. For many of these witnesses, although certainly not for all, these cognitive processes will lead them to look more favorably on international justice.

Evaluating Individual and Institutional Performance

The two elements that comprise the role of the individual experience in our theory of individual evaluations of international justice concern the extent of the trauma the individual lived through during the Balkan wars and the individual's attitudes regarding his or her testimony at the ICTY. The element we discuss here is the individual's assessment of his or her performance on the witness stand. The act of testifying before an international tribunal to relay what are likely the most traumatic events of one's life, in front of an assembly of international judges, lawyers and staff, and, of course, those accused of committing these severe violations of human rights, is likely to be an experience unlike anything these witnesses have ever undergone. As our survey has revealed, witnesses report feeling a range of emotions before and after appearing on the witness stand, from feeling "cooperative," "satisfied," "relieved," "positive," and "fulfilled" to feeling "tense," "obligated," and "confused" (King and Meernik 2017). Overall, the witnesses recall feeling more positive emotional states than negative ones, both before and after testimony. We asked the witnesses about two attitudes in particular regarding their testimony, attitudes we contend will be key to understanding how their individual testimonial experiences shape their views of international justice.

Witnesses were asked if they believed their testimony (1) contributed to providing justice and (2) contributed to the discovery of the truth about the wars in the former Yugoslavia. Over two-thirds of the witnesses (67 percent) agreed or strongly agreed that their testimony contributed to justice, and 71 percent agreed or strongly agreed that they believed their testimony contributed to the discovery of truth (King and Meernik 2017). Scholars have found that individuals are more likely to grant legitimacy and express approval of judicial institutions if they believe that they have some voice or influence in the institution (Doak 2015; Tyler 1990; Tyler and Darley 2000). In turn, research across a variety of fields (including sociology, political science, and criminal justice) has found that individuals are more likely to be satisfied with their testimony if they think the experience was positive (Clark 2014; Horn et al. 2009; Stepakoff et al. 2014; Stover 2005), cathartic (Brounéus 2010; Dembour and Haslam 2007; Mendeloff 2009; Stover 2005), important in truth telling (Doak 2011; Findlay and Ngane 2012) or provided the witness with an opportunity to tell their personal narrative (Hodžić 2010; Horn et al. 2009). Conversely, when individuals feel negatively about their testimony, when testifying leads to feelings of re-traumatization, or when witnesses feel disrespected by the courtroom actors, their satisfaction with justice more generally and with their own testimony declines. We suggest that testifying is more likely to be satisfying: if it was a meaningful encounter for the witness (Doak 2011); if the witness felt respected by court personnel; and if the witness perceived cross-examination as a positive experience (Horn et al. 2009).

We contend that individuals' attitudes regarding their own assessment of their role in the testimonial process plays a critical role in their evaluations of the tribunal more generally. Individuals who have a more positive attitude about one aspect of the testimonial process are more likely to report positive feelings about other elements of international justice. Psychological research has found that there are significant associations between positive moods and other behaviors, including cognitive flexibility (Isen 1990), creativity (Nadler, Rabi, and Minda 2010), and other types of success (Lyubomirsky, King, and Diener 2005). Those witnesses who have a more positive attitude about their testimony are more likely to also view the tribunal in a positive light.

We also contend that the cognitive processes we described earlier—confirmation bias and motivated reasoning—will influence some individuals in their assessments of the tribunal. Individuals who believe that their testimony contributed to the discovery of truth and the delivery of justice may also then perceive the ICTY in a positive light. That is, individuals who view their performance positively may generalize these attitudes toward the larger institution and its mission. Our reasoning here is similar to our previous argument regarding the impact of wartime trauma on witness support for the ICTY. We suggest that there is a tendency among individuals to ascribe or transfer their own sense of satisfaction with their performance to that of the larger institution to which they have contributed. In light of their substantial trauma during the war and of the personal costs entailed in their journey (both literally and figuratively) to The Hague, many individuals may feel a strong need to justify such suffering and sacrifice by viewing their own efforts and the work of the tribunal in a positive light. Therefore, as witnesses view their contributions to truth and justice more favorably, they are more likely to hold positive attitudes about the work of the ICTY.

A Model of Individual Evaluations of International Justice

Our tripartite model of how witnesses before the ICTY develop their assessments of the justice provided by that institution is premised on three distinct components. First, we argued that at the most fundamental level, individuals are strongly influenced by their identity. In the case of the former Yugoslavia, this identity is intimately bound up in their ethnicity which is comprised of other key identity features. It tends to be strongly correlated with religion (for Bosniak Muslims, Orthodox Serbs, Catholic Croatians, and Muslim Albanians), geography (even though this geography does not always respect national boundaries), and historical experience.[2] Hence, ethnic identity carries a great deal of powerful, complex, and emotionally laden baggage. We hypothesize that it exercises a direct influence on witness evaluations of international justice, as those groups whose narratives are more often validated in general at the ICTY should be more likely to support the tribunal. We also hypothesize that its influence is felt through the extent to which the outcomes of the ICTY—its verdicts and punishments—comport with individuals' expectations regarding the tribunal's performance. In chapter 3, we explain these components of the model in greater detail and conduct preliminary, descriptive tests of the validity of the identity explanation of support for international justice.

The second element of our theory is fairness. As research increasingly shows, individuals are willing to extend a great deal of support for justice and to grant it considerable legitimacy if they believe that its personnel and processes are behaving in a fair manner. People and procedures should be neutral, honest, objective, and worthy of a range of other adjectives that revolve around the integrity of the enterprise itself. In the course of their experiences with a justice system, individuals treated with respect and politeness and, most especially, allowed to state their cases and perceive that their input is valued will tend to view justice as fair and to support the enterprise, even when its outcomes do not comport with individual preferences. We expect this sort of logic to operate on individual attitudes toward international courts just as it does in regard to domestic courts. Research has shown that such attitudes toward international courts, particularly their perceived fairness, are often an extension of individuals' opinions of national courts (Voeten 2013; cf. Gibson and Caldeira 1995). Both microlevel fairness toward the individual witness personally and macrolevel fairness that the tribunal exhibits toward others should influence evaluations of international justice.

Personal experience during the Balkan wars and at the ICTY is the third component of our theory. We hypothesize that the witnesses in our sample who have suffered the most during the war and those who come away from their testimony believing they have contributed to truth and justice will be more likely to approve of the ICTY. Especially in a context in which individuals do not always fully understand the complex workings of an institution like the tribunal, they are more likely to utilize the most personally relevant and accessible decision cues to aid in their opinion formation. In particular, we believe that many individuals will have a strong need to view the ICTY as successful, to psychologically justify the physical and emotional costs that have been endured in the years leading up to their appearance(s) before the tribunal.

In sum, our model forecasts that witness evaluations of the ICTY are based on these principal psycho-social indicators. Though we also include a number of other control factors in our statistical models (e.g. gender, age, and education), we hypothesize these three principal sets of factors provide the dominant lenses through which witnesses evaluate international justice. Our model is designed to explain the attitudes of a sample of witnesses from the former Yugoslavia who have appeared before the ICTY, but we also believe the model is sufficiently generalizable to account for the opinions of witnesses and other stakeholders at other international ad hoc tribunals (e.g., the International Criminal Tribunal for Rwanda) as well as the permanent International Criminal Court.

Each of the key components of this model should be applicable in these other settings. Identity, while not always a factor in all conflicts or instances where governments engage in severe human rights repression, is often quite prominent. Whether involving race in South Africa, ethnicity in Rwanda, or religion in the Central African Republic, conflicts and violence rooted in identity are frequently the subject of transitional justice. We expect, then, that identity narratives play an important role in the manner in which individuals evaluate these transitional justice mechanisms. When international justice inserts itself into the middle of these conflicts, we expect that many individuals, not just witnesses, premise their assessments on the extent to which their narratives are affirmed or rejected by these institutions. We suggest that perceptions of fairness, too, exerts a powerful influence on individual evaluations, regardless of the nature of the conflict. As Tyler and Huo (Tyler 1990; Tyler and Huo 2002) and others have shown, the importance attached to fairness transcends personalities and national boundaries. Finally, we believe that the individual-level experiences that witnesses have undergone are universally important as well. All witnesses bring with them to these tribunals a fraught history of suffering and a subsequent period of coping with their loss, which cannot help but structure and influence their perceptions of these institutions responsible for sorting out who did what to whom in the course of this violence.

In the next three chapters, we derive a set of hypotheses from these three components and describe the findings we obtain from a series of primarily bivariate relationships between these variables and our dependent variables measuring the witnesses' evaluations of the justice brought by the ICTY. The principal focus of each chapter is the testing of these hypotheses in a multivariate model. The hypothesis testing culminates in chapter 5, where we combine the elements of our model and test all three components simultaneously. We believe that our IFE model will help build the foundation of a robust and comprehensive theory of justice, whose components are intended to be generalizable to other institutions of international justice and to shed important light on what it means to do justice for individuals who have experienced some of the greatest injustice.

THREE

Identity, Trial Outcomes, and International Justice

The types of conflicts over which international tribunals exercise jurisdiction are characterized by extreme levels of violence. When tens or hundreds of thousands of innocent people are killed, we know that this kind of violence must be driven be something much deeper and more powerful than differences over policy preferences. We have argued that the role of identity is critical in understanding not only why and how such death and destruction occur. It is also key to understanding people's perceptions of conflict and their reactions to judgments about responsibility. Identity in general and ethnicity in particular cannot account for all the causal streams that lead to war, but ethnic identity provides the foundation on which many of the violations of international law come before the international courts. Moreover, it is a powerful perceptual lens through which individuals make sense of complex and enormously consequential events. We contend that ethnic identity will exercise significant influence over how the witnesses evaluate the work of the International Criminal Tribunal for the Former Yugoslavia and that this theoretical lens can be utilized to understand opinions regarding other international courts.

We begin our analysis of the influence of identity on evaluations of the ICTY by looking at its simple and direct effects. Four ethnic groups were involved in the lion's share of the fighting in the Balkan wars: the Serbians, the Croatians, the Bosniaks, and the Kosovar Albanians. The Yugoslav government fought a brief war against Slovenia when it became the first republic to break away, and a later conflict in Macedonia led to one case at the ICTY, but, in general, the tribunal did not delve into those conflicts. Its caseload reflected the pattern of war atrocities where most such violations occurred in Bosnia, Croatia, and Kosovo. In the present analysis, we first measure ethnicity as a transnational identity concept (grouping all Serbians together and all Croatians together, regardless of their country of residence), and then we examine whether the ethnic groups have differences based on their state of residence. We also test several model specifications, to determine how best to capture the impact of ethnic identity on evaluations of international justice. In these analyses, ethnicity, which is measured as a series of dichotomous variables, functions as an overarching general concept through which the individual understands the work of the tribunal. In this sense, the individual's ethnic identity acts as a powerful filter that aids in the interpretation of complex events and unfamiliar institutions.

The second method by which we analyze the influence of ethnicity is through the prism of one critical component of the ICTY's work—the judgments and the sentences issued by the Trial Chambers. The ICTY's most essential mission is to provide retributive justice for violations of international law that occurred in the former Yugoslavia. Its trials and its punishments may not satisfy all victims and witnesses, but they are the principal and most visible means by which the tribunal signals to all of its stakeholders its ultimate legal and historical judgment of the events of the 1990s. Therefore, we suggest that the witnesses will be particularly concerned with the punishment meted out at the ICTY and that their evaluation of its work will be based partly on whether they believe ICTY sentences are sufficiently severe or lenient, depending on which type of witness they were (for the prosecution or for the defense). Hence, in our analysis, we look for an interaction between ethnicity and trial outcome that can help us understand witness evaluations of the ICTY, and we particularly examine whether support for the ICTY is contingent on the ethnic identity of the individual found guilty and sentenced. In this chapter, we detail the trial data we utilize to test these hypotheses, and we conduct a series of analyses to determine the impact of trial outcomes.

We begin this chapter by reviewing research on the role of ethnicity in opinions regarding international justice in general and as it pertains to the ICTY in particular. We offer a series of hypotheses on the direct impact of ethnicity on ICTY evaluations, introduce our four measures of ICTY evaluations, and review the basic bivariate relationships between ethnic identity and support for the ICTY. We then discuss the role played by trial outcomes in assessing one particular way in which ethnicity may influence witnesses' opinions of the ICTY. We discuss data on trial verdicts and sentencing and test the impact of these outcomes on witnesses' opinions, through a series of statistical tests. Later in this chapter, we utilize a multivariate modeling approach to help explain how ethnic identity influences witnesses' evaluations of the ICTY, as well as its role in shaping perceptions of sentences that further influence opinions of the ICTY.

Ethnic Identity and Evaluations of International Justice

Research from multiple fields (including psychology, sociology, and political science) document the power of identity—ethnicity, religion, nationality, and related concepts—in shaping individuals' perceptions of war and justice (Elcheroth 2006; Ford 2012; Staub 2006, 2013). Individuals perceive conflict, particularly when it involves divisions among identity groups, as a zero-sum game in which gains for the "other" necessarily entail a loss for one's own group. Divisions premised on identity are especially acute and salient when the issue concerns security. When the "other" is portrayed as an enemy from within that is seeking domination or as an external adversary with predatorial designs and territorial ambitions, individuals learn a conflict narrative—from the state and other powerful groups and conflict entrepreneurs—in which the actions of the other identity group are aggressive and criminal while one's own goals are defensive and appropriate. The ICTY not only must adjudicate the liability of individuals for specific crimes that have occurred during this fighting, but must act as the arbiter of a battle over historical facts and narratives. We expect that the ICTY will be judged not just by specific decisions but by the message and version of history it supports by virtue of the numbers from each ethnic group among the people it indicts, prosecutes, and sentences when found guilty.

The power of the ethnic lens has been especially prominent in research examining the opinions of the peoples of the former Yugoslavia regarding the ICTY (Ford 2012; Meernik 2015a; Orentlicher 2008). The findings, in almost all cases, are fairly similar across these studies. Bosnian Muslims, or Bosniaks, typically register the highest levels of support for the ICTY, while Serbians, particularly those from Bosnia-Herzegovina, tend to be least supportive. Croatians and Kosovar Albanians register varying levels of support, with the Albanians being more apt to support the work of the ICTY. Meernik (2015a) found that almost 90 percent of Bosniaks, 74 percent of Kosovar Albanians, and 60 percent of Croatians supported the ICTY and that approximately one-third of Serbians agreed or strongly agreed that they supported the tribunal. In a poll in Kosovo by the United Nations Development Program, approximately 69 percent of Kosovar Albanians agreed they were very or somewhat satisfied with the work of the ICTY in 2007, while that number jumped to 82 percent in 2012; only 35 percent of Serbians living in Kosovo were very or somewhat satisfied with the ICTY in 2007, and after 2012, when several Kosovar Albanian leaders on trial at the ICTY were acquitted and when a number of Serbians were convicted of crimes committed in Kosovo, only 2 percent of Serbians reported being satisfied with the tribunal.[1] In a study of public opinion among members of a victim's association in Bosnia-Herzegovina, Ivković and Hagan (2016b) also found that Bosnian Muslims were most likely to support the ICTY, followed by Bosnian Croatians and Bosnian Serbians.

The majority of those who have been indicted and convicted have been Serbians from Bosnia and Serbia proper, which has contributed to numerous Serbian allegations of bias and impropriety on the part of the ICTY. Serbians have accused the ICTY of overlooking crimes committed by Bosniaks, Croatianss, and Kosovar Albanians. In a study by the Organization for Security and Cooperation in Europe, 40 percent of Serbians believed that the ICTY was created to "put the blame for war sufferings on the Serbs," and 73 percent believed that the ICTY has different attitudes toward groups depending on their ethnicity (OSCE 2011, 16, 22). Bosniaks have not been unqualified cheerleaders for the ICTY; they, too, have criticized the tribunal for acquittals of key Serbian leaders, such as Momcilo Perisic and Vojislav Sesjl. As longtime observer and journalist Mirko Klarin has commented, support for the ICTY tends to be inversely related to the number of people from one's group who have been convicted in The Hague (Klarin 2009). In the present analysis, we focus on the role of ethnicity and, more specifically, the ethnic groups of the former Yugoslavia. We note however, that identity will likely play a critical role in shaping perceptions of international justice regardless of whether that identity is rooted in ethnicity, religion, nationality, or some other deeply felt trait. From this, we derive the following hypotheses from our theory and from prior research on ethnicity and international justice:

Hypothesis 1.1. Bosniaks will be more likely to express support of the ICTY in all aspects of its performance.

Hypothesis 1.2. Kosovar Albanians will be more likely to express support of the ICTY in all aspects of its performance.

Hypothesis 1.3. Serbians will be less likely to express support of the ICTY in all aspects of its performance.

Hypothesis 1.4. Croatians will be neither more nor less likely to express support of the ICTY in all aspects of its performance.

To investigate witness perceptions of international justice, we utilize their responses to four questions regarding their opinions of the ICTY's effectiveness, in four different areas described in chapter 2. Witnesses were asked if they "believe that *in general* the ICTY has done a good job" in: (1) ***establishing the truth*** about what happened in the former Yugoslavia; (2) ***determining*** who was responsible for the grave crimes committed in the former Yugoslavia; (3) ***punishing*** those responsible for the grave crimes committed in the former Yugoslavia; (4) ***preventing*** grave crimes from occurring again in the former Yugoslavia. We distinguish between those respondents who answered affirmatively with either "agreed" or "strongly agreed" (coded 1), and all others, including those who expressed no opinion (coded 0).

We begin by examining the support that the four principal ethnic groups—the Bosniaks, Croatians, Kosovar Albanians, and Serbians—have given to the ICTY in the areas of discovering the truth, determining responsibility, appropriately punishing the guilty, and contributing to deterrence. Subsequently, we analyze support in greater detail across nationality and ethnicity focusing in on the responses of those individuals who agreed or strongly agreed that the ICTY had generally done a good job in a particular mission.

In table 3.1, the differences among the four principal ethnic groups are quite stark across all four measures of the tribunal's impact. Bosniak witnesses are the most supportive group across all four categories, while the Serbian witnesses provide the lowest levels of approval regarding the

TABLE 3.1. Ethnicity and Support of ICTY Goals

Percentage Agreeing or Strongly Agreeing That the ICTY Has Generally Done a Good Job

ICTY Goals	Determine Truth	Establish Responsibility	Punish Those Responsible	Prevent Crimes from Occurring Again
Bosniaks	73	73	42	58
Croats	46	37	32	57
Serbs	15	13	16	43
Kosovar Albanians	72	52	39	43

ICTY's effectiveness in achieving its primary aims. The disparities in support are quite revealing. For example, on the question of whether the tribunal is doing a good job in determining responsibility for the crimes committed, 73 percent of Bosniaks agreed that it is, while only 13 percent of the Serbians indicated approval. Kosovar Albanian witnesses, whose ethnic brethren have largely been acquitted of any violations of international law, typically provide the second-highest levels of support. Croatian witnesses provide substantially lower levels of support than Bosniaks and Kosovar Albanians but somewhat higher levels than Serbians. Such findings largely corroborate what others have found (Ford 2012; Meernik 2015a; Orentlicher 2008), but there are also substantial differences of opinion depending on which goal respondents are asked to evaluate. Variation in support tends to be greatest on the "truth" and "responsibility" questions, while support is more consistently negative on the "punishment" question and more likely to be supportive on the "deterrence" question. The following words of a Croatian witness reveal both the impact of identity on ICTY evaluations and a longing for a better form of justice:

> The other thing that seems very important to me, what I see as the biggest mistake, shortcoming of the Tribunal is the fact that it advertised itself too much as a source of international law. And since the legal community accepted this very seriously, the major powers brought enormous pressure to bear on convictions, in my opinion the convictions of Gotovina and Markač and Perišić show this very clearly. Because it is absolutely clear that in future the question of the degree of permissible precision of artillery fire or whether somebody who aided the criminal but did not participate in the crimes should be responsible, for the crimes, is not important either for Croatia or for Serbia but for the US, Russia, China, Israel or somebody like that. And their pressure, I believe, influenced the Court, and not the "ours against theirs" thing that can be heard among Croatian and Serbian nationalists, because nobody took those nations seriously, in other words, there is a need for much more caution, which will hopefully be possible if the International Criminal Court—the International Permanent Criminal Court really starts to work because then there will be a practice and then things can be looked at in that framework.

We next break down support for the ICTY by ethnicity and nationality, to determine if Serbians and Croatians differ in their evaluations depend-

TABLE 3.2. Support for ICTY Performance in Establishing the Truth Percentages

Witnesses who believe that the ICTY has generally done a "good job in establishing the truth"

Response	Bosniak	Croat in BiH	Serb in BiH	Croat in Croatia	Serb in Serbia	Albanian in Kosovo	Other Ethnicities	No Response on Ethnicity
Strongly Agree / Agree	73	53	14	41	23	72	25	71
Strongly Disagree / Disagree	8	17	41	14	45	16	25	12
No Response / No Opinion	19	30	45	45	32	12	50	18

TABLE 3.3. Support for ICTY Performance in Determining Responsibility Percentages

Witnesses who believe that the ICTY has generally done a "good job in determining responsibility for grave crimes"

Response	Bosniak	Croat in BiH	Serb in BiH	Croat in Croatia	Serb in Serbia	Albanian in Kosovo	Other Ethnicities	No Response on Ethnicity
Strongly Agree / Agree	73	23	19	43	8	52	25	71
Strongly Disagree / Disagree	9	27	38	20	47	24	25	6
No Response / No Opinion	18	50	43	37	45	24	50	24

TABLE 3.4. Support for ICTY Performance in Allocating Punishment Percentages

Witnesses who believe that the ICTY has generally done a good job in "punishing those responsible for grave crimes"

Response	Bosniak	Croat in BiH	Serb in BiH	Croat in Croatia	Serb in Serbia	Albanian in Kosovo	Other Ethnicities	No Response on Ethnicity
Strongly Agree / Agree	42	27	24	33	13	40	50	35
Strongly Disagree / Disagree	26	33	41	31	49	32	25	29
No Response / No Opinion	32	40	36	35	38	28	25	35

TABLE 3.5. Support for ICTY Performance in Deterring Grave Crimes Percentages

Witnesses who believe that the ICTY has generally done a good job in "preventing grave crimes from happening again"

	Bosniak	Croat in BiH	Serb in BiH	Croat in Croatia	Serb in Serbia	Albanian in Kosovo	Other Ethnicities	No Response on Ethnicity
Strongly Agree / Agree	58	57	48	57	40	43	50	71
Strongly Disagree / Disagree	13	13	10	18	26	26	0	18
No Response / No Opinion	30	30	43	26	34	30	50	12

ing on where they reside in the former Yugoslavia. Several general observations are in order before we proceed to dissect how ethnicity and nationality influence evaluations of international justice. In tables 3.2 and 3.3, patterns of support for the ICTY in establishing the truth and determining responsibility are very similar, especially since these two goals are close to the heart of the essential business of war crimes tribunals. We expect that "truth" and "responsibility" as established by the ICTY will feature prominently in how these identity groups fundamentally perceive the work of the tribunal. Bosniaks and Kosovar Albanians still come out as the biggest supporters: well over 70 percent believe that the ICTY has generally done a good job in advancing the mission of telling the truth (table 3.2). Opinions do change on the measure of determining responsibility. While the Bosniaks provide almost the same level of support on this measure as they do on the truth variable, support from Kosovar Albanians drops from 72 percent on the truth variable to 52 percent on the responsibility variable (table 3.3). Serbians in Serbia and in Bosnia provide among the least support of any ethnic group. Only 22.6 percent of the former and 14.3 percent of the latter believe that the ICTY has done a good job in establishing the truth, while 7.6 percent of Serbians from Serbia and 19.1 percent of Bosnian Serbians agree or strongly agree that the ICTY has generally done well in establishing responsibility. Croatians in Croatia and in Bosnia are more supportive of the ICTY. On the truth measure, 53.3 percent of the Croatians living in Bosnia support the ICTY, while 41.2 percent of Croatians living in Croatia do. The numbers hold fairly steady for the latter group on the responsibility measure, as 43.1 percent express support, while only 23.3 percent of Croatians in Bosnia hold such views. Among those who did not indicate their ethnicity, there is significant support for the ICTY on both measures—70.6 percent in both cases. Among those from "other" groups (including Macedonians and Serbians from Croatia), their numbers are too small for meaningful analysis.

The data clearly demonstrate that no ethnic group is pleased with the punishments meted out by the ICTY (table 3.4). Bosniaks are most supportive of the ICTY's work (42.3 percent), 40 percent of Kosovo Albanians express approval, and the other ethnic groups generally cluster in a range of 23–35 percent. Serbians from Serbia are least supportive (though we do not comment on the four individuals from other ethnic groups), as only 13.2 percent believe that the ICTY has done a good job in determining punishment. In many ways, these findings are not a surprise. Punishment of the guilty is an emotionally charged issue. After having experienced so much violence and suffering and having made the difficult decision to share their experiences before an international audience, the witnesses are necessarily intensely concerned with what the tribunal does as a result of their testimony. The sentencing of the guilty is perhaps the most concrete manifestation of the outcomes of international justice and, as such, is fixated on by many observers looking to judge the judges. Many may believe that sentences handed out to their adversaries are too light and that those given to members of their group are too severe. Others may find it difficult to understand how individuals can plead guilty and be offered a lighter sentence in recognition of their confession. One witness explains,

> You know, it is painful for someone who has lost so much and who has gone through so many difficult experiences to arrive to a situation to barter with a criminal, to make all sorts of arrangements, deals, for some sort of punishments to be determined which are inappropriate and so on, I mean, that is painful.

Indeed, those who work for the ICTY have made many of the same charges (Harmon and Gaynor 2007). We tend to suspect that the punishment issue is a topic on which many witnesses and victims have an opinion that has been formed by a constellation of personal, political, and legal factors. We explore this issue in great depth in the next section of this chapter.

Our findings on witnesses' evaluations of the ICTY performance in helping to prevent such conflicts from occurring again—what we label as the "deterrence" mission—show that approval of the ICTY's work is strongest in this area (table 3.5). A majority of respondents agree or strongly agree that the ICTY has generally done a good job, with Bosniaks being the most likely to support the ICTY (58 percent). Serbians in Bosnia-Herzegovina and Serbia are the least supportive (47.6 and 39.6 percent, respectively), while Croatians in both Bosnia-Herzegovina and Croatia provide majority support on the deterrence goal, at roughly 57 percent each. Albanian support of the ICTY's ability to keep the peace is low (43 percent) in comparison to their support on the truth and responsibility measures. Given that the ICTY had been in existence for six years prior to the outbreak of major war in Kosovo in 1998–99, it is not too surprising that Kosovar Albanians are more critical of the ICTY's ability to advance deterrence.

In general, we find what we expected. Bosniaks and Kosovar Albanians provide the highest levels of support across the four measures, while Serbs, regardless of their country of residence, provide the least support. Croatians tend to fall somewhere in between. These findings provide us with a strong benchmark against which to test the impact of other factors on witnesses' evaluations of international justice. If the stark differences we see here continue to hold, we will wish to identify just how much of a unique contribution toward the overall explanatory power of the model can be made by the other factors. Our next step is to further explore the impact of identity on evaluations of international justice by looking to see if the various ethnic groups are influenced by trial outcomes as they pertain to their ethnic brethren and their ethnic adversaries.

Trial Outcomes and Approval

Earlier, we quoted a witness who argued that no matter what the ICTY might do to punish those the judges declare guilty, the punishment could in no way be commensurate with the victims' pain and suffering. One only has to read the judgments of the war crimes tribunals (to say nothing of the witness transcripts) to understand just how horrible the violence was and how true that witness's feeling is. Regardless of the truth of these sentiments on an existential level, we also know that individuals want retribution; they want the guilty to be punished severely. Regarding why ICTY punishments do not provide the kind of justice sought by the victims, one of the people surveyed, reasons,

> I've already said, they could have done much more about those mass graves. Also the sentences, they could have imposed more severe sentences, if not the death penalty, they should have imposed lon-

> ger prison terms. Albeit to the victims those sentences do not mean much, it is more important to find their loved ones who are missing than how severe the punishment is. To a mother there is no punishment that can bring satisfaction if she does not know where her son is, where her son's body is and that sort of thing. So this is where The Hague could have done much, much more. But again, I say, without the Tribunal, even as it is, it would have been much, much more difficult for Bosnia and Herzegovina.

As we demonstrated above, individuals often perceive the ICTY's justice through an ethnic identity filter. They tend to attribute responsibility for the crimes of the Balkan wars to their ethnic adversaries and to downplay, if not absolve, any wrongdoing by their side. If the witnesses in our sample perceive the tribunal in this fashion, we expect that they would like to see their ethnic adversaries sentenced severely and their ethnic brethren either declared innocent or, at least, punished lightly if found guilty. If this assumption is correct, we expect that their evaluations of the ICTY's work will be influenced by the extent to which the tribunal has meted out the kind of punishment they expect.

This interaction between ethnic identity and trial outcome is a variant of what might be termed "distributive justice" at the domestic level. As Tyler and Huo (2003) show in their analyses of people's views of their local criminal justice systems, individuals are not as likely to link their evaluations of criminal justice authorities, such as the police and judges, to the outcome of their case. Rather, in their opinions of the criminal justice system, individuals accord greater weight to the manner in which they were treated, especially the fairness of their treatment (a subject we explore in chapter 4). Scholars have long found evidence that individuals are concerned more about the fairness of a criminal justice system on the domestic level than about the outcomes these systems produce (Benesh 2006; J. Jackson et al. 2012; Kelly 1984; Tyler 1990; Tyler and Huo 2002; see Tyler and Jackson 2003 for an extensive list of studies that reach similar conclusions), although others find that perceptions of the fairness of courts make little or no difference in public support of courts and their legitimacy (Gibson 1989; Gibson and Caldeira 1995). Tyler (2003, 294) finds that "44 percent of the variance in people's willingness to accept decisions is uniquely shaped by procedural justice and motive-based trust, while only 1 percent of the variance is uniquely shaped by outcome judgments." Others find that outcomes do matter (Bartels and Johnston 2013) and this may be especially true regarding support for the ICTY (Stover 2005). This effect, however, may be contingent on the type of case, which element of the criminal justice system is evaluated (Wood and Tilley 2015), the passage of time, and controversy over particular outcomes (Ura 2014). It may also be that outcomes, in tandem with fairness, are what matter as others have found (Moorhead, Sefton, and Scanlan 2007, 89; see especially Ivković and Hagan 2011).

We begin our exploration of the impact of outcome, as interacted with ethnic identity, by examining the data on trial outcomes. Based on the verdicts and punishment delivered in the many ICTY cases in trials involving the four principal ethnic groups (Bosniaks, Serbians, Croatians and Kosovar, Albanians), is there reason to assume that some groups, especially the Bosniaks and Albanians, will be more inclined to support the work of the ICTY? To address this question, we utilize data from a long-running project on the trial outcomes of the international tribunals (Meernik 2011: the reader is encouraged to consult this source for an extensive description of these data). We examine the number of accused (table 3.6), the verdicts (table 3.7), the sentences at trial (table 3.8), and the sentences on appeal (table 3.9) for individuals from each of these four ethnic groups.

There has been no doubt that the ICTY's indictments and prosecutions have focused on Serbians and Bosnian Serbians; the evidence that has emerged from the Balkan wars has demonstrated that their forces committed the majority of the crimes as well as some of the most heinous offenses, including the genocide at Srebrenica (Research and Documentation Center [Sarajevo] 2008; Scheffer 2012). We see this reflected in the data in all four tables. As we see in table 3.6, Serbians comprise a significant majority of the individuals whose cases were brought to conclusion at trial (excluding both cases where the individual died before the trial was completed and cases that were referred to local courts). Approximately 63 percent of the individuals who went to trial were Serbian, while roughly 22 percent were Croatian, 8 percent were Bosniak, 5 percent were Kosovar Albanians, and two individuals were from Macedonia. Roughly 92 percent of Serbians and Croatians were convicted, as we see in table 3.7, while smaller percentages among the other ethnic groups were found guilty. This suggests that Serbian criticisms of the ICTY may have some basis in fact. Before reaching such conclusions however, it is useful to compare ICTY convictions with those from US domestic courts. According to the federal government's statistics for fiscal year 2013, "96.9 percent of all convicted defendants pleaded guilty."[2] Using the most recent data available for fiscal year 2013 and looking only at federal criminal cases that go to trial, we find that defendants are acquitted at trial 13.8 percent of the time. The

TABLE 3.6. Ethnicity of Those Charged by the ICTY

Ethnicity of Defendant	Frequency	Percentage
Serb	69	63
Croat	24	22
Bosniak	9	8
Kosovar Albanian	6	5
Macedonian	2	2

TABLE 3.7. Ethnicity and ICTY Trial Outcomes

Verdict	Serb	Croat	Bosniak	Kosovar Albanian	Macedonian	Total
Number Acquitted	5	2	2	5	1	15
Percentage of Acquittals	33.3	13.3	13.3	33.3	6.6	100
Percentage Acquitted (by Ethnicity)	7.3	8.3	22.2	83.3	50	13.6
Guilty	65	22	7	1	1	95
Percentage of Guilty	67.7	23.16	7.37	1.05	1.05	100
Percentage Guilty (by Ethnicity)	92.8	91.7	77.8	16.7	50	86.4
Total Defendants	70	24	9	6	2	110

TABLE 3.8. Ethnicity and Sentence Length at Trial

Ethnicity of Defendant	Mean Sentence	Standard Deviation
Serb	253.5	166
Croat	209.7	106.7
Bosniak	93.4	84

TABLE 3.9. Ethnicity and Sentence Length after Appeal

Ethnicity of Defendant	Mean Sentence	Standard Deviation
Serb	260.7	157.6
Croat	146.3	105.4
Bosniak	95	88.2

ICTY is not too far off the mark in its conviction rates and is actually more likely to acquit when we consider that both guilty convictions and pleas are included in that 92 percent guilty outcome rate. At the same time, though, we see that Bosniaks are found or plead guilty 78 percent of the time, while the trials involving Kosovar Albanians mostly result in acquittals. However, there have been legitimate allegations of witness tampering in the Kosovar Albanian trials (Borger 2016).

When we examine the sentences (measured in months),[3] we find distinct differences among the punishments received by individuals from the various ethnic groups (tables 3.8 and 3.9). Serbians receive sentences of 253 months on average; Croatians are generally given somewhat lighter sentences of 209 months on average. There is a substantial decrease in sentence length for Bosniaks (93 months on average) (there were too few sentences for Kosovar Albanians and Macedonians to calculate averages). The average sentences that defendants receive on appeal are fairly similar. Serbian sentences, despite being adjusted in several cases (e.g., the case of Momcilo Perisic, a prominent Serbian leader who was acquitted on appeal), remain fairly stable. They still average approximately 260 months. There are few changes in the sentences given to Bosniaks on appeal. Turning to Croatians, we see a substantial decline in the average sentences from the ICTY Appeals Chamber. The average drops from 209 months to 146 months. In fact, in cases involving such Croatian military leaders as Tihomir Blaskic and Ante Gotovina, the ICTY has substantially or entirely, reduced the sentences handed down by the Trial Chamber.

At first glance, this may appear to suggest disparate treatment of the Serbians especially and perhaps, to a lesser extent, the Croatians. Research has generally shown, however, that other factors—such as the gravity of the crime, the number of guilty counts, and the level of power exercised by the accused—dominate models of judicial sentencing (Holá, Bijleveld, and Smeulers 2011, 2012; Holá, Smeulers, and Bijleveld 2009, 2011; King and Greening 2007; King and Meernik 2011; Meernik 2003, 2011; Meernik and King 2003; Meernik, King, and Dancy 2005). Nonetheless, the disparate sentences have led ethno-nationalists to charge bias and have caused other critics to complain of inconsistency (Drumbl 2007; Harmon and Gaynor, 2007; Henham 2003, 2007a; Olusanya 2005). As we analyze witness evaluations of the ICTY, we do not adjust our view of witnesses cognitive processes to account for the findings of social science research, but continue to assume (until our hypotheses are disconfirmed) that witnesses are more likely to hold to their dominant cultural-historical narratives about who did what to whom.

Describing these typical trial outcomes has been fairly simple and straightforward, but how do we link witness evaluations to trial outcomes? As we have argued and as research has shown, individuals from the former Yugoslavia tend to evaluate the ICTY on the basis of both the severity of the sentences meted out to their ethnic adversaries and the leniency granted to their own defendants. The critical issues we must address when attempting to explore the link between outcomes and opinions are which sentence(s) the witnesses are most likely to recall and which they are most likely to consider important in their evaluations. The good news is that we have several options for operationalizing variables to measure what the witnesses might consider to be important and what might then influence their evaluations. The (slightly) bad news is that not one of these options is perfect—each has its strong and weak points.

The most vexing issue we must address is the simple fact that unlike many domestic criminal trials in which a single individual is put on trial for a criminal offense and in which the (living) victims expect a certain verdict and sentence, there are a multiplicity of defendants and trials at the ICTY. A single witness might testify in a trial with three to seven defendants or may testify in multiple trials with multiple defendants. There are three hundred witnesses in our sample, but only seventy-eight testified in just one trial with one defendant. Given that most witnesses testified in trials involving more than one defendant and/or testified in multiple trials, the critical question we must answer is, what are these witnesses (or any interested observer) looking at regarding the ICTY sentences when they evaluate the work of the tribunal? Is the most salient outcome the verdict in the first trial in which a witness testifies? Do first impressions matter the most, or do more recent experiences at the ICTY exercise more impact? Does a witness focus on the average of all sentences handed down in the last trial in which the witness took part? Do witnesses construct some type of opinion in the aggregate about the propriety of the sentences defendants have received in the various trials in which they testified? Perhaps the most salient outcome is the sentence handed down to a particular individual who has come to represent, in the witnesses' mind, the key figure they hold most liable or toward whom they have the greatest animus. Perhaps the most important sentence is the one handed down in a particularly meaningful case for a witness personally.

We focus on several measures of trial outcomes that we believe are likely to resonate with witnesses, while we are cognizant that these are educated conjectures and may not represent what is truly important to any particular person. We examine (1) the total number of acquittals in trials of first instance (i.e., the original trial, not the appellate outcome), (2a) the average sentence handed down to each defendant (or defendants) in the first trial and (2b) the average sentence in the last trial in which a witness testified, and (3a) the average sentence handed down to each defendant by the ICTY Appeals Chamber from the first trial and (3b) the average appellate sentence from the last trial in which a witness testified. We drill down further in the data to control for whether the witness testified on behalf of the prosecution or the defense, as well as for the ethnicity of the witness. We expect that prosecution witnesses would generally prefer that defendants whom they are testifying against receive more severe sentences. These fact witnesses are generally called to testify about an event that they witnessed or personally experienced. Thus, we assume that most of these individuals will want to see the perpetrators locked up and sent away for a long time. While there may be some individuals who testify for the prosecution unwillingly and are favorably disposed toward the defendant, we would have no way of ascertaining witness preferences. We include analyses in which we restrict the population to prosecution and defense witnesses for each of the ethnic groups, to ascertain whether they exhibit any particular proclivity to express support or disapproval of the ICTY's performance.

We chose these measures with careful consideration. We decided to examine the acquittals because these verdicts are so prominent and often generate outrage on one side of an ethnic divide (e.g., the acquittal of hardline Serbian nationalist, Vojislav Seselj) and cause for celebration on the other (e.g., the Croatian general Ante Gotovina received a hero's welcome in Croatia after he was essentially acquitted on appeal). We would expect the prominence of such decisions to figure substantially in the witnesses' awareness and evaluation of the ICTY. We believe that the first sentence handed down at a trial and the revised (if any) average sentence that the Appeals Chamber delivers for that trial will be salient to the witnesses for a couple reasons. First, for many witnesses (n = 195), this is the only trial in which they testified. Second, there is some truth to the old adage that first impressions matter. Hence, even for those individuals who go on to testify in other trials, their first experience at the ICTY may be the most meaningful and memorable. We also look at the average of sentences in the last trial in which the individual testified and the average sentence in that trial after appeals. We include this measure because the last trial will be the most recent for each individual and, thus, should be particularly prominent in the witnesses' views of the tribunal. We considered using the average sentence across all trials in which the individual testified, but we decided that such a measure would not be useful. Aggregating across so many trials and defendants would entail combining too many trials and too much diversity into one measure. For example, an individual might testify in one trial involving mid-ranking officials who might receive "moderate" sentences, and the same individual might also testify in a trial of major political leaders who might receive a severe sentence. Combining all averages could potentially dilute the impact of any one trial. We are also not convinced that individuals process information by considering all outcomes rather than just those that are salient. We offer the following hypotheses:

Hypothesis 1.5. The greater the number of acquittals in trials in which a witness testified on behalf of the prosecution is, the less likely the individual is to support the ICTY.

Hypothesis 1.6. The greater the number of acquittals in trials in which a witness testified on behalf of the defense is, the more likely the individual is to support the ICTY.

Hypothesis 1.7. The greater the average sentence length is in the first trial (the original trial and the appeal) in which a witness testified on behalf of the prosecution, the more likely the individual is to support the ICTY.

Hypothesis 1.8. The greater the average sentence length is in the first trial (the original trial and the appeal) in which a witness testified on behalf of the defense, the less likely the individual is to support the ICTY.

TABLE 3.10. Correlation Matrix of Trial Outcomes and Witness Support of the ICTY Truth Mission

Has the ICTY done a good job in establishing the truth?	All Acquittals for Witnesses	Average Sentence in First Trial	Average Sentence in Last Trial	Average Sentence on Appeal from First Trial	Average Sentence on Appeal from Last Trial
All OTP Witnesses	−0.035	.155*	0.186*	0.231*	0.272*
All Defense Witnesses	0.04	−0.127	−.222*	−0.362*	−0.323*
All Bosniak OTP Witnesses	−0.162	0.038	0.017	−0.148	−0.134
All Serb OTP Witnesses	−0.066	−0.092	0.178	0.089	0.315
All Croat OTP Witnesses	0.046	0.21	0.215	0.312*	0.331*
All Kosovar Albanian OTP Witnesses	0.186	−0.163	0.09	0.287	0.452
All Bosniak Defense Witnesses	0.166	0.188	0.111	0.136	0.101
All Serb Defense Witnesses	0.052	−0.174	0.191	−0.139	−0.114
All Croat Defense Witnesses	0.025	0.138	0.199	−0.027	0.101
All Kosovar Albanian Defense Witnesses	n/a	n/a	n/a	n/a	n/a

Hypothesis 1.9. The greater the average sentence length is in the last trial (the original trial and the appeal) in which a witness testified on behalf of the prosecution, the more likely the individual is to support the ICTY.

Hypothesis 1.10. The greater the average sentence length is in the last trial (the original trial and the appeal) in which a witness testified on behalf of the defense, the less likely the individual is to support the ICTY.

TABLE 3.11. Correlation Matrix of Trial Outcomes and Witness Support of the ICTY Mission to Determine Responsibility

Has the ICTY done a good job in determining who was responsible?	All Acquittals for Witnesses	Average Sentence in First Trial	Average Sentence in Last Trial	Average Sentence on Appeal from First Trial	Average Sentence on Appeal from Last Trial
All OTP Witnesses	−0.085	.174*	0.207*	0.265	0.293*
All Defense Witnesses	−0.041	−0.107	−0.262*	−0.359*	−0.353*
All Bosniak OTP Witnesses	0.041	−0.037	−0.052	−0.074	−0.103
All Serb OTP Witnesses	−0.191	0.32	0.376*	0.16	0.354
All Croat OTP Witnesses	0.008	0.145	0.215	0.277	0.334*
All Kosovar Albanian OTP Witnesses	0.206	−0.225	−0.096	0.209	0.279
All Bosniak Defense Witnesses	0.166	0.188	0.111	0.136	0.101
All Serb Defense Witnesses	−0.156	0.166	−0.156	−0.168	−0.208
All Croat Defense Witnesses	0.218	−0.017	0.161	−0.252	−0.097
All Kosovar Albanian Defense Witnesses	n/a	n/a	n/a	n/a	n/a

TABLE 3.12. Correlation Matrix of Trial Outcomes and Witness Support of the ICTY Punishment Mission

Has the ICTY done a good job in punishing those responsible?	All Acquittals for Witnesses	Average Sentence in First Trial	Average Sentence in Last Trial	Average Sentence on Appeal from First Trial	Average Sentence on Appeal from Last Trial
All OTP Witnesses	−0.033	0.052	0.004	0.211*	0.224*
All Defense Witnesses	0.004	0.005	−0.053	−0.161	−0.134
All Bosniak OTP Witnesses	0.075	0.031	−0.098	0.06	0.035
All Serb OTP Witnesses	−0.282	0.118	0.324	0.151	0.354
All Croat OTP Witnesses	−0.15	0.216	0.225	0.356	0.360*
All Kosovar Albanian OTP Witnesses	0.249	−0.336	−0.215	0.135	0.213
All Bosniak Defense Witnesses	.218	0.304	0.255	0.178	0.222
All Serb Defense Witnesses	−0.146	0.054	0.035	−0.035	0.02
All Croat Defense Witnesses	0.144	0.043	−0.005	−0.181	−0.15
All Kosovar Albanian Defense Witnesses	n/a	n/a	n/a	n/a	n/a

In Tables 3.10–3.13, we provide the correlation coefficients between the multiple measures of trial outcomes described above and our four measures of ICTY support—whether the ICTY generally did a good job in providing the truth, determining responsibility, allocating punishment, and helping to deter future violence (we refer to these as the "truth measure," the "responsibility measure," the "punishment measure," and the "deterrence measure"). Those correlation coefficients that reached statistical significance are noted with an asterisk. The findings are fairly consistent across all four measures of ICTY support. The total number of acquittals in all trials in which an individual testified is never statistically significant. We combined all acquittals into this measure, given that they are relatively infrequent outcomes, but we also examined whether the number of acquittals in the first trial in which an individual testified and the last trial in which they appeared would influence support for the ICTY. We still found no statistically significant relationships (results not shown). We also analyzed whether the even rarer acquittals on appeal might influence opinions of the ICTY, but there were too few such cases to conduct realistic analyses. As we will note throughout, one of our concerns in tracking relationships between outcomes and evaluations is that we may not be capturing what are the most salient outcomes for the individual. We assume, in this case, that acquittals in trials in which they testified would be most meaningful, but it may be that an acquittal in a high-profile case (e.g., that of Seselj or Gotovina) might be more prominent in their decision-making.

TABLE 3.13. Correlation Matrix of Trial Outcomes and Witness Support of the ICTY Deterrence Mission

Has the ICTY done a good job in preventing grave crimes from occurring again?	All Acquittals for Witnesses	Average Sentence in First Trial	Average Sentence in Last Trial	Average Sentence on Appeal from First Trial	Average Sentence on Appeal from Last Trial
All OTP Witnesses	–0.063	0.148*	–0.003	0.062	–0.006
All Defense Witnesses	–0.14	0.014	–0.028	–0.026	–0.073
All Bosniak OTP Witnesses	0.103	0.096	–0.13	–0.235	–0.35
All Serb OTP Witnesses	–0.167	0.162	0.303	0.118	0.099
All Croat OTP Witnesses	0.095	0.068	–0.109	0.018	–0.012
All Kosovar Albanian OTP Witnesses	–0.232	–0.032	0.126	0.157	0.273
All Bosniak Defense Witnesses	0.408	0.085	0.409	0.086	0.219
All Serb Defense Witnesses	–0.225	–0.004	–0.016	0.169	0.081
All Croat Defense Witnesses	0	–0.016	–0.15	–0.031	–0.076
All Kosovar Albanian Defense Witnesses	n/a	n/a	n/a	n/a	n/a

The impact of the average sentences handed down in the first and the last trials in which the witness testified is more consequential. These statistically significant relationships, however, only occur when we look at the group of all witnesses for the prosecution. When we consider the average sentence handed down for those defendants found guilty in the first trial in which an individual testified and for the last trial in which they testified, there are positive relationships with the truth measure (table 3.10), the responsibility measure (table 3.11), and the deterrence measure (table 3.13) (although not significant in the case of the average sentence in the last trial) for all witnesses for the Office of Prosecution (OTP). The greater the average length of the sentence is in the first and last trials, the more likely the witness is to express approval of the ICTY performance regarding these three missions. It is ironic that the only area in which the average trial sentence is not related to ICTY performance is punishment—the most germane of the four areas. Even if prosecution witnesses are more apt to associate longer sentences with support for the ICTY in its more general goals of providing justice and deterring violence, they are still displeased with its sentencing patterns in general, as we saw earlier.

Looking at defense witnesses, there is a consistently, negative relationship between sentence length and satisfaction with the ICTY, as we had hypothesized. Those individuals who testify on behalf of the defendants might typically prefer that their punishment, if any, be light (again, this is an inference). We only find, however statistically significant relationships in the case of support for the ICTY's truth and responsibility missions, and mostly when we consider the average sentence handed down in the last trial in which the individual testified.

These relationships between sentences at trial and the measures of ICTY support hold primarily for the prosecution witnesses and to a lesser extent for the defense witnesses. The correlation coefficients for the ICTY support measures and sentence length at trial are not statistically significant for any of the ethnic groups. The only exception to this finding concerns Serbian witnesses for the prosecution, who are more inclined to indicate approval of the ICTY for the responsibility measure. Perhaps the number of observations, which can be quite small in number (as in the case of Kosovar Albanian defense witnesses), is insufficient for establishing relationships. It is also possible that what unites most prosecution witnesses and defense witnesses, regardless of ethnicity, is the desire to see the defendants punished severely or lightly, respectively.

Looking deeper, whether an individual testifies for the prosecution or the defense depends heavily on ethnicity. For example, 91 percent of the

Bosniaks in our sample and 87 percent of the Kosovar Albanian witnesses testified for the OTP (results not shown); only 13 percent of each group testified for the defense. Conversely, 37 percent of the Serbian witnesses appeared on behalf of the OTP, while two-thirds testified for the defense. As we might expect, Croatians fall between the two extremes and are split fairly evenly between the two sides (there are also thirteen witnesses who testified for both the OTP and the defense). Therefore, it is important to always bear in mind that ethnic identity plays a key role in determining on whose behalf a witness testifies.

The findings regarding the effect of the average sentences for the first and last trials in which the witnesses appeared are largely replicated when we examine the average sentences handed down after the final appeals. In fact, a majority of sentences are not changed on appeal,[4] so we would not expect too much variation in results between the Trial Chamber variables and those measuring the sentences of the appellate chamber. There are positive relationships between Appeals Chamber sentences regarding the first and last trials in which a witness appeared for the prosecution, when we examine the results for the truth measure (table 3.10); for the responsibility measure (table 3.11), although this correlation coefficient for the appellate sentence in the first trial just misses statistical significance; and even for the punishment measure (table 3.12). For witnesses who testified on behalf of the defense, there are also negative correlation coefficients between the sentences handed down on appeal and the truth measure (table 3.10) and the responsibility measure of ICTY success (table 3.11). Lastly, there is one exception to the general finding that there are no statistically significant relationships between sentence length and ICTY support when we interact ethnicity with witness type (prosecution or defense). When sentences are longer, Croatian prosecution witnesses are more likely to approve of the ICTY efforts to provide truth and determine responsibility. As we remarked earlier, several Croatian defendants were released on appeal, while many of the Serb defendants accused of crimes against Croatians were convicted.

The purpose of this exercise has been largely exploratory. We sought to determine if there was any prima facie evidence of a relationship between the verdicts and punishments delivered by the ICTY and witnesses' evaluations of the ICTY's success in realizing its most basic mandate goals. Our hypotheses have been partially confirmed, as we saw there was evidence that on two of the variables by which we measured witnesses' opinions of the work of the tribunal, longer sentences were associated with increased approval for the ICTY from the witnesses who testified for the prosecution and with decreased approval among the defense witnesses. Such findings only partially corroborate the work of many scholars who have argued that individuals are concerned more about the treatment they receive from a criminal justice system than about the outcomes (Benesh 2006; J. Jackson et al. 2012; Kelly 1984; Tyler 1990; Tyler and Huo 2002). When viewed in this simple and direct manner, outcomes do matter to some individuals. Yet these simple, bivariate correlations represent the beginning of our analysis of the impact of identity and its interaction with sentences, rather than the conclusion.

Building a More Sophisticated Model of Evaluations of International Justice

We here begin the development of our statistical model of the witnesses' opinions regarding the work of the Yugoslav Tribunal. The first step in this process is to properly model the impact of ethnic identity on evaluations. We have argued that identity constitutes a lens—perhaps the most important lens—through which individuals in the former Yugoslavia as well as many other conflict zones perceive and judge the violence of conflict and the postwar political environment, including the efforts of international criminal justice. Powerful narratives that speak to the history of a group, inspire sociocultural practices, and guide the policies of political and military leaders shape the perceptions of individuals as well.

We estimated a series of prohibit models to assess the impact of sentencing on the evaluations of prosecution witnesses and defense witnesses. Because we found that, for the most part, the impact of trial and appellate sentencing (whether measured at the occasion of the first trial/appeal or the last trial/appeal) were fairly similar across the various measures of ICTY approval, we have chosen to focus on the impact of the sentence at appeal for the last trial in which the individual testified. This will also be the most recent input witnesses will have into their evaluations of the four types of measures. For most individuals, there is no difference between the first and last trial, as they testified only once. We also include dichotomous variables for each of the four principal ethnic groups—Bosniaks, Serbs, Croats, and Albanians. The reference category includes those with other ethnic backgrounds and those who chose not to specify an ethnic identity on the survey.

In this model, we include a control for the type of trial in which the witness testified, to distinguish among trials that focus on high-ranking defendants, low-ranking defendants, and individuals who fall somewhere in between. Every defendant's level of responsibility was first measured on a three-value scale of power. Low-level war criminals, principally ordinary soldiers and prison camp guards, are coded 1; midlevel officials, such as prison camp commanders, military officers below the rank of colonel, and political figures below cabinet-level status, are coded 2; and high-level officials, including military officials at or above the rank of colonel and political officials of cabinet-level status or higher, are coded 3 (Meernik 2011). While most trials feature individuals of comparable rank, not all do. So our analyses use a measure of the percentage of high-level officials who were defendants in the trials in which individuals testified. We use this measure as a control for the types of sentences that individuals are likely to receive, as research has consistently shown that more powerful individuals are given more severe punishment (Holá, Smeulers, and Bijleveld 2009; King and Meernik 2011; Meernik 2011). We provide the models for prosecution witness evaluations in tables 3.14–3.17 and the analogous estimates for defense witnesses in tables 3.18–3.21.

TABLE 3.14. Support for the ICTY Truth Mission for OTP Witnesses

	Coefficient	Standard Error	*Z* Score	*P* Value	Marginal Impact
Last Trial Sentence on Appeal	0.001	0.001	1.730	0.083*	0.000
Percentage Big Fish	–0.364	0.305	–1.200	0.232	–0.142
Bosniaks	–0.164	0.360	–0.460	0.649	–0.064
Serbs	–1.380	0.430	–3.210	0.001***	–0.494
Croats	–0.654	0.379	–1.730	0.084*	–0.256
Albanians	0.033	0.475	0.070	0.945	0.013
Constant	0.674	0.408	1.650	0.098	

Note: $N = 169$.
* $p < ..1$, ** $p < .05$ one-tailed test *** $p < .01$.

TABLE 3.15. Support for the ICTY Responsibility Mission for OTP Witnesses

	Coefficient	Standard Error	*Z* Score	*P* Value	Marginal Impact
Last Trial Sentence on Appeal	0.001	0.001	1.860	0.062*	0.000
Percentage Big Fish	–0.098	0.299	–0.330	0.744	–0.039
Bosniaks	0.064	0.345	0.180	0.854	0.025
Serbs	–0.919	0.413	–2.230	0.026**	–0.344
Croats	–0.564	0.369	–1.530	0.127	–0.222
Albanians	–0.087	0.453	–0.190	0.848	–0.035
Constant	0.144	0.397	0.360	0.717	

Note: $N = 169$.
* $p < ..1$, ** $p < .05$ one-tailed test *** $p < .01$.

TABLE 3.16. Support for the ICTY Punishment Mission for OTP Witnesses

	Coefficient	Standard Error	*Z* Score	*P* Value	Marginal Impact
Last Trial Sentence on Appeal	0.001	0.001	2.350	0.019***	0.001
Percentage Big Fish	–0.343	0.292	–1.180	0.240	–0.128
Bosniaks	–0.154	0.335	–0.460	0.646	–0.057
Serbs	–0.663	0.428	–1.550	0.122	–0.218
Croats	–0.032	0.368	–0.090	0.930	–0.012
Albanians	–0.041	0.454	–0.090	0.929	–0.015
Constant	–0.270	0.391	–0.690	0.490	

Note: $N = 169$. *
* $p < ..1$, ** $p < .05$ one-tailed test *** $p < .01$.

TABLE 3.17. Support for the ICTY Deterrence Mission for OTP Witnesses

	Coefficient	Standard Error	*Z* Score	*P* Value	Marginal Impact
Last Trial Sentence on Appeal	0.000	0.001	–0.640	0.521	0.000
Percentage Big Fish	–0.358	0.286	–1.250	0.211	–0.141
Bosniaks	–0.274	0.340	–0.810	0.419	–0.108
Serbs	–0.594	0.396	–1.500	0.134	–0.233
Croats	–0.492	0.366	–1.350	0.179	–0.194
Albanians	–0.689	0.451	–1.530	0.126	–0.268
Constant	0.922	0.389	2.370	0.018	

Note: $N = 169$.

TABLE 3.18. Support for the ICTY Truth Mission for Defense Witnesses

	Coefficient	Standard Error	*Z* Score	*P* Value	Marginal Impact
Last Trial Sentence on Appeal	–0.002	0.002	–1.300	0.195	–0.001
Percentage Big Fish	–0.677	0.454	–1.490	0.136	–0.180
Bosniaks	0.104	0.781	.130	0.894	0.153
Serbs	–2.524	0.607	–4.150	0.000***	–0.657
Croats	–0.995	0.549	–1.810	0.070*	–0.220
Constant	1.780	0.770	2.310	0.021	

Note: $N = 113$.
* $p < ..1$, ** $p < .05$ one-tailed test *** $p < .01$.

TABLE 3.19. Support for the ICTY Responsibility Mission for Defense Witnesses

	Coefficient	Standard Error	Z Score	P Value	Marginal Impact
Last Trial Sentence on Appeal	–0.003	0.002	–1.830	0.068*	–0.001
Percentage Big Fish	–0.281	0.457	–0.610	0.539	–0.068
Bosniaks	1.740	0.687	2.530	0.011***	0.597
Serbs	–0.798	0.526	–1.520	0.129	–0.193
Croats	0.173	0.467	0.370	0.712	0.043
Constant	–0.077	0.606	–0.130	0.899	

Note: $N = 113$.
* $p < ..1$, ** $p < .05$ one-tailed test *** $p < .01$.

TABLE 3.20. Support for the ICTY Punishment Mission for Defense Witnesses

	Coefficient	Standard Error	Z Score	P Value	Marginal Impact
Last Trial Sentence on Appeal	–0.001	0.001	–0.550	0.582	0.000
Percentage Big Fish	–0.258	0.367	–0.700	0.482	–0.068
Bosniaks	–0.212	0.578	–0.370	0.714	–0.051
Serbs	–0.822	0.466	–1.760	0.078*	–0.215
Croats	–0.210	0.439	–0.480	0.632	–0.053
Constant	–0.134	0.513	–0.260	0.795	

Note: $N = 113$.
* $p < ..1$, ** $p < .05$ one-tailed test *** $p < .01$.

TABLE 3.21. Support for the ICTY Deterrence Mission for Defense Witnesses

	Coefficient	Standard Error	Z Score	P Value	Marginal Impact
Last Trial Sentence on Appeal	0.000	0.001	0.300	0.767	0.000
Percentage Big Fish	0.020	0.303	0.070	0.947	0.008
Bosniaks	–0.147	0.560	–0.260	0.793	–0.058
Serbs	–0.756	0.427	–1.770	0.077*	–0.294
Croats	–0.131	0.434	–0.300	0.762	–0.052
Constant	0.372	0.463	0.800	0.423	

Note: $N = 113$
* $p < ..1$, ** $p < .05$ one-tailed test *** $p < .01$.

Across each of the models for prosecution witnesses, the impact of ethnicity is fairly consistent but unimpressive, as very few of the coefficients for the ethnic variables are statistically significant. Only in tables 3.14 (truth measure) and 3.15 (responsibility measure) is there evidence of the impact of identity on evaluations: Serbians are more likely to disapprove of the ICTY's efforts in these two areas. The coefficients for the Serbian variables are statistically insignificant in tables 3.16 (punishment) and 3.17 (deterrence). The coefficients for the Bosniak, Croatian, and Albanian variables are statistically insignificant in all four of these models for prosecution witnesses.

The coefficients for the variables measuring the average sentence after appeal for the guilty individuals in the last trial in which a witness testified are statistically significant in each of the first three models, while the coefficient is statistically insignificant in the model of support for the ICTY's efforts at preventing wars from breaking out again in the former Yugoslavia (the deterrence measure, in table 3.17). The greater the sentence is, the more likely prosecution witnesses are to support the ICTY. But the size of these impacts is not especially substantial. Among the first three models, in which sentence length is a statistically significant variable, the marginal impact coefficients are generally around 0.0004–0.0005. Thus, if the mean sentence for defendants in a trial were to increase by ten years (120 months), the probability of support would only increase approximately 5 percent. The impact of outcomes on evaluations of justice exercises only a minor or modest effect here, as has been found in other research (Tyler 1990; Tyler and Huo 2002). The effect of the statistically significant marginal impact coefficients for the ethnicity variables are greater. For example, Serbian witnesses are approximately 49 percent less likely to approve of the ICTY's performance in establishing the truth (table 3.14). However, both because these models are not fully developed yet (the final and complete models are tested in chapter 5) and given the rather narrow population we are analyzing (prosecution witnesses at the ICTY), we do not here speculate or extrapolate further on these results.

Estimating the same set of models for defense witnesses yields somewhat different results. The coefficient for the Serbian variable is statistically significant and negative in three of the four models—those involving the truth (3.18), punishment (3.20), and deterrence measures (3.21), although the coefficient is statistically significant at the 0.1 level when using a two-tailed test in the latter two models (punishment and deterrence). As a group, Serbians are distinctly unlikely to approve of the ICTY's work, despite the different measures we use and regardless of whether they are witnesses for the prosecution or the defense. One witness in the survey argued about the perceived bias of the ICTY,

> If they, if it is the Court that is supposed to get to the truth and convict all those who violated international principles and committed crimes, then that should really be done throughout the entire territory. As a human being, I find it unacceptable that there are two measures one for one side, one for this or that side.

In the estimates for defense witnesses, we also see that Croatians are less likely to express support for the ICTY's efforts with regard for truth, and the coefficient for this variable is significant at the $p< 0.1$ level (table 3.18). This is actually true in both the OTP and Defense witness models. The coefficient for the Bosniak variable is positive and statistically significant in the responsibility model (table 3.19). We were not able to create and use a variable for Albanian defense witnesses, as there were so few of them (3) in our sample.

The findings regarding the sentencing measure do not reveal much. The coefficient for the variable is statistically significant in only the responsibility model (table 3.19), and even that is only to the 0.1 significance level. The greater the average sentence is in the last trial in which they testified, the less likely defense witness are to approve of the ICTY's efforts at establishing responsibility for the crimes committed in the former Yugoslavia. For every ten-year increase in sentencing, the probability that a defense witness approves of the ICTY's performance in determining responsibility decreases by approximately 12 percent (recall that the last trial sentence variable is measured in months, not years). This finding confirms one aspect of our hypotheses, but in general, our findings seem to indicate that trial outcomes are not especially relevant to defense witnesses. Perhaps because, as a group, they tend to be Serbian primarily and Croatian secondarily, they are not necessarily inclined to be supportive of the ICTY regardless of the trial outcome. Sentences that are perceived as inappropriate might serve to only buttress negative attitudes toward the ICTY. In the open-ended question portion of the survey, one defense witness stated,

> I would add just this: it is a pity that the opportunity was missed to establish the true factual situation. It was a good opportunity,

> but unfortunately it was not taken. All the facts and circumstances should have been established from the break-up of Yugoslavia to the final conclusion of these armed conflicts with the NATO aggression. Only then would we have a complete picture and the factual situation would be left to history. This way only part of the facts regarding obviously serious crimes has been illuminated, or partially illuminated, before the Tribunal, but everything that happened before has remained in fog and darkness. I don't have anything more to say.

For our control variable of the percentage of high-level individuals on trial, the coefficient is negative for truth, responsibility, and punishment, but not for deterrence, and it is *never* statistically significant.. It would seem, however, that given the consistently negative impact exercised by this variable, witnesses who testify in high-profile trials are not generally pleased with the international justice delivered by the tribunal. Perhaps because of high expectations that these powerful generals and politicians will be sentenced to lengthy terms of incarceration, if not given life sentences, the witnesses are bound to be displeased with any other type of trial outcome. Some may even believe that the "real" ringleaders of these atrocities have escaped justice, as one witness from Bosnia and Hercegovina suggests

> It is my personal opinion that some people who appeared before the Hague Tribunal, i.e. in court, are less important and it is even believed that they should not have been there at all. Other people, who were more responsible for the events which took place in those parts, should have been there.

Finally, we recognize that we have lost a number of observations for witnesses who testified in trials where the defendant died before a verdict at trial could be rendered. Witnesses testified in two such cases, those of Slavko Dokmanovic and Slobodan Milosevic. We might suspect that individuals who testified in these trials would be frustrated by the lack of closure. Indeed, after Slobodan Milosevic died, there was much discussion that he had "escaped justice." Are these witnesses less likely to approve of the ICTY's performance? We created a variable that measured simply whether the trial resulted in a verdict. The correlation coefficients for this variable were statistically insignificant across all measures of ICTY support and regardless of whether the witness testified for the prosecution or the defense (results not shown).

Conclusion

A central finding in the emerging research on public attitudes in the former Yugoslavia regarding international criminal justice is that support for the ICTY depends significantly on ethnic identity. Individuals from ethnic groups whose socio-historical narratives have been generally affirmed in the judgments of the ICTY—principally the Bosnian Muslims and the Kosovar Albanians—have given the tribunal significantly higher levels of support, while those from ethnic groups whose narratives have largely been discredited by the tribunal—the Serbians—give it fairly low marks. As other research has shown, Serbians often view the ICTY as a tool of the West, especially the hegemonic United States. Support from the Croatian population tends to fall somewhere between these high and low levels of approval. Our results largely confirm these findings, but they also show that among our sample of witnesses, the side for which the individual is testifying matters a great deal. Those testifying for the prosecution are generally more inclined to support the ICTY, while defense witnesses tend to be less supportive. Moreover, the more severe the sentence is, the greater satisfaction prosecution witnesses have with ICTY performance across our four metrics.

Ultimately, however, even these twin factors—witness type and sentence length—should be viewed in the context of ethnic identity. An overwhelming majority of Bosniak and Kosovar Albanian witnesses testify for the prosecution, while a minority of Serbian witnesses and a slight majority of Croatian witnesses appeared on behalf of the OTP. The positive correlation between sentence length and support for the ICTY depended on whether the witness testified for the prosecution. Our findings support the proposition that the ethnic fault lines of the former Yugoslavia extend all the way to The Hague. Ethnicity formed the basis of the political parties, the foundation of their political and military programs, while ethnicity and its geographic divisions determined where the fighting took place and provided the inspiration for those most heinous acts of violence that were the basis of the ICTY's caseload. The work of the ICTY could not help but reflect these divisions. As we argued in chapter 2, the cases before these international tribunals are generally (though not always) concerned with violence that has roots in identity. Across the violence in Rwanda, The Sudan, Uganda, the Congo, the Central African Republic, and Kenya, we tend to find identity playing a major role. To be sure, there are other forces at work, such as greed (e.g., in the Congo) and grievance (in Uganda), while identity issues were not critical in other conflicts (e.g., in Sierra Leone). Nonetheless, all such violence occurs among groups, and these groups, whether political or identity-driven in nature, have a powerful influence over individuals. All groups want international justice to affirm their narrative and their cause. Ethnic identity happens to exercise an especially deeply felt impact on individuals and thus plays a prominent role in how individuals perceive international justice.

We believe that the concept of identity provides a powerful tool through which to understand opinions about international criminal justice and that its impact is not confined to the ICTY. Hence, scholars studying legitimacy and support for both international justice and national trials should begin by identifying the key fault lines along which a conflict breaks. One witness stated,

> But in any case, the Hague Tribunal is a political court. And yes, it did not justify its existence. The majority, not just me and not just in this state, but also when you hear people in Croatia, in Bosnia and Herzegovina and possibly in Kosovo-Metohija, most will say the same thing, that in some way the Tribunal was a court of selective justice. But it is up to those who set it up to think about it.

To be sure, the role of ethnic identity has been deeply entrenched in Balkan conflicts dating back centuries. Nonetheless, given the increasing importance of identity in today's world and especially in today's most bitter conflicts and wars, we suggest that the results of the present analysis are generalizable to other international and domestic courts.

While identity is a critical foundation shaping public views about war, atrocity, and justice, it is not, however, the only factor that matters. In chapter 4, we continue the work of developing our theory of public evaluations of international justice, by analyzing the impact of fairness. Chapter 5 makes the case for the importance of individual experience and then brings all these factors together to provide a comprehensive and final analysis of witness evaluations of the work of the Yugoslav Tribunal.

FOUR

Fairness

Fairness, like justice, is developed in cultural, political, and individual contexts that embody different meanings and values for different people. From an early age, we acquire a sense of fairness about what is appropriate treatment of other people and about who is deserving of what and how much. Fairness may have a strong component of selfishness, especially early in life, as it may be viewed as a relative gains competition, in which one evaluates the fairness of a "thing" or a process in terms of the sufficiency of the rewards one gains (Tyler 1990). With age, the meanings of what is fair and who is entitled to fairness expands. As we have discussed previously, fairness is a critical component of individual evaluations of justice, particularly in the work of Tyler (1990) and other scholars who have investigated the notion that what matters most to individuals is not what justice gives them but how justice treats them (Benesh 2006; J. Jackson et al. 2012; Kelly 1984; Tyler 1990; Tyler and Huo 2002; see Tyler and Jackson 2003 for an extensive reference list). Fairness is the second core component of our theory of individual evaluations of international justice.

Our survey of the witnesses asked several questions about how they perceived the fairness with which they, other witnesses, and defendants were treated. Thus, we can assess how both personal treatment and perceived treatment of others influence witnesses' opinions regarding the ICTY and international criminal justice. Do the witnesses care more about how they were treated as individuals during the course of their testimony—experiences for which they have personal and direct knowledge—or are their opinions of the ICTY more affected by their perception of the tribunal's treatment of others of their ethnic group and members of adversarial groups? These are the key questions that we explore in this chapter.

First, we briefly review some of the more pertinent findings of the literature on fairness and justice. From this literature, we derive a series of hypotheses, which we then begin assessing by examining the bivariate and, then, more complex relationships between witnesses' views of ICTY fairness and their evaluations of the tribunal's success in realizing its four key goals. Later in this chapter, we test these hypotheses in our multivariate models of support for the Yugoslav Tribunal. We conclude the chapter by discussing how these findings contribute to our knowledge of the relative importance of the process and fairness of justice versus the outcomes of judicial systems.

The Meaning of Fairness in Justice

Fairness matters a great deal to those who come into contact with domestic criminal justice systems (see Gibson 1989 for a contrary view). Tyler (1990) and others (Benesh 2006; Tyler and Huo 2002) find ample evidence that people are concerned more about their treatment by courts and court officers than about trial outcomes, even when those outcomes are negative. Exactly what does fairness entail? At the most general level, it pertains to the quality of the procedures that are used over the course of an interaction between an individual and the judicial system. Procedural fairness is further described by Tyler and Jackson (2012, 5) as including "treating people with dignity and respect, showing concern for people's rights and cultural backgrounds, using procedures that are judged to be unbiased and neutral, and giving everyone the opportunity to be heard." Tyler (1990) has further theorized about and tested for the impact of what he calls "process control"—the extent to which an individual believes he or she has some degree of control over his or her relationship with the criminal justice system and its treatment of the individual's situation. People tend to perceive the justice process as fairer to the extent that an individual is allowed to contribute to it and have his or her voice heard. Tyler writes, "When respondents react to their experiences with legal authorities, they focus more on their opportunities to state their case than they do on their influence over decisions" (Tyler 2006b, 126; see also Moorhead, Sefton, and Scanlan 2007; Voeten 2013). Tyler and Huo (Tyler 1990; Tyler and Huo 2002) demonstrate that trust in the motives of those in the criminal justice system is critical.

Not all scholars, however, are so convinced of the importance of fairness in evaluations of justice systems. Gibson (1989, 485) writes, "Perceptions of the fairness of the *decisionmaking* processes within these institutions have virtually no impact on willingness to accept the institutional decision as final and binding" (emphasis in original) While Gibson's study was focused more on compliance with judicial decisions, the US citizens he polled indicated that they were more likely to comply with decisions with which they agreed. One might also argue that the utility of fairness in evaluations of justice assumes some level of knowledge of or experience with these procedures. While many citizens may possess such knowledge and experience regarding courts that are visible or with which they interact (e.g., to report a crime, to act as a juror, or to appear regarding a traffic violation), the same cannot be said about knowledge regarding the rather arcane procedures of international justice. Indeed, beyond those who practice or study international criminal law, few people are likely to have much awareness of how international tribunals operate. The question becomes whether this lack of knowledge inhibits the development of opinions on fairness. We suggest that it does not.

We contend that because fairness is such a fundamental concept that individuals continually employ, often regardless of knowledge or experience of what the term *fairness* means, we should not assume that they are unwilling to rely on their own perceptions and opinions to evaluate fairness. Precisely *because* it is such a core belief that develops from an early age, individuals apply their judgments about it regardless of whatever socialization, experience, or other thoughts they might have.

While fairness comprises multiple components, such as respect, politeness, and a belief that those in authority are acting with good motives, one fairness element seems particularly important both in previous research and in our own preliminary analyses of our witness survey data. That element is the opportunity to state one's case. Individuals want the opportunity to fully present their story to the responsible officials and to know that those officials are listening. When individuals are cut off before they finish or when they perceive that their evidence is being treated in some sort of assembly-line fashion (without appreciation of its importance to the individual) or that the listeners did not actually understand what the individuals were conveying, levels of satisfaction with courts decline (Gosling 2006, cited in Moorhead, Sefton, and Scanlan 2007). Treating witnesses with respect is especially important given the tremendous stress of the testimonial process. As one witness related,

> Well, to tell the truth, testifying is a very difficult process, but if you ask me whether I would do it again, I would do it again. But it is a very difficult process and you can never even imagine to what extent it actually crushes you; if there was something negative, then it would be some wounds that had to be nursed and closed afterwards again, and you had to move on but, in general, I have no objection to any segment of that process.

While the case for the inclusion of fairness in our model is strongly buttressed by this extensive research, there is another reason why fairness is key to understanding how the witnesses in our sample feel about the Yugoslav Tribunal. We consistently found that this topic was the subject of many of their spontaneous comments about what aspects of the trials in which they testified were most meaningful. Time and again, the witnesses made clear that what was important to them in their treatment by the judges, the prosecution, and the defense was being allowed to tell their story without interruption and without hostile questioning. When they felt they were not given proper respect by the prosecution, defense, or judges, witnesses made clear they felt mistreated. For example, one witness reported,

> It did not really go as I imagined it would. I mean, because quite a few times it . . . it happened to me during the testimony itself that, that I felt as an enemy to both the prosecutors and those defenders, meaning the lawyers of those accused, because they expected me to say some something that I did not know. I mean, and from that aspect I felt really empty. Then I tried, I mean, to find comfort in the judges, to look at them, for them to tell me, to protect me, as, in a sense of "do not harass him any longer, leave him alone on that subject," so that it was, I mean, when the testimony was finished, I mean, I was thinking: "have I made a mistake, or not?"

When asked to comment about their treatment by the Office of the Prosecutor, most witnesses focused on whether the OTP cared about their well-being, whether the OTP was professional and acted properly toward them, whether they were allowed to testify without interruption, and whether the prosecution protected them from hostile cross-examination by the defense. When asked to comment about their treatment by the defense, the most frequent response concerned their impression that the defense cared about their well-being and acted professionally toward them. Most interviewees only had good things to say about their treatment by the Trial

Chamber judges and highlighted how the judges let them finish answering their questions and that they appreciated it when the Trial Chamber intervened on their behalf. Similarly, they have welcomed positively Trial Chamber statements made at the conclusion of the evidence and acknowledging the witness's personal suffering (Stepakoff et al. 2015). Therefore, we contend that witness perceptions of the fairness with which they were treated will be important in their evaluations of the justice brought by the ICTY. We also note that we focus on the fairness with which witnesses were treated by the Office of the Prosecutor and the defense. We do not include witnesses' perceptions of the fairness of the Trial Chamber, as the witnesses are nearly unanimous in their satisfaction of their treatment by the judges, as we describe below.

We also consider the witnesses' perceptions of the treatment accorded to other witnesses and the defendants. We suggest that witnesses have both the knowledge and the motivation to be attuned to how the tribunal treats these individuals. In addition to the potential for witnesses knowing other witnesses (especially in trials where other witnesses may be friends, neighbors, and coworkers who witnessed the same atrocities), witnesses may also interact with other witnesses while in The Hague awaiting to testify or after they have testified, but before they head home. These interactions and communities of interest can serve to heighten awareness of how the ICTY has treated others, making such knowledge more salient in the witnesses' evaluation of the tribunal. Furthermore, given the importance of identity issues in the wars of the former Yugoslavia and in the adjudication of the cases before the ICTY, we believe that witnesses will be interested in how others from their ethnic group and from the other groups are treated. It would seem to be a natural human instinct to evaluate one's own standing by comparing how one is treated by authority figures with the treatment accorded to others. We would expect that such assessments of the relative fairness of the ICTY toward oneself and toward others would occur and be utilized to further judge the tribunal. Therefore, we expect that the witnesses in our sample will consider the degrees to which both they and others have been treated fairly by the tribunal.

In particular, we assess the role of perceptions of the fairness with which both other witnesses and the defendants were treated by the ICTY. We further break down these two types of fairness to distinguish between fairness accorded to members of one's own ethnic group and the fairness with which witnesses and defendants from other ethnic groups are perceived to be treated. We suggest the following hypotheses:

Hypothesis 2.1. Witnesses who believe they were treated fairly by the Office of the Prosecution will be more likely to approve of the ICTY's performance.

Hypothesis 2.2. Witnesses who believe they were treated fairly by the defense will be more likely to approve of the ICTY's performance.

Hypothesis 2.3. Witnesses who believe that the ICTY has treated witnesses of their ethnicity fairly will be more likely to approve of the tribunal's performance.

Hypothesis 2.4. Witnesses who believe that the ICTY has fairly treated witnesses who are not of their ethnicity will be more likely to approve of the tribunal's performance.

Hypothesis 2.5. Witnesses who believe that the ICTY has treated defendants of their ethnicity fairly will be more likely to approve of the tribunal's performance.

Hypothesis 2.6. Witnesses who believe that the ICTY has fairly treated defendants who are not of their ethnicity will be more likely to approve of the tribunal's performance.

Analyzing Fairness and Justice

In our survey of the witnesses, we posed several questions to the participants about the fairness with which they were treated and their perceptions of how the tribunal treated others. Witnesses were asked to respond to the statement "Overall, I believe I was treated fairly by the (trial chamber judges; the Office of the Prosecutor, the Defense and the Victims and Witnesses section)." Their possible responses were "strongly agree," "agree," "disagree," "strongly disagree," "don't know," and "no opinion." The results are found in table 4.1. The vast majority of witnesses (93 percent) agreed or strongly agreed that they were treated fairly by the Trial Chamber, 79 percent believe they were treated fairly by the OTP, and 71 percent indicated that they were treated fairly by the defense. The results further show that of all the ICTY actors, the witnesses were most satisfied with their treatment by the Victims and Witnesses Section; almost 96 percent of interviewees believed they were treated fairly by the VWS. We also looked at whether responses to these questions depended on which party called the witnesses to testify (results not shown). We find that 93 to 96 percent of both OTP and defense witnesses indicated that they were treated fairly by both the judges and the VWS. Yet, while 88 percent of the witnesses called by the Office of the Prosecutor believed they were treated fairly by the OTP, only 63 percent of the defense witnesses expressed that opinion of the OTP (results not shown). Opinions are reversed when examining perceptions of how witnesses were treated by the defense. Among defense witnesses, 89 percent believed they were treated fairly by the defense, while only 60 percent of the OTP witnesses believed they were treated fairly by the defense (results not shown). Despite these differences, however, most witnesses view their own personal treatment by these key ICTY actors favorably.

Because the issue of fairness is so critical in public opinion regarding justice in general, we drill down further into the data, especially those instances where the witnesses were given the opportunity to provide additional comments about how they were treated by the various parties. The witnesses' opinions of their treatment by the parties are often influenced by their perceptions of courtroom dynamics and their preparation for the difficult act of testifying (Stepakoff et al. 2014, 2015). One witness summarized this daunting responsibility as follows:

> "I can never . . . walk through town not even for 5 minutes without encountering either the parents of those who were killed or their children or wives or brothers or sisters, and for as long as I live I will never, have peace of mind because of what happened. That is why I considered it my duty to go and testify about what happened and, God forbid, if this were to happen again I would go once more and testify.

The calling party usually determines what topics will be covered during the testimony, but some witnesses may find it hard to focus on a certain segment of their war experience and disregard other parts that they consider important. VWS personnel noticed that sometimes witnesses consider the courtroom as the right arena to tell the whole truth about what they survived, and they may feel offended when they are interrupted while talking about very important life events. The VWS noted that when asked to reply only with "yes" or "no" to a series of questions posed by the parties and/or

TABLE 4.1. Interviewee Perception Percentages about Treatment by the ICTY

Witness Response	Treated Fairly by Judges	Treated Fairly by OTP	Treated Fairly by Defense	Treated Fairly by VWS
Strongly Agree / Agree	93	79	71	96
Strongly Disagree / Disagree	3	11	17	0
No Response / No Opinion	4	9	12	4

Trial Chamber, witnesses may feel that the complexity of their experience and the emotional suffering attached to it is not being properly acknowledged. Often, the witnesses believe they have not been able to tell what they believe to be the very crucial part of their story. One witness contends,

> As far as I'm concerned, did not give [*sic*] the true picture of what I had seen. I was able to say something here and there, but not what I thought I would be saying. They led me to answer questions that I believe were not relevant at all at that point, because I saw many things, many worse things than the ones they led me to talk about.

Other research confirmed such observations (Wald 2002).

Witnesses are often surprised when an opposing party tries to undermine their credibility. Some felt outraged and reported to the VWS that they felt as if they were the ones in the dock. In particular, witnesses who testify about their own experience of abuse and violence (sexual violence, torture, loss of closed family members, etc.) may be deeply hurt during cross-examination if they feel that the opposing party is questioning their evidence or their experiences. Moreover, witnesses can be severely distressed when the questioning goes into details they might have preferred to forget. Summing up the frustration of many, one witness asserted,

> I would maybe just add that the Defense should not be given much space for some provocative, you know, questions or something like that, you know. Because, after all, it affects the witnesses. He (the witness) is under a lot of stress anyway, the memories that are coming back after so many years and all, it should be at least relatively sanctioned, so that they are not given so much space for, for, for the witness harassment and things like that.

The Trial Chamber has the role of controlling the proceedings and addressing violations of the code of conduct during the cross-examination. Similarly, they have positively welcomed statements made by the chamber at the conclusion of their evidence and acknowledging the witness' personal suffering (Stepakoff et al. 2015). Additionally, many witnesses ask, at the end of their testimony, if they can make a final statement to the court. The VWS experience is that such statements are usually short and that witnesses appreciate it when they are given permission to speak at the conclusion of their testimony (Bandes 2009).

In general, the witnesses give the ICTY fairly high marks for the fairness with which they were treated by the principal actors in that institution—the judges, the prosecutors, the defense attorneys, and the staff of the VWS. The witnesses have firsthand knowledge, obviously, of their own experiences with the tribunal, but how do they respond when asked about the fairness with which the ICTY has treated others? Should we expect witnesses to generalize from their own experiences with the ICTY to assume that other witnesses from their ethnic group and the other groups of the former Yugoslavia are treated fairly? What should we expect when the witnesses are asked about the treatment accorded the defendants? To answer these questions, we asked the witnesses in our sample to determine whether they agreed or disagreed with the following statements: "*In general*, I believe that the ICTY has treated witnesses *of my own ethnicity* fairly"; "*In general*, I believe that the ICTY has treated witnesses who are *not of my own ethnicity* fairly"; "*In general*, I believe the ICTY has treated defendants *of my own ethnicity* fairly"; and "*In general*, I believe the ICTY has treated defendants who are *not of my own ethnicity* fairly." The breakdown of their responses is in table 4.2.

Approximately 63 percent of the individuals in our sample believed that witnesses of their ethnic group were treated fairly by the ICTY, and 48.3% believed that witnesses from other groups were treated fairly. Interviewees were less likely to believe that witnesses from other ethnic groups were treated fairly, and they were more apt to feel that those from their ethnic group were treated fairly. This finding runs counter to what many researchers have found, which is that individuals seem more likely to perceive that their group as receiving less favorable treatment than the "other" (Clark 2014).

Theorizing about why and how witnesses see fairness in terms of the "other" may mean that witnesses in our sample see fairness as a matter of degree not kind and on a continuum with lesser and greater levels of "fairness." It is also possible that some witnesses may perceive a deficit of fairness as a problem in which minimal standards of fairness are not maintained and in which individuals are not treated with the respect, politeness, and due process that the law and the institution guarantee. Fairness is a benchmark to be met and is more function of process and treatment. Perhaps some witnesses consider a surfeit of fairness, which we might term "favoritism." Here the perception is about "unfairness," and witnesses might believe that some witnesses and defendants are treated *too* fairly and given *better* treatment. The view of fairness here is that such treatment is unfair not so much to other witnesses and defendants, but to the quest for justice. For example, some interviewees indicated that the ICTY treats defendants fairly when imposing a sentence proportionate to the crimes committed. Some reported that defendants of "other" ethnic groups have received disproportionately positive treatment (e.g., supervised release or not being held accountable), which they believe creates too much "fairness" and is undeserved. One witness explained,

> No war is good, please understand that. But, in—in Kosovo and Metohija it was a civil war. And—the war was caused by K—K—KLA, the Liberation Army of Kosovo, and there is no evidence for any of them and no one is being brought to account—no one is being held responsible, what witnesses there were—those who came forward—these guys killed them! And nothing is being done about it.

Other witnesses indicated that defendants are treated fairly when they are given proper legal assistance and detention facilities. While scholars tend to define and measure fairness as an issue regarding the degree to which the institutions of justice strive to maintain a minimum "floor" of fairness consisting of basic procedural guarantees, these witnesses (and perhaps others) view fairness as encompassing benefits as well as rights. Fairness may mean both the absence of bias *and* the presence of favoritism. About the treatment in prison of those found guilty, one witness contended,

> Those prisons virtually do not resemble the prisons, and then after those, those so-called custodies, they go to some countries to serve those very short sentences and the one-third *[of the sentence]* is taken off. And for the killing of hundred people, they are free after ten, twelve years. Which is inconceivable. It is inconceivable for the victims themselves."

Future research in this area could certainly help determine if fairness is a more complex and multifaceted concept than we have previously considered. We see in table 4.2 that while 33 percent of the witnesses in our

TABLE 4.2. Fairness of Treatment Percentages by the ICTY to Defendants and Witnesses

Witness Response	Treated Defendants of My Ethnicity Fairly	Treated Defendants Not of My Ethnicity Fairly	Treated Witnesses of My Ethnicity Fairly	Treated Witnesses Not of My Ethnicity Fairly
Strongly Agree / Agree	33	26	63	48
Strongly Disagree / Disagree	28	29	7	5
No Response / No Opinion	39	45	30	46

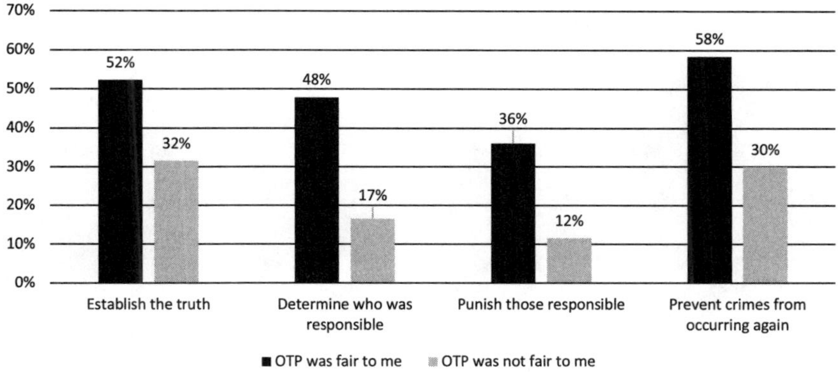

Figure 4.1. Perceived fairness of Prosecution and support for the ICTY's effectiveness

sample believed that defendants of their own ethnicity were treated fairly by ICTY, that number dropped to 26 percent when the question pertained to whether "other" ethnicities have been treated fairly by the tribunal. We note that the split between agreement and disagreement about ethnic treatment is a limited range, indicating that witnesses are fairly evenly divided about fairness. There are also sizable numbers across all four questions about fair treatment ranging from 30 percent to 46 percent who are unsure and have no opinion.

We next review the basic bivariate relationships between our four measures of the ICTY's effectiveness and our measures of fairness. We begin by examining whether individuals' perceptions of their treatment by the prosecution and the defense helps predict their evaluations of the tribunal. We chose not to analyze the fairness responses that pertained to the Trial Chamber and the VWS, as those responses were so overwhelmingly positive. The results are presented in figure 4.1.

As we would expect, approval of the ICTY's job performance in each of the four areas is associated with witnesses' perceptions regarding whether they felt they were treated fairly by the Office of the Prosecution. In every case, support is higher among those who felt fairly treated. The differences in support among those who felt fairly treated and those who did not is around 28 to 31 percent in all the categories with except on the punishment measure, where the difference is approximately 24 percent. We see majority approval of the ICTY among those who felt fairly treated on the truth measure and the deterrence measure. Even among those who felt fairly treated by the OTP, there are majorities who still do not approve of the ICTY's performance in determining responsibility and allocating punishment.

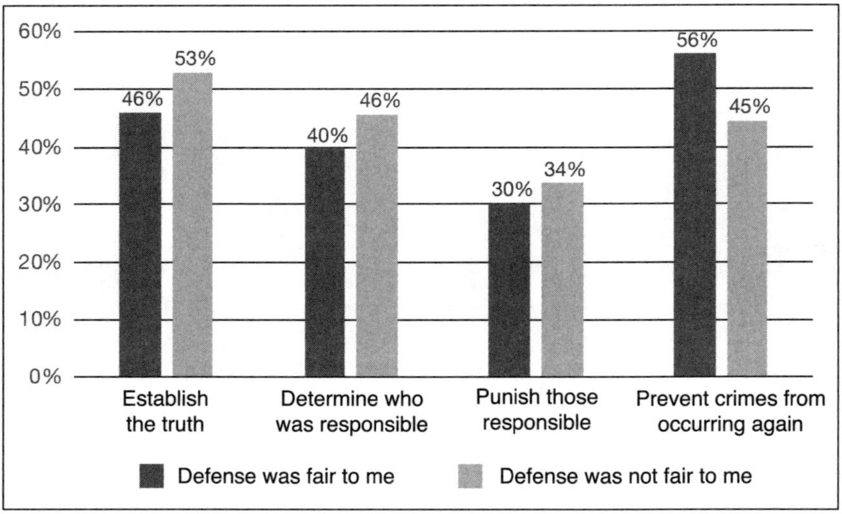

Figure 4.2. Perceived fairness of Defense and support for the ICTY's effectiveness

Figure 4.2 shows rather different relationships. First, the differences in approval of the ICTY's job performance do not vary nearly so much between those who believe the defense treated them fairly and those who do not. Furthermore, only on the measure of ICTY deterrence do we see majority support for the tribunal among those who indicated that the defense treated them fairly. On the other three measures, support is higher for the ICTY among those who indicated that the defense did not treat them fairly. We might suspect that many of the defense witnesses most likely to believe they were treated fairly by the defense—typically Serbian witnesses and less so Croatian ones—are the same witnesses less inclined to support the ICTY. Conversely, those witnesses who seem more likely to believe that they were treated unfairly by the defense—principally the Bosniak and Kosovar Albanian witnesses for the OTP—would be more likely to support the ICTY. Individuals care about how they are treated and whether they are treated with the respect and fairness they deserve. These factors influence their willingness to approve of the work of international justice across various measures of its success. We next turn to the issue of fairness toward others.

As we have discussed, the witnesses in our sample have had repeated and direct interactions with multiple actors at the ICTY, from the staff of the VWS who support their visit while in The Hague, to the attorneys of the prosecution who have been in touch with the witness numerous times through the course of arranging their testimony, to the judges who guide how they are questioned on the witness stand. Witnesses likely do not have as much firsthand knowledge about the experiences of other witnesses and the defendants. Nonetheless, we argue the powerful role played by fairness in opinion formation regarding justice means that witnesses still form opinions about what fairness means to themselves and others. This in turn leads them to still feel comfortable reaching conclusions about fairness, even toward others.

There are several decision-making strategies that the witnesses might utilize to reach conclusions about the fairness with which others are treated. Witnesses might base such assessments on general impressions of the ICTY that are gleaned from newspapers, television, and other media outlets. Furthermore, they might anchor these opinions in what they have heard from others, including other witnesses, opinion leaders at home, and other people with whom they have interacted at home and in The Hague. They may use their own experiences as a decision cue and generalize from those interactions and the fairness with which they were treated by the various actors at the ICTY to the experiences of other witnesses, regardless of ethnicity.

To examine this, we ran a correlation matrix of all of our measures of fairness and found a small, positive, statistically significant correlation (ranging from 0.09 to 0.19) between whether individuals think they were treated fairly by the OTP and their evaluations of the fairness granted to the groups of other witnesses and to the defendants (results not shown). Interestingly, the correlation between the witnesses' evaluations of the OTP and their assessment of the fairness with which the ICTY has treated witnesses of their ethnicity is the smallest and is statistically significant at just the 0.1 level. There were no statistically significant relationships between witnesses' evaluations of their treatment by the defense counsel and the other four measures of fairness.

We further explored whether these relationships were once again contingent on which party called the witnesses to testify (results not shown). Among the prosecution witnesses, the correlation coefficients remain small, positive, and statistically significant. There was no significant relationship between their evaluations of the fairness with which they were treated and their perception of the fairness by which defendants from other ethnic groups were treated. There are still no statistically significant relationships among the defense witnesses. While by no means conclusive, this brief foray into understanding how witnesses construct evaluations of how the

ICTY has treated others is suggestive. Some part of their evaluation may be based on personal experience, but there is clearly more to this puzzle. Witnesses do not reflexively give the ICTY the same fairness marks when considering its treatment of other witnesses and the defendants as when they are evaluating their personal experience.

One possible accounting of the method by which witnesses evaluate the ICTY's treatment of other witnesses and the defendants would focus on the most reliable of decision cues, ethnicity. In chapters 2 and 3, we detailed how identity issues play a powerful role in structuring individuals' perceptions of the causes, consequences, and aftermath of the wars of the former Yugoslavia. These ethno-nationalist narratives, premised on enduring historical and cultural stories and experiences, play a powerful role in shaping how individuals perceive and evaluate the work of international justice. To the extent that these narratives are affirmed by the judges of the ICTY, we have found individuals more likely to give favorable evaluations of the tribunal. We suspect something similar may be happening with regard to assessments of the perceived fairness of the tribunal and that the familiar patterns we have seen before will emerge here; that is, we might expect Bosniaks and Kosovar Albanians to perceive the ICTY as generally fair, Serbians to view it as unfair, and the perceptions by Croatians to fall somewhere between the two ends of the spectrum. We ran the correlations between our four measures of fairness and the four ethnic groups, and the results (in table 4.3) largely support our expectations.

Bosniaks are more likely to give the ICTY positive evaluations of its fairness toward others, while Serbians are less likely to be as supportive. All of the correlation coefficients for the former group are positive and statistically significant, while all the correlations for the latter are negative and statistically significant except for Serbians' views of the ICTY's treatment of witnesses who are from other ethnic groups. Our sample yielded no statistically significant relationships among Croat witnesses and only one statistically significant relationship among Kosovar Albanians. Those

TABLE 4.3. Correlations between Perceptions of Fairness and Ethnicity

Perceptions of Fairness	Bosniaks	Serbs	Croats	Kosovar Albanians
Fair to Defendants of My Ethnicity	0.247*	–0.328*	0.052	0.091
Fair to Defendants Not of My Ethnicity	0.181*	–0.186*	0.046	–0.087
Fair to Witnesses of My Ethnicity	0.140*	–0.113*	0.015	0.039
Fair to Witnesses Not of My Ethnicity	0.218*	–0.066	0.013	–0.178*

Note: $N = 300$.

witnesses are unlikely to believe that the ICTY is fair to witnesses from other ethnic groups. It is possible that Croatian and Kosovar Albanian witnesses may also believe that the ICTY is being too fair toward witnesses from other ethnic groups and providing them better treatment than should be expected. Nonetheless, these results again highlight the important role played by ethnic identity in the perceptions and evaluations of international justice.

We turn next to examining how perceptions of the fair treatment accorded others influences witnesses' evaluations of the ICTY's effectiveness. We consolidated our four exogenous factors into four dichotomous variables, coded 1 for those who (strongly) agreed that the ICTY gave fair treatment to (1) witnesses of their ethnicity, (2) witnesses from the other ethnic groups, (3) defendants of their ethnic group, and (4) defendants from other ethnic groups; those who indicated otherwise were coded 0. The results are presented in figures 4.3–4.6. The first two figures pertain to the tribunal's treatment toward witnesses and show that there are substantial differences in the level of support given to the ICTY by those who do or do not believe the tribunal has been fair to witnesses of their ethnicity and witnesses from other ethnic groups. The difference is most stark when we look at the truth and responsibility indicators (and to a lesser degree punishment), where figure 4.3 shows respective gaps of thirty-three and thirty-six points in witness support for the ICTY among those who do or do not believe that the tribunal has been fair to witnesses of their ethnic group. Among those who believe the ICTY was fair, 60 percent approve of its effectiveness in telling the truth, and 55 percent approve of the ICTY's ability to determine who was responsible for committing crimes in the former Yugoslavia. The differences decrease in size when we look at witnesses' support for ICTY punishment, where only 41 percent of those who thought it was fair approved of its job performance. While 61 percent of those who thought the ICTY was fair to witnesses of their ethnicity approved of the ICTY's efforts at deterrence, 39 percent of those who thought the ICTY was unfair still approved of its work in this area.

Similar patterns hold when the witnesses are queried about ICTY fairness toward witnesses from other ethnic groups (fig. 4.4). Between those who do and do not believe the ICTY was fair to witnesses from other ethnicities are gaps of twenty-six points on the truth measure (61 versus 35 percent, respectively) and thirty-two points on the responsibility measure (58 versus 26 percent, respectively). Also between those groups are gaps of twenty-nine points when we look at the punishment measure of ICTY effectiveness and eighteen points on the deterrence measure.

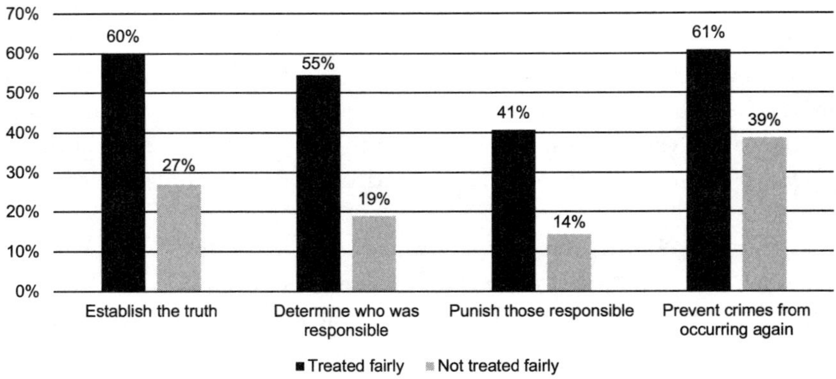

Figure 4.3. Perceptions of ICTY fairness toward witnesses from one's ethnic group and support for the Tribunal

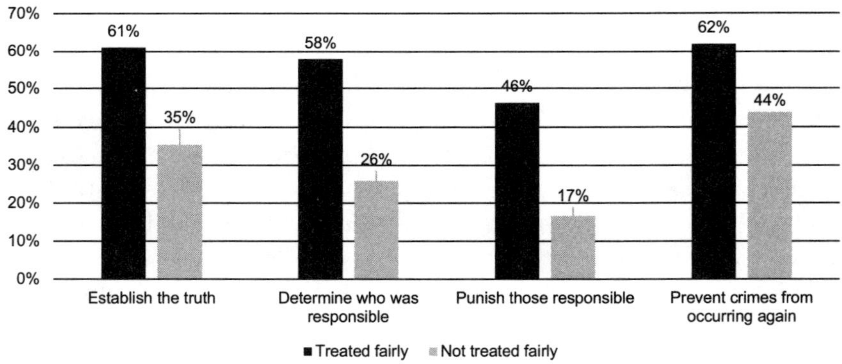

Figure 4.4. Perceptions of ICTY fairness toward witnesses from other ethnic groups and support for the Tribunal

When we turn our attention to the witnesses' views on the fairness with which defendants from their ethnic group and other ethnic groups have been treated, the results follow the same basic pattern and are even more pronounced in some cases (figs. 4.5 and 4.6). Among those witnesses who believe that the ICTY has treated defendants from their ethnic group fairly (fig. 4.5), we see that majorities support the work of the ICTY across all four dimensions of truth, responsibility, punishment, and deterrence (77, 77, 51, and 67 percent, respectively). The differences in support for the ICTY among those who do or do not believe that the ICTY has been fair range from a low of 21 percent (on the deterrence measure) to a high of 46 percent (on the responsibility measure).

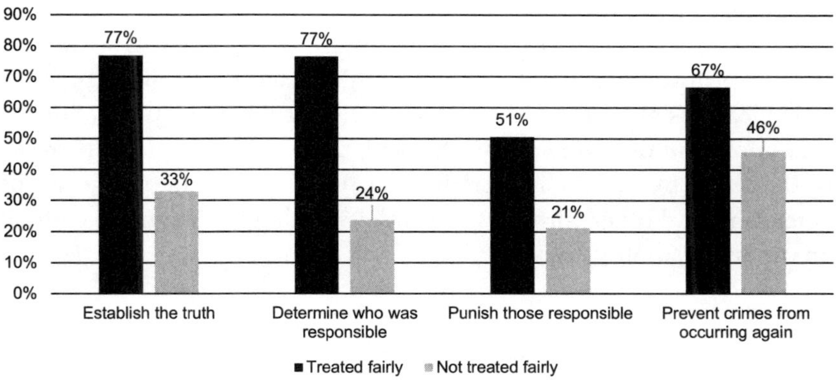

Figure 4.5. Perceptions of ICTY fairness toward defendants from one's ethnic group and support for the Tribunal

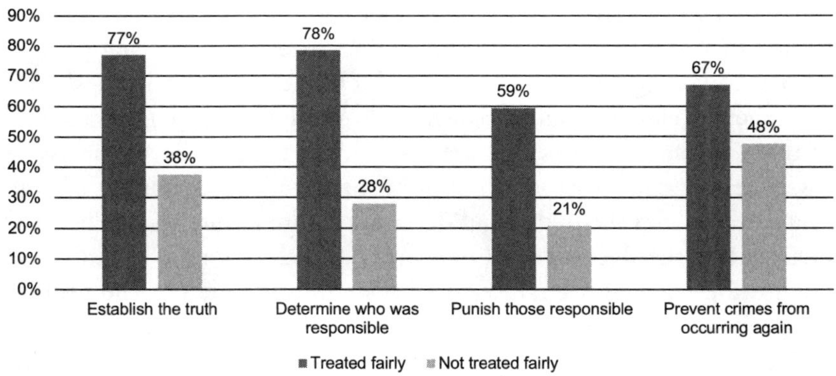

Figure 4.6. Perceptions of ICTY fairness toward defendants from other ethnic groups and support for the Tribunal

The relationships stay largely the same when we look at witness perceptions of the fairness with which the ICTY has treated defendants from other ethnic groups (fig. 4.6). Support is high among those who see the ICTY as fair (77%, 78%, 59%, and 67%) on the four measures of ICTY support and remains quite similar to the results we see in figure 4.5. The witnesses maintain fairly constant attitudes on the ICTY's treatment of defendants in the context of their overall evaluations of the tribunal's effectiveness. The distribution of responses from figure 4.5 to figure 4.6 are quite similar.

We take away two principal lessons from this brief analysis. First, fairness matters. Given the stark differences in whatever kind of fairness we analyze—whether toward witnesses or defendants, toward the individual's ethnic group or other ethnic groups—it is clear that witnesses' evaluations of international justice are significantly influenced by multiple measures of fairness. Hence, we expect fairness to play a prominent role in our multivariate analysis. Second, there are very similar patterns in the levels of witness support for the ICTY across the categories of defendants and other witnesses. With these findings in mind, we embark on our multivariate analysis.

Multivariate Analysis

The stark differences in support for the work of the ICTY depending on whether a witness perceived the tribunal to be treating other witnesses and the defendants fairly provide prima facie evidence that the findings of those who study fairness in US and other court systems may also hold at the international level. Our next step in the process of identifying whether fairness plays a significant and substantial role in evaluations of the ICTY is to further develop our multivariate models. We use the same four measures of these evaluations—whether the individual witness believes the ICTY has generally done a good job in advancing truth, determining responsibility, punishing the guilty, and deterring future crimes—and the set of independent variables we used in chapter 3, with some modifications. In the previous chapter, we ran separate analyses for witnesses who testified for the prosecution and those who were called by the defense teams. We utilize the same types of analyses in this chapter, but we begin by testing the impact of fairness on the entire sample of witnesses. We use the critical ethnic identity variables for Bosniaks, Serbians, Croatians, and Kosovar Albanians in all the model estimations.

In the interest of avoiding problems of multicollinearity in our model estimation, we determined that we would combine our similar measures of witness perceptions of fair treatment by the ICTY to other witnesses and the defendants. We created additive measures for the two variables that sought witness views on ICTY fairness toward witnesses of their own ethnicity and witnesses of other ethnic groups, as these measures correlated at .69. Similarly, because of the .67 correlation between the measures seeking witness opinions regarding whether the tribunal was fair to defendants of the witnesses' ethnic group and defendants from other groups, we combined those variables to create an additive measure. The correlation between witness opinions on whether the prosecution or the defense gave fair treatment to them personally was statistically insignificant, so we chose to keep these measures separate. The results for our first set of prohibit estimates involving all sample witnesses and the truth, responsibility, punishment, and deterrence measures are found in Tables 4.4–4.7, respectively. They generally show significant support for the importance of perceptions of diverse measures of fairness in the witness evaluations of the ICTY's efforts at advancing truth, determining responsibility, delivering punishment, and helping to prevent future conflict.

We see that witness views of their treatment by OTP are positively related to their opinions about the work of the ICTY. In all but table 4.4,

TABLE 4.4. Fairness and Support for the ICTY Truth Mission

	Coefficient	Standard Error	*Z* Score	*P* Value	Marginal Impact
OTP Fair to Me	0.061	0.215	0.280	0.776	0.024
Defense Fair to Me	0.004	0.188	0.020	0.982	0.002
ICTY Fair toward Witnesses	0.301	0.105	2.870	0.004***	0.120
ICTY Fair toward Defendants	0.438	0.119	3.700	0.000***	0.175
Bosniak	–0.120	0.308	–0.390	0.696	–0.048
Serb	–1.485	0.314	–4.730	0.000***	–0.514
Croat	–0.698	0.300	–2.320	0.020**	–0.267
Albanian	0.018	0.385	0.050	0.962	0.007
Constant	–0.048	0.340	–0.140	0.888	

Note: N = 295.
* $p < ..1$, ** $p < .05$ one-tailed test *** $p < .01$.

TABLE 4.5. Fairness and Support for the ICTY Responsibility Mission

	Coefficient	Standard Error	*Z* Score	*P* Value	Marginal Impact
OTP Fair to Me	0.548	0.251	2.180	0.029**	0.196
Defense Fair to Me	0.036	0.201	0.180	0.856	0.014
ICTY Fair toward Witnesses	0.294	0.109	2.690	0.007***	0.113
ICTY Fair toward Defendants	0.644	0.122	5.280	0.000***	0.247
Bosniak	0.356	0.312	1.140	0.255	0.138
Serb	–1.063	0.325	–3.270	0.001***	–0.362
Croat	–0.519	0.311	–1.670	0.095*	–0.189
Albanian	0.028	0.382	0.070	0.941	0.011
Constant	–1.097	0.379	–2.890	0.004	

Note: N = 295.
* $p < ..1$, ** $p < .05$ one-tailed test *** $p < .01$.

where we estimate a model of opinions about the ICTY's success in establishing the truth of what happened in the former Yugoslavia, the coefficient for the variable is positive and statistically significant. According to the marginal impact coefficients, when witnesses believe that the OTP has treated them fairly, they are 19 percent more likely to express approval of the ICTY's efforts to establish responsibility, 17 percent more likely to approve of the tribunal's performance in meting out punishment, and approximately 25 percent more likely to believe that the ICTY has done a good job preventing grave crimes from occurring again. The results for the variable measuring whether the individual believed the defense treated him

TABLE 4.6. Fairness and Support for the ICTY Punishment Mission

	Coefficient	Standard Error	*Z* Score	*P* Value	Marginal Impact
OTP Fair to Me	0.573	0.245	2.340	0.019**	0.171
Defense Fair to Me	-0.025	0.188	-0.130	0.895	-0.008
ICTY Fair toward Witnesses	0.377	0.110	3.440	0.001***	0.127
ICTY Fair toward Defendants	0.331	0.109	3.030	0.002***	0.111
Bosniak	-0.293	0.304	-0.970	0.334	-0.094
Serb	-0.624	0.313	-1.990	0.046**	-0.192
Croat	-0.317	0.304	-1.040	0.297	-0.102
Albanian	0.087	0.378	0.230	0.819	0.030
Constant	-1.302	0.371	-3.510	0.000	

Note: N = 295.
* $p < ..1$, ** $p < .05$ one-tailed test *** $p < .01$.

TABLE 4.7. Fairness and Support for the ICTY Deterrence Mission

	Coefficient	Standard Error	*Z* Score	*P* Value	Marginal Impact
OTP Fair to Me	0.635	0.201	3.170	0.002***	0.248
Defense Fair to Me	0.363	0.174	2.080	0.037 **	0.144
ICTY Fair toward Witnesses	0.226	0.097	2.330	0.020**	0.090
ICTY Fair toward Defendants	0.113	0.108	1.040	0.297	0.045
Bosniak	-0.428	0.293	-1.460	0.144	-0.170
Serb	-0.587	0.290	-2.020	0.043**	-0.231
Croat	-0.276	0.291	-0.950	0.342	-0.110
Albanian	-0.614	0.367	-1.670	0.094*	-0.237
Constant	-0.610	0.329	-1.850	0.064	

Note: N = 295.
* $p < ..1$, ** $p < .05$ one-tailed test *** $p < .01$.

or her fairly are something like a mirror-image opposite. Where the OTP fairness measure was statistically significant in all but one of the models, the coefficient for the defense fairness is statistically significant in only one model—the ICTY's deterrence mission (table 4.7). The marginal impact coefficients show that witnesses who indicate that the defense team treated them with fairness are 14 percent more likely to approve of the ICTY's performance in deterring future crimes.

Why would fairness by the prosecution predict individual support for the ICTY better than the witnesses' treatment by the defense? While the models themselves do not allow us to reach any conclusions regarding this question, we can make inferences based on reasonable assumptions. Perhaps the most obvious explanation is that witnesses may tend to view the work of the prosecution and the whole work of the ICTY as interrelated. Indeed, the Office of the Prosecutor is a unit within the ICTY, established by the UN Security Council resolution that authorized the ICTY. Hence, it should come as no surprise that the witnesses who report a positive experience with the OTP are more likely to approve of the ICTY's efforts to realize the four measures of success, as both opinions may be part of a more comprehensive view of the tribunal in its entirety. Conversely, the witnesses' impressions of their treatment by the defense may not matter as much in their evaluations of the tribunal, as they see a more distinct separation between the defense and the tribunal as an institution. Indeed, the defense teams mostly worked, literally and figuratively, outside the ICTY's headquarters in The Hague, so it would be quite rational for the witnesses to see little connection between the tribunal's work and their own treatment by the defense.

The results for our measures of witness perceptions regarding how fairly the ICTY has treated other witnesses and the defendants are positive and statistically significant across all the models but one—the deterrence mission. Those witnesses who believe the ICTY has fairly treated witnesses of their ethnicity and from other ethnic groups are more likely to hold positive views about the tribunal's performance across all four measures of success. The marginal impact coefficients for this variable are also quite consistent across all four tables. Those individuals who are more likely to indicate belief that the ICTY is fair toward witnesses are approximately 9 to 12 percent more likely to approve of the ICTY's performance. These same relationships hold for the witnesses' perceptions of the ICTY's fairness toward defendants. The coefficients for this variable are positive and statistically significant in each model except in the deterrence model estimates (table 4.7). The marginal impact coefficients are generally larger—

but also more variable in the effect, ranging from a low of 0.11 in the punishment model (indicating an increase of 11 percent in the likelihood of an individual approving of the ICTY's performance) to a high of 0.24 in the responsibility model (or 24 percent).

We draw two principal inferences from these findings. First, the results indicate that fairness is a multifaceted concept and that witnesses care about how the ICTY treated both them personally and other witnesses and the defendants. Much of the research on the impact of fairness on public opinion has focused on individuals' assessments of the fairness of institutions of criminal justice toward them personally (Tyler 1990; Tyler and Huo 2002). Our results suggest that fairness considerations can also incorporate the perceived treatment of individuals and groups beyond the survey participant. We do not yet know whether the relationship between the witnesses' views of ICTY treatment of these others is an independent assessment of the ICTY's operations or should be viewed as one of several components of individual's overall evaluation of the tribunal's work.

We also note that all of these measures are a product of the witnesses' recollections of the ICTY. Hence, it is possible that the relationship between the fairness measures and the witnesses' evaluations of the tribunal are more correlational than causal. In particular, witnesses' opinions about the fairness with which the ICTY has treated defendants may be related to their overall evaluations of the tribunal, since they are unlikely to have nearly the same level of knowledge regarding such matters as they would have of their own treatment by the ICTY. Despite these caveats, however, we believe that the evidence thus far indicates a significant and substantial relationship—whether correlational or causal in nature—between opinions about fairness and opinions regarding the ICTY's performance. Before reaching any final conclusions, we must analyze these relationships when we incorporate information about sentences into the model and break down the analyses by witness type (prosecution or defense).

Before doing so, we note lastly for the ethnicity measures, only the coefficients for the Serbian variable are statistically significant across all four models. As we saw in chapter 3, Serbians are less likely to approve of the ICTY's performance on any metric, and these results continue to remain consistent. Indeed, Serbians are as much as 51 percent less likely to believe that the ICTY is doing a good job in establishing the truth, while they are still unlikely, albeit less so, to approve of the tribunal's efforts in establishing responsibility, providing punishment, and deterring future violence. The coefficient for the Croatian variable is negative and statistically significant for only the truth measure (table 4.4). The Bosniak and Kosovar

Albanian variables do not appear to be as meaningful, as their coefficients never attain statistical significance.

In table 4.8, we provide the coefficient estimates and standard errors of the variables in each of the four models of witness evaluations of the ICTY for those witnesses who testified for the Office of the Prosecutor and table 4.9 provides these estimates for the defense witnesses (statistically significant relationships are noted). In these models, we also include our measure of the average length of sentence for each of the defendant(s) as determined by the ICTY Appeals Chamber for the last trial in which a witness testified. This measure generally was statistically significant in our model estimates in chapter 3, where it indicated that the longer the average sentence was, the more likely the witness was to approve of the ICTY's performance. We begin here by noting that the coefficients for this variable never reach statistical significance in these estimates. Once we control for witness perceptions of fairness, considerations about sentencing and trial outcomes do not seem to matter as much. Moreover, the coefficients for the variable measuring the percentage of "big fish" against whom the individual testified in his or her last trial never attains statistical significance. Hence, these results generally are supportive of the research of Tyler and others that fairness considerations matter more than outcomes in evaluations of justice.

When we consider just those who testified on behalf of the OTP, fairness emerges as the more statistically significant and powerful predictor of witness attitudes toward the ICTY realization of its mandate objectives. The coefficients for witnesses' perceptions of the fairness with which other witnesses have been treated are statistically significant in all of the four models, while their views of the ICTY's treatment of defendants are statistically related to their evaluations of the tribunal in each model except the deterrence estimates. Among these prosecution witnesses, however, their opinions of the fairness accorded them by the defense makes no or little difference, while the coefficients for the measure of their attitudes about OTP fairness are statistically significant in only the responsibility and deterrence models.

While our models of ICTY evaluations by the OTP witnesses provide fairly consistent results among all the variables, the analogous estimates for defense witnesses (table 4.9) are not nearly so clear. First, the coefficients for the variables measuring witness perceptions of how they were treated by either the prosecution or the defense are not statistically significant in any of the models. Similarly, the coefficients for the indicator of ICTY fairness toward other witnesses are not statistically significant

TABLE 4.8. Fairness and Evaluations of the ICTY Mission for OTP Witnesses

	Truth		Responsibility		Punishment		Deterrence	
	Coefficient	Standard Error	Coefficient	Standard Error	Coefficient	Standard Error	Coefficient	Standard Error
OTP Fair to Me	0.325	0.402	**0.927**	**0.531***	0.916	0.548	**0.647**	**0.368***
Defense Fair to Me	0.205	0.251	0.211	0.257	0.086	0.240	**0.567**	**0.223*****
ICTY Fair toward Witnesses	**0.364**	**0.150*****	**0.389**	**0.149****	**0.540**	**0.158*****	**0.259**	**0.142***
ICTY Fair toward Defendants	**0.629**	**0.172*****	**0.712**	**0.164*****	**0.325**	**0.141****	0.165	0.141
Bosniak	−0.595	0.424	−0.351	0.417	−0.529	0.391	−0.481	0.366
Serbs	**−1.640**	**0.492*****	**−1.048**	**0.484***	−0.665	0.481	−0.618	0.430
Croats	**−0.886**	**0.444****	**−0.798**	**0.446***	−0.004	0.424	−0.444	0.396
Albanian	−0.146	0.527	−0.256	0.519	0.091	0.501	−0.754	0.474
Last Trial Sentence on Appeal	0.001	0.001	0.001	0.001	0.001	0.001	−0.001	0.001
Percentage Big Fish	−0.444	0.351	−0.100	0.354	−0.324	0.325	−0.468	0.309
Constant	−0.050	0.592	−1.350	0.697	−1.863	0.712	−0.103	0.537

Note: $N = 169$. Statistically significant coefficients are bold.
*p < ..1, **p < .05 one-tailed test ***p < .01.

TABLE 4.9. Fairness and Evaluations of the ICTY Mission for Defense Witnesses

	Truth		Responsibility		Punishment		Deterrence	
	Coefficient	Standard Error	Coefficient	Standard Error	Coefficient	Standard Error	Coefficient	Standard Error
OTP Fair to Me	−0.431	0.361	0.380	0.545	−0.217	0.338	0.292	0.279
Defense Fair to Me	0.195	0.577	−0.770	0.729	0.743	0.605	0.521	0.444
ICTY Fair toward Witnesses	0.248	0.204	0.438	0.262	0.226	0.193	**0.332**	**0.164****
ICTY Fair toward Defendants	0.273	0.236	**0.909**	**0.280*****	**0.484**	**0.219****	−0.013	0.212
Bosniak	−0.023	0.807	1.253	0.803	−0.661	0.672	−1.104	0.743
Serbs	**−2.733**	**0.692*****	**−1.788**	**0.941***	**−1.061**	**0.573***	**−1.519**	**0.623****
Croats	−1.252	0.595	−0.618	0.644	−0.726	0.533	−1.060	0.637
Albanian	−1.427	1.080	0.000	(omitted)	0.000	(omitted)	0.000	(omitted)
Last Trial Sentence on Appeal	−0.002	0.002	**−0.007**	**0.003****	−0.001	0.002	0.000	0.001
Percentage Big Fish	**−0.929**	**0.522***	**−1.673**	**0.954***	−0.460	0.417	−0.102	0.322
Constant	1.852	1.001	1.278	1.351	−0.593	0.886	0.405	0.849

Note: $N = 113$. Statistically significant coefficients are bold.
*p < ..1, **p < .05 one-tailed test ***p < .01.

except in the estimates for the deterrence measure. Yet those witnesses who believe the ICTY treated the defendants fairly are more likely to approve of the ICTY's performance in determining responsibility and punishing the guilty. It's almost as if the OTP witnesses perceive fairness toward defendants as related to success in preventing future conflict, while fairness toward witnesses means holding those responsible accountable through proper punishment in the here and now.

The only other finding of note is that we see a negative relationship between sentence length and approval of the ICTY's efforts to establish responsibility for the crimes committed in the former Yugoslavia. Defense witnesses are less likely to approve of the ICTY's performance in this area the greater the sentence is. As most defense witnesses are likely called because they can and desire to contribute testimony that might exonerate the defendant(s), this is as expected. From the different results we obtain when we separate out prosecution and defense witnesses, it is clear that the relationship between fairness (however measured) and support for the tribunal is contingent. Defense witnesses may be predisposed to distrust the tribunal to such an extent because of perceptions that the ICTY as a whole is unfair to their ethnic group and that the fairness with which they are treated as individuals cannot overcome these entrenched attitudes.

Conclusion

In this chapter, we set out to better understand how witnesses' evaluations of justice are affected by their views regarding the fairness with which the ICTY treated the witnesses personally, other witnesses, and defendants. The evidence we have analyzed has illuminated the nature of fairness and has helped color in this picture of the role played by fairness in evaluations of the work of the Yugoslav Tribunal. Nonetheless, that is only a beginning step in the evolving construction of our understanding of what fairness means in the context of international justice. With that spirit in mind, we here assess our analysis's contributions to elucidating both the notion of fairness and how witnesses to international crimes conceive of this value. As we review these findings, we also suggest how our understanding of fairness could be further bolstered by additional research.

We must begin by bearing in mind that although the witnesses have their own personally and socially constructed meanings for fairness as a general value, the meaning of "fairness" takes on a particular resonance within the context of the history and wars of the former Yugoslavia. The process and the outcomes of international justice in general and of the ICTY in particular are also evaluated according to a variant of fairness that, for most individuals in the former Yugoslavia, centers on the extent to which there is congruence between the history as understood by the victims and witnesses, on the one hand, and the history as affirmed in the judgments of the Trial Chamber, on the other. The greater the congruence between these histories is, the greater the level of support given to the tribunal will be. We make this point not to assert that fairness rooted in identity issues and narratives provides us a complete and definitive conception of fairness or evaluations of the ICTY, but to acknowledge the pervasive role played by this factor. Regarding the overall fairness of the ICTY and what it means for those who testify, one witness commented,

> I think that The Hague Tribunal did not meet the expectations, at least mine, my expectations were that it would judge fairly, and that, that justice can heal. And that justice leads to reconciliation. This is the way it should be. I am not fully convinced that justice has led to the truth. Because now we are, even after all this, how long has it been? About fifteen years have passed since The Hague Tribunal has been actively working, and there, I have a feeling that nothing has changed. Almost nothing.

Even independent of identity issues, fairness is a multifaceted concept that plays an important role in shaping witness evaluations of international justice. The results from the survey data indicate that witnesses care about how the actors of the tribunal—the Trial Chamber, the OTP, the defense, and the VWS—treated them and witnesses and defendants from their own and other ethnic groups. Our findings suggest the strongest relationships, however, between fairness evaluations that apply to others rather than to the witnesses themselves. The differences in support given to the ICTY across the four metrics of truth, responsibility, punishment, and deterrence are greater between those who believe the ICTY treated other witnesses and the defendants fairly and those who do not. The coefficients for these variables also tend to be more likely to reach statistical significance and to exercise a greater impact on ICTY evaluations, according to our model estimates. Nonetheless, we would not conclude definitively that the witnesses place greater emphasis on the treatment of others over treatment to themselves. It is possible that opinions regarding ICTY fairness toward other witnesses and the defendants are endogenous to evaluations of the tribunal across our four measures. That is, we cannot rule out the possibility that this conception of institutional fairness might also be viewed as a fifth metric of ICTY success and might thus reflect many of the same contours of opinion about the tribunal that are reflected by the other four measures.

Perhaps the most important finding of this research regards our assessment of the comparative contribution of outcomes versus fairness in witness evaluations of the ICTY. While the initial evidence in chapter 3 suggested that the leniency/severity of the sentences handed down to the guilty parties was related to witness opinions about the tribunal, we find that once we account for fairness in the individual decision-making process, the impact of outcomes is much more attenuated. We found consistent evidence that witness views of ICTY fairness toward them individually and especially toward other witnesses and defendants played a more meaningful role in opinions about the ICTY and that the effects of sentences on these opinions was significantly reduced even among prosecution witnesses. These findings bolster the work of many scholars who have long studied fairness in the US system of criminal justice (J. Jackson et al. 2012; Tyler 1990; Tyler and Huo 2002), as well as those who have studied its role in other systems (Moorhead, Sefton, and Scanlan 2007). The power of fairness to shape attitudes and behavior should not be underestimated, as we see illustrated in the following powerful words from a witness:

> When I finished my testimony, I felt a great, great, great relief, because I knew that the Tribunal would be fair and that it would reach such decisions as those against whom I had testified probably deserved. . . . And when I, as a citizen, come and show up at the municipality, or some other institution or other, wherever they are in these structures of power, I am—I am the one who is be humble. Instead of him being the one, I am once again the one."

In the next and last analytical chapter of this book, we describe the role played by witnesses' individual experiences before, during, and after their testimonies. The factor of experience is then combined with the model we have developed thus far, for our final set of estimates of public support for the ICTY. The impact of fairness in the context of our fully specified model can then be assessed.

FIVE

Wartime Experiences and Witness Efficacy

Thus far in this book, we have studied the ICTY witnesses as shaped by external forces that influence how they view the work of international criminal justice. Ethnic identity narratives exert a powerful socializing role that can structure and guide how witnesses perceive the tribunal, just as the work of the actors who make up the ICTY can lead individuals to develop more or less positive views of the tribunal's performance, depending on how the witnesses perceive they have been treated. In this final analytical chapter of the book, we explore the wartime experiences of the witnesses and how their background and their sense of personal efficacy influence their views about the tribunal.

The most pivotal of all the witnesses' experiences are those events of the wars of the 1990s in the former Yugoslavia that not only are the basis of their testimony at the ICTY but are also likely the most traumatic episodes of their lives. Individuals deal with the horrors of war in many ways. Some may use ways that lead to recovery and stability in their lives, while others may adopt less than optimal coping mechanisms (e.g., the use of drugs and alcohol) that interfere with their recovery. For many witnesses, the very opportunity to testify about these experiences can play an important role in their coping strategies. A great deal of research has examined whether testifying in open court (or perhaps in front of a truth commission) aids or impedes this psychological recovery process (Stepakoff et al. 2015; Brounéus 2010; Doak 2011; King and Meernik 2017; Hamber 2009; Mendeloff 2009; Stover 2005). Indeed, given what we learned about the importance of the fairness with which individuals are treated by court personnel, it is possible to understand how a particularly exacting prosecutor or an aggressive cross-examination by a defense lawyer might present problems for witnesses who feel that the veracity of their account is being challenged or who are prevented from describing what they believe are the most important details of their experiences. It is even possible that some witnesses may come away from testifying feeling angry or upset or may undergo some type of re-traumatization on the witness stand.

Our focus here on the witness experience centers first on whether the type and range of wartime trauma that these individuals have undergone led them to develop positive or negative attitudes about international justice. A particularly fascinating line of research, surveyed by Bauer et al. (2016), looks at various, multi-field inquiries showing that many individuals emerge from wartime violence with more prosocial attitudes. By some accounts, the atrocities of war lead some people to direct their energies toward social interactions that might help prevent such violence from occurring again, in much the same way as victims of other unfortunate events seek to galvanize attention and resources to prevent others from experiencing their problems (e.g., on issues like gun violence, drunk driving, and cancer). In this chapter, we seek to build on this research by analyzing the impact of wartime experiences on evaluations of the ICTY, to determine if those who have lived through the worst are more apt to see the best in the tribunal.

Comprising the second component we examine in this chapter in relation to the witnesses' personal experiences are their attitudes about their contribution to the work of the tribunal. Each witness who appears before the ICTY provides, through testimony, a piece of the larger puzzle about who was responsible for committing violations of international law. Each witness contributes the truth as he or she has experienced it, and each therefore contributes to the delivery of justice. Just as the witnesses evaluate the efforts of the ICTY to bring truth and justice, so they are asked about their own contributions toward the delivery of those consequences. We expect to find that the greater the sense of one's own personal efficacy is, the more likely the witness is to express more favorable attitudes regarding the ICTY's performance.

In this chapter, we first describe the various types of traumatic experiences the witnesses lived through during the Balkan wars. We do some preliminary testing of the impact that the level and type of trauma the witnesses experienced has on their evaluations of the ICTY. We then similarly analyze the role that witnesses' evaluations of their own performance in the courtroom has on their views of the tribunal's performance. Later in the chapter, we bring these individual-level components of our model together with the variables we assessed and analyzed in the previous chapters, to provide the final and comprehensive statistical estimates of our model of witness evaluations of the ICTY.

Wartime Experiences

The type and range of suffering the witnesses endured during the wars of the former Yugoslavia were significant and substantial. Indeed, our data cannot begin to convey the kinds of horrific atrocities through which many of these witnesses personally lived. Previous studies have shown that the people of the former Yugoslavia underwent extreme deprivation and trauma, although these experiences were not evenly distributed throughout the region (Scheffer 2012; Research and Documentation Center 2008). The following words of one witness speak volumes:

> I thought that it was the obligation of us all who survived the things that happened during the wartime events on, on, on, on the territory of Bosnia and Herzegovina to say it and to put it on the record, to do it both for ourselves, the survivors, and for the generations who to come. Some friends advised me to appear before the Tribunal as a witness with protective measures, which I refused, because I believed and I still do believe that all the witnesses should appear in the open before the Tribunal. Why hide from something you went through, from something you have seen with your own eyes, from something you experienced so dramatically, and why put that experience of yours behind? Why put some, some, screen in front of that experience of yours?

In keeping with emerging research on resilience and prosocial attitudes among individuals who have endured significant levels of violence, we hypothesize that greater levels of trauma are associated with a greater likelihood of support for the ICTY. We contend, to briefly restate the arguments we developed in chapter 2, that individuals who have undergone greater wartime suffering may possess a stronger need to see the ICTY succeed and to believe that it is accomplishing the four goals asked about in our survey.

In their review of the literature, Bauer et al. find that people who are exposed to violence are more likely to become cooperative, participate in social activities, take leadership roles, and give altruistically and that this positive impact of exposure to violence holds up across gender and age and among victims as well as perpetrators.

> The evidence suggests that war affects behavior in a range of situations, real and experimental. People exposed to more war-related violence tend to increase their social participation, by joining more local social and civic groups or taking on more leadership roles in their communities. They also take actions intended to benefit others in experimental laboratory games, such as altruistic giving. (Bauer et al. 2016, 3)

While there is likely to be a parochial dimension to these prosocial attitudes, with individuals cooperating more with those in their community, which may presage divisions among groups of people, this research demonstrates that prosocial behavior emerges across a wide variety of conflicts, as an "evolved response to external threats" (Bauer et al. 2016, 4). This type of victim resilience shows through quite clearly in the statement of one witness who commented on how he was able to go on living and eventually testify despite the traumatic experiences of the wartime era.

> How do I derive any positive aspects from that in terms of courage? To answer this question correctly, listen . . . perhaps I ought to put it as simply as possible, which means that when you have been through a number of storms it is clearly easier to bear the next storm. Because you get a little harder, you have more experience, you know that there is sunshine after the rain, and after the sunshine, there is the rain again, so that, in that sense, you must accept it, with a lot of optimism, particularly from that side in order to preserve the mental health of both yourself and your family. Because without the optimism and hope I think that a person cannot go and testify before the Hague Tribunal, especially as a prosecution witness.

Elcheroth and Spini (2009, 190) found that communities that experience violence on a level like the people of the former Yugoslavia underwent "become more critical toward local authorities and more supportive of international institutions that prosecute human rights violations." In situations of severe danger, individuals develop a common perception of threat, which may subsequently lead to increased support for human rights and humanitarian norms (Spini, Elcheroth, and Fasel 2008). Elcheroth (2006) finds as well, however, that individuals who have experienced trauma are less likely to desire retribution as a reaction to the violence they suffered.

The research cited by Bauer and his colleagues, which finds that individuals who have been exposed to such violence are more likely to develop prosocial attitudes, suggests several possible explanations. Individuals who experience the insecurity of war may act collectively as a form of social defense and may continue to engage in such activities after the fighting has ended, to insure the continued safety of their community. Bauer et al. (2016, 24–25) write that "evolutionary researchers from several disciplines have argued that our species' long history of intergroup competition may have favored adaptive psychological responses that promote the success of an individual's group relative to other groups—especially relative to antagonistic outgroups." Individuals may also be led to develop prosocial attitudes because of changes they personally undergo as a result of war. Individuals may reexamine their priorities in life, may decide to take action to ensure that such violence does not occur again, or may engage in other forms of post-traumatic growth or resilience. As Bauer and his colleagues (2016) note, however, we know a great deal more about the incidence of prosocial behavior after war than we do about its causes.

We synthesize insights both from research contending that exposure to violence in war can foster prosocial attitudes and from work finding that such violence can lead to a desire for prosecution of those who commit acts of violence, to suggest that such individuals are more likely to be supportive of the work of international justice. For those witnesses in our sample who have experienced greater levels and types of trauma, we have reason to believe that such exposure would tend to increase support for the ICTY. Such violence may lead them to be especially desirous of prosecution and punishment for those who are responsible, to satisfy a desire for retribution or as closure to a painful chapter in their lives. However, the desire for such prosecution does not necessarily lead a witness to develop a favorable opinion of the ICTY. Witnesses may be pleased that such justice efforts take place, but they may prefer that they take place at a local level or, perhaps, that efforts focus on the actual perpetrators of such crimes rather than on their distant superiors.

Nevertheless, we suggest that if, for some number of individuals, the suffering and violence of war leads them to develop a more positive, social outlook, their more expansive outlook on life might also lead them to appreciate the need for and benefits of international justice; that is, the development of a prosocial outlook may extend to communities beyond the individual's immediate surroundings and encompass larger social projects, such as the justice of the international tribunals. This research agenda regarding prosocial attitudes in the aftermath of violence, especially toward international institutions, is quite new, and our expectations may not reflect the actual witness experience. Therefore, we embark on this line of inquiry to better understand whether those who have experienced such violence are more apt to be satisfied with the work of the international tribunal, and we suggest the following hypothesis:

> *Hypothesis 3.1. The greater the number and type of traumatic wartime events a witness experiences are, the greater the likelihood is that the witness will approve of the performance of the ICTY.*

For our survey, the witnesses were asked to indicate whether they "experienced," "witnessed," "heard stories" about, or had no knowledge of multiple types of trauma that civilians and military personnel experienced during the armed conflict.[1] In table 5.1, we present the results from the

TABLE 5.1. Wartime Trauma Experienced and Witnessed

Trauma	Experienced	Witnessed
Artillery Fire / Shelling	234	129
Frightening Situation	211	114
Close to Death	208	151
Combat Situation	185	152
Lack of Food/Water	185	140
Murder of Family, Friends, or Acquaintances	158	101
Exposed to Propaganda	151	111
Lack of Shelter	138	155
Ethnic Cleansing	127	132
Family, Friends, Relatives Went Missing	125	84
Forced Separation from Family	116	105
Mine Explosion	112	114
Psychological Abuse	106	87
Unnatural Death of Family/Friend	103	66
Ill Health / No Medical Care	101	132
Detention/Imprisonment	94	125
Serious Injury	92	168
Forced Isolation	77	80
Murder of Stranger(s)	71	93
Physical Assault by Stranger	68	82
Torture	66	80
Physical Assault by Familiar Person	47	63
Kidnapped	22	39
Sexual Assault by Stranger	7	15
Sexual Assault by Familiar Person	3	11

Note: $N = 300$.

data on the events the witnesses personally experienced or personally witnessed (King and Meernik 2017). The results are ranked from highest to lowest based on the "experienced" category.

The results in table 5.1 reveal the extent and diversity of the types of trauma the witnesses in our survey experienced. Indeed, it bears keeping in mind that for every data point, there is an individual story of extreme suffering, such as torture, kidnapping, and sexual assault. The data in table 5.1 also show that the witnesses experienced some types of traumatic experiences more often than others. For example, over two hundred of the witnesses in our sample reported that they experienced shelling, being close to death, and feeling as if their lives were in danger. Furthermore, 185 interviewees indicated that they experienced combat situations, as well as a lack of food and water. Even the least frequently occurring types of trauma—the two types of sexual assault—were experienced by ten individuals in our sample. When we sum up the total of all experiences reported by the witnesses, we find that they collectively reported directly experiencing a total of 2,876 events (2,813 of these were specifically asked about on the questionnaire, while the remaining events were described in short answers provided by the interviewees and are not listed in the table, because they were reported by fewer persons). In addition, on average, female witnesses in our sample reported experiencing 11.8 wartime traumas, while male witnesses reported 9.5 such experiences.

The violence of the wars in the former Yugoslavia was not evenly distributed. Instead, the extreme acts of violence and many of the prosecutions at the ICTY tended to cluster around particular types of crimes and certain geographic regions, such as eastern Bosnia and the border between Croatia and Serbia. The violence tended to feature attacks by Bosnian Serb paramilitary forces and regular military forces against Bosniaks and, later, by Serbian forces that attacked Kosovar Albanians (who were also fighting Serbia). Other ethnic groups also committed crimes, but their offenses tended to be much less frequent and far less severe. In fact, 80 percent of the civilians who died during the Bosnian war were Bosniaks (Borger 2016, xxii).

To better understand the extent to which wartime suffering was contingent on ethnic identity, we created a quintile percentage ranking of the range of traumatic experiences the witnesses reported experiencing. Table 5.2 breaks down exposure to trauma by these quintiles and along ethnic lines. Individuals who fall into the first quintile experienced the fewest traumatic experiences (zero to three), while those in the fifth quintile experienced the most such events (sixteen or more). Individuals in the second, third, and fourth quintiles experienced four to seven, eight to ten, and eleven to fifteen such events, respectively. It is clear that some ethnic groups were exposed to much more violence and trauma than others. Bosniaks reported experiencing the highest level of trauma—38 percent of Bosniaks fall into the fifth (or highest) quintile for experiencing trauma. In total, two-thirds of all Bosniaks fall into the fourth and fifth quintiles. Kosovar Albanians also experienced high levels of wartime trauma and tend to fall into the two highest categories of trauma—65 percent are in the fourth and fifth quintiles. Serbians report the least level of trauma among the groups. For example, only 8 percent of Serbians reported experiencing the highest level of trauma, in the fifth quintile. When we conducted *t*-tests on the ethnicity variables and range of trauma experienced, we found that Bosniaks and Kosovar Albanians were statistically more likely to report higher levels of trauma (their respective correlation coefficients are 0.29 and 0.13), while Serbians (with a correlation coefficient of -0.36) were analogously less likely to report high levels of wartime suffering. There was no statistically significant relationship between amount of trauma and Croatian ethnicity.

While these descriptive data can help illustrate the distribution of wartime trauma that the witnesses underwent during the Balkan wars, we are also interested in the types of experiences they had, whether any of these experiences tend to cluster together, and whether these types of experiences might help us better understand witnesses' attitudes toward the Yugoslav Tribunal. We conducted factor analyses to determine if there are clusters of experiences that characterize the types of traumas the witnesses report. The analyses indicated five distinct dimensions of trauma as reported by the witnesses, given that we chose just those factor loadings where the eigenvalue was at least 1 (King and Meernik 2017). The first group comprises several variables that collectively describe wartime experiences pertaining to detention. Those specific experiences include (1) being held in detention and (2) being imprisoned. We label this factor category "detention." The second grouping pertains to human loss, where witnesses indicated that

TABLE 5.2. Ethnicity and Wartime Trauma Percentages

Level of Trauma Experienced	Bosniak	Croat	Serb	Kosovar Albanian	Other
5th Quintile	38	23	8	30	20
4th Quintile	29	20	11	35	13
3rd Quintile	13	19	14	17	30
2nd Quintile	15	23	32	17	23
1st Quintile	4	15	35	0	13

Note: $N = 300$.

they experienced situations that involved (1) missing family, friends, or relatives; (2) the murder of family, friends, or acquaintances; and (3) unnatural deaths of family members or friends. We label this category "suffering of family and friends." The third set of factors measure wartime deprivation and include (1) ill health without access to medical care, (2) lack of shelter, and (3) lack of food and water. We label this category "deprivation." The fourth factor, which we label "sexual assault," involves either (1) rape or sexual assault by a familiar person and/or (2) rape of sexual assault by a stranger. Finally, the last group of variables that clustered together, which we termed "war violence," include (1) combat situations, (2) artillery fire or shelling, (3) being close to death, and (4) mine explosions.

We begin with several bivariate analyses that look at the total number of wartime traumas the witnesses reported experiencing and their support for the ICTY. In each case, with the exception of the deterrence measure, the greater the number of wartime traumas witnesses reported experiencing is, the greater the likelihood is that they will support the ICTY. The correlation coefficients between the amount of trauma experienced and support for the ICTY's truth, responsibility, and deterrence missions are 0.20, 0.19, and 0.14, respectively. It is possible, however, that the relationship between the number of such experiences and support for the ICTY is not strictly linear. There may be certain, particular thresholds at which ICTY support becomes significantly more or less likely. Utilizing our quintile measure of the five levels of traumatic experiences, we find that those witnesses who fall into the first quintile and experienced the fewest indicators of trauma (we can say nothing about the severity of the trauma) are statistically less likely to approve of the manner in which the ICTY is providing truth, determining responsibility, and meting out punishment, according to the correlation coefficients (results not shown). Those who fall into the top percentile and report the highest numbers of traumas are more likely to approve of the ICTY's performance on the truth and responsibility measures. Table 5.3 displays the percentage levels of approval given to the ICTY across the four measures. The correlation coefficients for the

TABLE 5.3. Level of Wartime Trauma and Support for ICTY Goals Percentages

Level of Trauma Experienced	Truth	Responsibility	Punishment	Deterrence
5th Quintile	31	33	28	26
4th Quintile	20	19	25	20
3rd Quintile	14	16	18	12
2nd Quintile	25	20	19	25
1st Quintile	10	11	10	16

Note: N = 300.

four goals and the quintile ranking of wartime trauma are statistically significant, as we found earlier when looking just at the simple number of experiences (results not shown). Those who experienced the most trauma were more likely to express favorable opinions regarding the ICTY's contributions to truth, determining responsibility, providing punishment and deterring future crimes.

We also went through this exercise for the five factors of detention, suffering of family and friends, deprivation, sexual assault, and war violence, to assess their role in witness opinions. Interestingly, we found that only the factor of detention was consistently and positively related to evaluations of the Yugoslav Tribunal (results not shown). The correlation coefficients are statistically significant and range from 0.13 in the case of the deterrence measure to 0.23 for the truth measure. None of the other factors is related to the four measures of approval, although there is a negative relationship between experiences of wartime violence and support for the ICTY deterrence mission. Those who most directly experienced the violence of war are those who see little evidence that the ICTY has helped to prevent grave crimes from occurring again in the former Yugoslavia. At this point in our analysis, we would not want to conclude that the number of wartime traumas an individual experienced matters more than which type of traumas they underwent. We have no basis for suspecting that certain types of trauma have different impacts on victims and lead them to develop varying opinions regarding the performance of the ICTY. Indeed, between the amount, type, or duration of the trauma and opinions about international justice, there may be complex relationships that also encompass the types of experiences the witnesses testify about and the extent to which they have recovered emotionally and physically from these experiences. It is too early to conclude what role wartime trauma plays in witness evaluations, until we are able to test this hypothesis in a multivariate model. Before doing so, we clarify that there is likely a need for more fine-grained analyses of such questions.

Efficacy and Approval of the ICTY

Our survey of ICTY witnesses not only asked individuals for their thoughts about the ICTY's contributions to truth and justice but also solicited their views on their own contributions toward these goals. These are critical questions, as witness testimony is absolutely essential for the ICTY's success and for the effectiveness of the other international tribunals. Witness disapproval of the ICTY's performance is certainly not helpful and is damaging to its legitimacy, and if witnesses do not believe that their testimony made any difference, convincing other and future witnesses to undertake the extraordinary journey to The Hague and risk the possibility of threats to their safety and the security of their families becomes considerably more difficult. The witnesses often referred to their commitment to the truth and the consequences of their testimony for the future. As one witness so philosophically stated,

> So, one has to look at oneself in the mirror and say what is it that I can do, what is the truth, and that truth stays forever so that his grandchild tomorrow can say, my grandfather testified properly and honestly, because those events happened like that and one day the truth will be written.

The interests of justice and witness participation would seem to be best served if the witnesses knew that their testimony made a difference.

We hypothesize that witness efficacy—whether witnesses believe that their testimony has made a difference—will be a critical determinant of the witnesses' attitudes regarding whether they believe that the ICTY has generally done a good job in achieving its mandate goals. We suggest that those who believe that their testimony made a difference are also likely to believe, given their perception of effective input into the judicial process, that the ICTY has performed in such a way as to validate their contribution. As we suggested in chapter 2, we have reason to believe that witnesses' substantial sunk costs may lead them to engage in cognitive processing that makes them more likely to want to see the ICTY succeed. This sort of decision-making, which combines elements of motivated biases, wishful thinking, and reasoning by association (i.e., "If I feel good about my performance on the witness stand and believe I contributed to truth and justice, then surely the institution that welcomed my involvement should also be doing well"; see Ask and Granhag 2005; Garland and Newport 1991; Kunda 1987, 1990; Nickerson 1998; Taber and Lodge 2006), may lead some individuals to be more predisposed to approve of the ICTY's performance, because of their own sense of success on the witness stand. Therefore, we offer the following hypotheses:

Hypothesis 3.2. Witnesses who believe that they have contributed to providing truth to the ICTY will be more likely to approve of the performance of the tribunal.

Hypothesis 3.3. Witnesses who believe that they have contributed to providing justice to the ICTY will be more likely to approve of the performance of the tribunal.

Our survey asked the witnesses to respond to the analogous statements "*Overall*, reflecting back I believe that my testimony at the ICTY has contributed to the discovery of the truth about the wars in the former Yugoslavia" and "*Overall*, reflecting back on my entire testimony I believe that my testimony at the ICTY contributed to providing justice." The results are in table 5.4. The witnesses' responses to these statements are fairly uniform. Among all those surveyed (including those who did not know or did not offer an opinion), 67 percent agreed or strongly agreed that their testimony contributed to providing justice, and 71 percent agreed or strongly agreed that their testimony helped contribute to the discovery of the truth, while very few individuals (strongly) disagreed with this statement. Though nearly a quarter of the respondents did not express an opinion on this subject, the overwhelming majority of those who did choose an answer believe that their testimony made a difference.

This is good news for the ICTY, but what can we learn about how this sense of efficacy influences opinions about the tribunal? We can find the beginning of an answer in figures 5.1 and 5.2. The results among those who support the ICTY are similar in both figures. Among those who believe that their testimony contributed to the delivery of justice, the level of support given to the ICTY varies from highs of 62 percent and 63 percent on the truth and deterrence measures, respectively, to a low of 43 percent on the punishment measure. Among those who do not believe that their testimony made a difference in providing justice, the support ranges from a low of 8 percent for the responsibility and punishment goals to a high of 17 percent for the truth measure. The distribution of responses in support for the ICTY is similar when we analyze the witnesses' responses regarding their perceived efficacy on the truth measure. Those who believe that they contributed to the discovery of truth are quite likely to hold favorable attitudes regarding the ICTY's performance on the truth and deterrence measures (61 percent of them in both cases), while witness support on the

TABLE 5.4. Individual Attitudes about Witness Contribution to Justice and Truth Percentages

Witness Response	Contributed to Justice	Contributed to Truth
Strongly Agree / Agree	67	71
Strongly Disagree / Disagree	8	5
Don't Know / Did Not Respond	25	24

Note: $N = 300$.

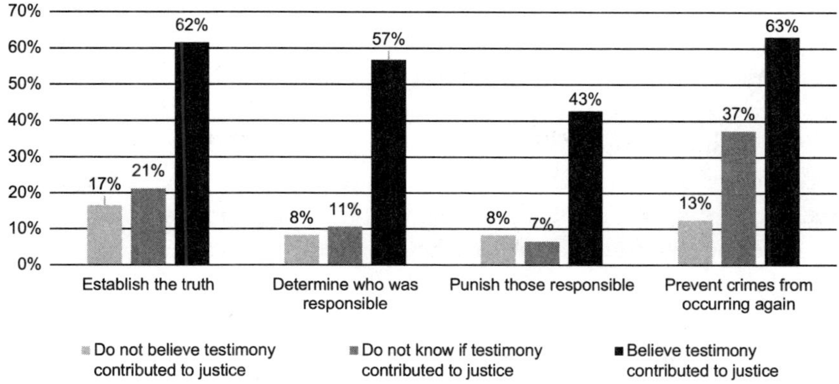

Figure 5.1. Efficacy, Justice and Support for the ICTY
N = 300

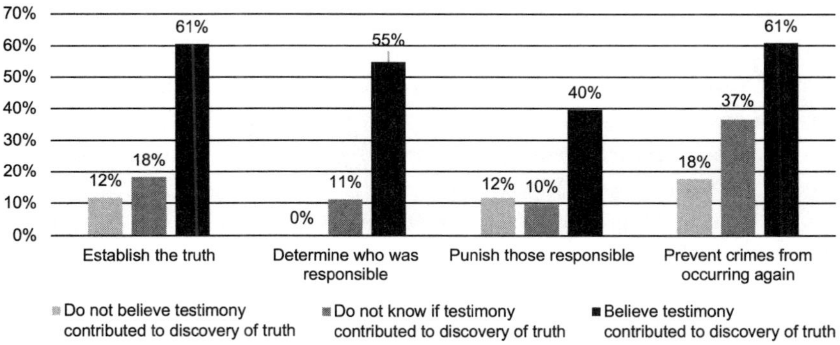

Figure 5.2. Efficacy, Truth and Support for the ICTY
N = 300

punishment measure still lags (at 40 percent). In general, though, the witnesses who feel the most positively about their contributions to the provision of truth and justice are also the ones most likely to support the ICTY. From these preliminary analyses, there is reason to believe that wartime trauma and feelings of personal efficacy are related to opinions about the ICTY's performance.

Final and Comprehensive Analyses

Having articulated and separately tested the three components of our model of individual support for international justice, we now bring these elements together in a series of multivariate models that will provide us with a more rigorous and comprehensive understanding of what factors are most critical in these evaluations by the witnesses. The first set of estimates includes (1) the four dichotomous measures of ethnic identity; (2) the variables measuring how individuals perceive they were personally treated by the Office of the Prosecution and the defense; (3) the composite measures of how individuals believe (a) that other witnesses (both from their ethnic group and the other ethnic groups) were treated by the ICTY and (b) that defendants from their ethnic group and other ethnic groups were treated by the tribunal; (4) our additive measure of the number of traumatic wartime experiences the witnesses underwent (with additional analyses utilizing the five trauma groupings); and (5) the variables measuring whether individuals believed they contributed to truth and justice. We also conduct separate analyses that make use of our variables pertaining to the sentences handed down by the ICTY to determine whether these punishments make a difference in the evaluations of the prosecution and defense witnesses. Finally, we include three control variables. The first is a dichotomous measure of gender, coded 1 for females and 0 otherwise. The second is a measure of how old the witness is in years, and the third is an ordinal measure of education that ranges from little or no education (coded 1) to a PhD (coded 9).

The probit estimates are presented in tables 5.5.–5.8 and follow the standard organization we have used in previous chapters, providing the estimates for the truth, responsibility, punishment, and deterrence measures of support, in that order. The measures of goodness of fit indicate that three of the four models provide a reasonably good fit. The exception is the model of individual approval of the ICTY's deterrence mission, which has generally proven to be the most vexing of the four measures and is typically the exception in many of our earlier analyses. We suspect that the difficulty we have had in explaining witness attitudes on this variable that measures whether the individual believes that "the ICTY will help in ***preventing*** grave crimes from occurring again in the former Yugoslavia" may be related to the varying interpretations witnesses may give to the key terms in this statement. Two aspects of this measure merit attention here. First, the statement refers to the future, about which many individuals may be uncertain: they may not have a general good sense for the likelihood of conflict in the future, to say nothing of the ICTY's ability to influence such events. Second, while the witnesses may know a good deal about the ICTY's efforts to provide truth, determine responsibility, and mete out punishment (through their own personal experiences as well as their general knowledge of the judicial processes of the tribunal), they may know less about deterrence, as the deterrence mission is rather distant, literally and figuratively, from the ICTY's work in The Hague. It has been difficult for scholars to establish connections between international justice and deterrence. Since the witnesses may also find it difficult to reach conclusions on this subject, their answers may not follow the usual patterns we see with the three other measures. Therefore, we suggest that the responses to this question, to the extent they are informed by some sort of consistent set of determinants, may reflect witnesses' perceptions of factors outside of international justice, such as regional and international political developments.

The model in which the dependent variable measures whether the individual (strongly) agreed that the ICTY has done a good job "in general in ***establishing the truth*** about what happened in the former Yugoslavia" shows a very good fit (table 5.5). The pseudo-R^2 is 0.32, and the percentage of cases correctly predicted is 76 percent, with a 50 percent reduction in error over the null model, for predicting the model category in every case. Table 5.6 presents the results for the dependent variable that measures whether the individual agrees or strongly agrees that "in general, the ICTY has done a good job in ***determining*** who was responsible for the grave crimes committed in the former Yugoslavia." Both the pseudo-R^2 of 0.42

TABLE 5.5. Complete Model of Witness Evaluations of the ICTY Truth Mission

	Coefficient	Standard Error	*Z* Score	*P* Value	Marginal Impact
Bosniak	–0.086	0.334	–0.260	0.798	–0.034
Serb	–1.365	0.339	–4.030	0.000***	–0.476
Croat	–0.564	0.316	–1.780	0.074*	–0.216
Kosovar Albanian	–0.002	0.414	0.000	0.997	–0.001
OTP Fair to Me	–0.141	0.235	–0.600	0.550	–0.056
Defense Fair to Me	–0.036	0.213	–0.170	0.865	–0.014
ICTY Fair toward Witnesses	0.301	0.113	2.650	0.008***	0.119
ICTY Fair toward Defendants	0.302	0.127	2.370	0.018**	0.120
Experiences	–0.008	0.017	–0.500	0.617	–0.003
Contributed to Truth	0.585	0.249	2.350	0.019**	0.225
Contributed to Justice	0.355	0.240	1.480	0.140	0.139
Female	–0.091	0.259	–0.350	0.724	–0.036
Education	–0.079	0.056	–1.410	0.160	–0.031
Age	–0.003	0.009	–0.380	0.705	–0.001
Constant	0.165	0.718	0.230	0.818	

Note: $N = 279$. $R^2 = 0.32$. Percent Corrected Predicted = 76%.
* $p < ..1$, ** $p < .05$ one-tailed test *** $p < .01$.

TABLE 5.6. Complete Model of Witness Evaluations of the ICTY Responsibility Mission

	Coefficient	Standard Error	*Z* Score	*P* Value	Marginal Impact
Bosniak	0.314	0.346	0.910	0.365	0.117
Serb	−0.887	0.363	−2.450	0.014**	−0.288
Croat	−0.384	0.338	−1.140	0.256	−0.133
Kosovar Albanian	−0.054	0.417	−0.130	0.896	−0.020
OTP Fair to Me	0.482	0.294	1.640	0.101*	0.162
Defense Fair to Me	−0.087	0.232	−0.370	0.708	−0.032
ICTY Fair toward Witnesses	0.341	0.123	2.760	0.006***	0.124
ICTY Fair toward Defendants	0.488	0.133	3.670	0.000***	0.177
Experiences	−0.011	0.018	−0.610	0.542	−0.004
Contributed to Truth	0.658	0.295	2.230	0.026**	0.221
Contributed to Justice	0.667	0.273	2.440	0.015**	0.226
Female	−0.049	0.283	−0.170	0.863	−0.018
Education	−0.061	0.062	−1.000	0.319	−0.022
Age	−0.010	0.010	−1.060	0.289	−0.004
Constant	−0.981	0.808	−1.210	0.224	

Note: $N = 280$. $R^2 = 0.42$. Percent Corrected Predicted = 83%.
* $p < ..1$, ** $p < .05$ one-tailed test *** $p < .01$.

TABLE 5.7. Complete Model of Witness Evaluations of the ICTY Punishment Mission

	Coefficient	Standard Error	*Z* Score	*P* Value	Marginal Impact
Bosniak	−0.213	0.334	−0.640	0.524	−0.065
Serb	−0.292	0.353	−0.830	0.408	−0.089
Croat	−0.119	0.332	−0.360	0.719	−0.037
Kosovar Albanian	0.144	0.412	0.350	0.727	0.047
OTP Fair to Me	0.274	0.267	1.030	0.305	0.082
Defense Fair to Me	0.005	0.211	0.030	0.980	0.002
ICTY Fair toward Witnesses	0.383	0.122	3.150	0.002***	0.122
ICTY Fair toward Defendants	0.222	0.118	1.890	0.059*	0.070
Experiences	0.012	0.017	0.710	0.480	0.004
Contributed to Truth	0.130	0.279	0.460	0.642	0.040
Contributed to Justice	0.948	0.292	3.240	0.001***	0.263
Female	0.161	0.259	0.620	0.534	0.053
Education	−0.107	0.058	−1.860	0.064*	−0.034
Age	0.006	0.009	0.620	0.539	0.002
Constant	−1.935	0.775	−2.500	0.013	

Note: $N = 280$. $R^2 = 0.24$. Percent Corrected Predicted = 78%.
* $p < ..1$, ** $p < .05$ one-tailed test *** $p < .01$.

and the percent correctly predicted (83 percent) for that variable are the highest of any of the four models. The proportionate reduction in error over the null model is also quite high, at 59 percent. The results for the punishment model, where the witnesses were asked whether "in general, the ICTY has done a good job in ***punishing*** those responsible for the grave crimes committed in the former Yugoslavia," provide a reasonably good fit (table 5.7). The adjusted R^2 is 0.24, and the model correctly predicts 78 percent of the cases, for a 29 percent reduction in error. Lastly, the model explaining opinions about the ICTY's performance in preventing grave crimes from occurring again predicts 68 percent of the cases correctly, while the proportionate reduction of error is 33 percent; the pseudo-R^2 is 0.14. We here discuss the findings regarding each of the independent variables across the four models.

Of the four ethnic groups we examine, the evidence is inconsistent regarding the impact of their identity on ICTY evaluations. In other research, Bosniaks and Kosovar Albanians were generally found to be more supportive of the ICTY (as we find in other results when we examine these bivariate relationships), but we find that these groups are statistically unlikely to express approval for any of the four measures of success we use when we include a more comprehensive set of exogenous factors in the model. In fact, in our model of deterrence (table 5.8), we even find

TABLE 5.8. Complete Model of Witness Evaluations of the ICTY Deterrence Mission

	Coefficient	Standard Error	*Z* Score	*P* Value	Marginal Impact
Bosniak	–0.619	0.322	–1.920	0.055	–0.242
Serb	–0.451	0.316	–1.430	0.153	–0.178
Croat	–0.290	0.310	–0.940	0.349	–0.115
Kosovar Albanian	–0.737	0.395	–1.870	0.062	–0.280
OTP Fair to Me	0.503	0.214	2.350	0.019**	0.198
Defense Fair to Me	0.449	0.193	2.320	0.020**	0.177
ICTY Fair toward Witnesses	0.210	0.104	2.020	0.043**	0.083
ICTY Fair toward Defendants	0.074	0.117	0.630	0.527	0.029
Experiences	0.004	0.015	0.280	0.777	0.002
Contributed to Truth	0.235	0.222	1.060	0.289	0.094
Contributed to Justice	0.406	0.220	1.840	0.065*	0.161
Female	–0.078	0.235	–0.330	0.741	–0.031
Education	–0.120	0.051	–2.330	0.020**	–0.048
Age	0.008	0.008	1.020	0.308	0.003
Constant	–0.851	0.674	–1.260	0.206	

Note: $N = 280$. $R^2 = 0.14$. Percent Corrected Predicted = 68%.
* $p < ..1$, ** $p < .05$ one-tailed test *** $p < .01$.

that Bosniaks and Kosovar Albanians are *unlikely* to express approval of the ICTY's efforts in preventing future crimes from occurring again (not marked as significant because it would be inconsistent with our hypotheses in chapter 3 about identity). All other things being equal, Bosniaks are approximately 24 percent less likely to express support on this measure, according to the marginal impact coefficient. Perhaps Bosniaks feel a greater threat about their current situation which contributes to their belief that future violence is possible (Clark 2014) or it may be that once one fully accounts for the holistic picture of the witness experience, evaluations about deterrence are more pessimistic. Similarly, Kosovar Albanians are also less likely to approve of the ICTY's work in realizing its deterrent mission (table 5.8). As we noted in chapter 3 this is not such a surprise given that the Kosovar Albanians continued to face outbreaks of violence in 1998–99 well after the ICTY had begun entering judgments.

As we have found throughout this research, Serbians are distinctly unsupportive of the Yugoslav Tribunal, especially in its efforts to provide truth (table 5.5) and determine responsibility (table 5.6). In these sets of estimates, Serbian witnesses are 48 percent and 29 percent less likely to express approval on these two measures, respectively. The coefficients are negative and statistically significant. Many were quite blunt in their condemnation of international justice, with one saying, "Practically, The Hague Tribunal is a political court, which was formed to convict Serbs and to take Kosovo from them." Many of their criticisms of the tribunal are summed up in the following words of one witness who found much about international justice lacking:

> If one side is on trial, in this instance the Serbian side, then it is incomplete. Soldiers, officers, policemen and leaders of one side are being tried. If at the same time Albanians are not on trial in the same courtroom for terrorism, and I mean members of the so-called KLA, then the case is incomplete and instead of searching for the truth, it is the guilt that is being sought after. . . . I wish to emphasise that NATO aggression against Yugoslavia was underway at that time. Not a campaign, as they call it, not the bombing as referred to elsewhere, but pure aggression. They have never been held accountable for it. Even Wesley Clark refused to take part in the process of giving evidence and he never showed up as a witness although he had been called by the defence. What does that infer? It corroborates what I said at the beginning, and that is that the aim was not to

> find out a full and veritable truth about the causes about what had been happening and what the consequences were.

Croatian witnesses are also unlikely to indicate approval of the ICTY's efforts to provide the truth about what happened in the former Yugoslavia, although the coefficients for this variable do not reach conventional levels of statistical significance. Their comments, are quite revealing, however, for many do possess a certain level of distrust toward the ICTY and its supporters. One said,

> I was under the impression that this was first and foremost a political court and that was how I considered it. I did not consider it to be a means to getting to the truth and I had a hard time imagining myself as a witness in these political games, that in my personal opinion were being played by the various European countries who were either directly or indirectly pressuring the court in The Hague.

The findings regarding the impact of ethnicity provide both good news and bad news for our model estimation. On the one hand, the relative lack of statistical significance among the coefficients indicates that the hypotheses we derived in chapter 3 are mostly not confirmed. On the other hand, in terms of developing a model of individual support for institutions of international criminal justice, that these Yugoslav-specific variables are generally not reaching conventional levels of statistical significance indicates that this model may well be generalizable to other nations that have become subject to international criminal tribunals and courts. The model fit does not appear to be overly driven by the impact of the ethnic variables that are specific to this particular tribunal. Nonetheless, we should not conclude that ethnicity as a more general measure of identity is not critical in witness evaluations.

We know that ethnicity pervades many other judgments and aspects of the work of the ICTY, just as we might expect it to exercise such a role in other institutions of transitional justice. For example, Bosniaks are more likely to indicate a belief that they have contributed to truth and justice (King and Meernik 2017), while Serbians are less likely to hold such attitudes. Earlier in this chapter, we saw that Bosniaks and Kosovar Albanians were more likely to have experienced high levels of traumatic wartime events. Hence, some portion of the impact of the ethnicity variables may be registering in other measures we use, especially given the consistent evidence we have seen previously for the powerful influence of ethnicity. Hence, we conclude that the impact of ethnicity is attenuated and may be influencing witness opinions of the ICTY's performance indirectly, through its relationships with other key concepts in the model. We revisit this issue shortly, when we conduct further analyses using a multilevel modeling approach, and when we discuss the role of identity in greater detail in this book's concluding chapter.

Our measures of whether the witnesses believe that they were personally treated fairly by the prosecution and the defense are almost all statistically insignificant in the truth, responsibility, and punishment models (tables 5.5–5.7) but are significant and positive in the deterrence model (table 5.8). At a loss to explain this anomaly, we suggest that in the absence of direct or helpful knowledge regarding the impact of the ICTY on deterrence, a number of individuals may have utilized their perceptions of ICTY fairness as a heuristic or clue as to its efforts toward preventing future conflict. Again, we believe that witness evaluations of the ICTY's contributions toward deterrence may follow a different pattern than their views about the three other goals, which focus much more on traditional aspects of the work of justice.

The results pertaining to witness beliefs about the fairness with which the ICTY has treated other witnesses and the defendants provide a much more consistent and substantively meaningful guide in explaining their evaluations of the tribunal. The coefficients for these two measures are positive and statistically significant in all models but one, as the variable measuring witness opinions regarding ICTY fairness toward defendants is not statistically significant in the deterrence model. For every unit increase in these measures (they range from 0, for witnesses who do not believe that the ICTY has been fair to witnesses/defendants of their ethnicity or those from other groups, to 2, for witnesses who believe that the tribunal has been fair to both groups of witnesses / defendants), the probability of believing that the ICTY has contributed to truth telling increases by 12 percent (identical for both variables). In the responsibility model, the marginal impact of the variable of fairness toward witnesses increases the likelihood of support by 12 percent (table 5.6), while the impact of the variable of fairness toward defendants raises the probability of support by 17 percent. In the punishment model (table 5.7), the corresponding marginal impacts are 12 percent for the witness variable and 7 percent for the defendant variable. Hence, the overall effect of the measure of witness perceptions of the fairness with which the ICTY treats defendants is remarkably consistent.

Fairness matters a great deal in the witnesses' evaluations of the

ICTY. One witness stated, "When I finished my testimony, I felt a great, great, great relief, because I knew that the Tribunal would be fair and that it would reach such decisions as those against whom I had testified probably deserved." Other research has consistently found that people tend to value fairness substantially, often even more than the outcomes of court cases (Tyler 1990; Tyler and Huo 2002). We must await the final set of analyses here before reaching such conclusions, but the evidence thus far indicates that the perception of fairness toward others—whether witnesses or defendants—matters a great deal. Equally as interesting, we also find that perceptions of the ICTY's general fairness toward others matters more than the witnesses' perceptions of the prosecution's and the defense's treatment of them. Earlier, we suggested that this may occur because witnesses hold linked opinions regarding our four measures of success and fairness; that is, fairness may be endogenous to the dependent variables. Again, we cannot rule out this possibility until we have more in-depth data on witness attitudes regarding specific cases and other more detailed information on their opinions. We do believe, however, that this evidence, coupled with a long history of prior research reaching similar conclusions, gives us a reasonable degree of confidence that fairness is a critical, as well as complex, factor in evaluations of international justice.

Two other variables assume a prominent role in these analyses. Witnesses who believe that they have contributed to providing truth and justice to the ICTY are more likely to approve of the ICTY's performance across our four measures. Witnesses who believe that their testimony has helped contribute to justice at the ICTY are more likely to express approval of the ICTY's performance in establishing responsibility, meting out punishment, and deterring future crimes. The marginal impact of this variable ranges from 16 percent in the deterrence model to 26 percent in the punishment model. The witnesses' reasoning is elucidated in the following quote from one who was talking about the horrors of war and the need to do something about these experiences:

> And that is the thing, you somehow feel, despite having, having seen terrible things—hundreds of people killed and expelled—yes, you are dealing with the fact that you have seen who did what to whom, and nobody has been convicted for it, well that's a real sin. I wanted to . . . my testimony to leave a positive mark. Not only for it to remain on paper or recorded on some audio tape, but to leave a trace, for someone to bear responsibility for this.

In addition, the coefficients for the analogous variable measuring whether the witness believed that he or she helped in the discovery of the truth are statistically significant in the truth and responsibility models. In each case, individuals who hold such beliefs are 22 percent more likely to believe that the ICTY has performed well in these areas. Those individuals who believe that their testimony has made a difference are among the most supportive of the ICTY. This illustrates the critical value of ensuring that the witnesses are made to feel that their testimony is important and valued. One witness said of the testimonial process,

> For me it was a positive, emotionally charged experience. I was visibly shaken during the whole of my testimony, but I was also satisfied that I had a chance to get all this off my chest, that I helped these international experts establish who had committed a crime, to convict the people who had done that.

The variable measuring the number of traumatic wartime experiences the witnesses endured does not reach statistical significance in any of the models. We also tested to determine if the type of traumatic experience was a better predictor of support for the tribunal. The performance of the five factors across the four models indicates that the specific types of traumatic experiences, such as detention and deprivation, generally do not help us explain support for the ICTY (results not shown). Only the coefficients for the factor measuring war violence are statistically significant. It is negatively related to support for the ICTY in the truth and deterrence models. We did not find any other specific factor to be statistically related to the ICTY performance measures. Perhaps for witnesses, *how* they and others are treated in being able to tell what they have been through is more important than *what* they have been through which brought them there to testify.

Among the control variables, education levels are negatively related to support for the ICTY in its punishment of the guilty and in its impact on deterrence, while none of the other coefficients are statistically significant. We cannot say whether this relationship occurs because those with higher education levels have a heightened awareness of the shortcomings of the tribunal or whether those with higher education levels may be more distrustful or critical of the efforts of the international community. We tested to determine if those individuals who indicated a greater degree of knowledge about the ICTY after they testified were also less likely to support the tribunal. After re-estimating the models, we found a positive relationship between ICTY knowledge and support for the ICTY's work in punishing the guilty, but that was the only finding of statistical significance (results not shown).

In the next phase of our analysis, we reran the models utilizing our variables measuring sentence length and the percentage of defendants who were high-ranking government or military leaders. We noted in chapter 3 that we ran separate analyses for the prosecution witnesses and for the defense witnesses, with the expectation that the former group would be more likely to seek lengthier sentences, while the latter group might be expected to prefer lighter punishments. The results (not shown) indicated otherwise. In the model estimations for prosecution witnesses, neither the coefficients for the sentencing variable nor those for the variable measuring percentage of "big fish" were statistically significant, although the relationships involving the other variables in the models described above mostly held. We were not able to run the models for the defense witnesses, because the limited degrees of freedom resulting from a smaller sample size meant that there was insufficient variation on the dependent variable, such that numerous cases were overdetermined. We dropped out some of the variables that contained missing cases, to determine if the resulting increased sample size might allow the model to be estimated. While we were able to generate estimates in this manner, we found that, here too, sentence length and involvement in trials with high-ranking defendants made no difference in impacting witnesses' evaluations of the ICTY. Thus, the preliminary results we found in chapter 3, suggesting that sentence length might influence these opinions, turns out to have been the result of the more abbreviated model we used. When controlling for all relevant factors in a more fully specified model, trial outcomes do not appear to play a significant role in the witnesses' opinions regarding the effectiveness of the ICTY. In this book's conclusion, we return to this theme and to the debate over whether the process and fairness of justice matters more than the outcomes.

We also sought to determine if there might be a better way to model the impact of ethnic identity on witness evaluations. Given the assumption that ethnic identity exercises a powerful and pervasive influence in the beliefs and attitudes of individuals, we elected to further model its impact through the use of a hierarchical or multilevel statistical model. Multilevel modeling has been used extensively in recent years to estimate the impact of larger units or groups in which individuals reside and that influence their behavior and opinions. For example, if we wish to explain student learning, we should take into account that students learn within a particular classroom environment, nested within a particular school, in a particular school system. Variables at each of these educational levels—such as the quality of the individual instructor, the curriculum plans of the school, and the resources of the school system—will shape certain aspects of student learning. Multilevel modeling techniques have been used in a variety of studies of individual attitudes (Anderson and Singer 2008; Arzheimer 2009; van der Meer, van Deth, and Scheepers 2009; Weldon 2006). We use such a technique here to assess the impact of ethnicity on witness evaluations, using the four, principal ethnic groups (Bosniaks, Serbians, Croatians, and Kosovar Albanians) and a fifth category of all others, as the filter through which we estimate those factors that we hypothesize exercise a more direct influence on opinions.

We begin by testing the model for just the prosecution witnesses and for just the defense witnesses, both to test the fit of the model when we include averages for sentence length and to determine if a mixed-effects modeling strategy is appropriate. The results are in tables 5.9 and 5.10, where statistically significant variables and coefficients are bolded. The results do not indicate that there is a need for a multilevel model. In fact, the likelihood ratio that indicates the appropriateness of a multilevel model was statisti-

TABLE 5.9. Multilevel Model of Support for ICTY Goals for Prosecution Witnesses

	Truth		Responsibility		Punishment		Deterrence	
	Coefficient	Standard Error	Coefficient	Standard Error	Coefficient	Standard Error	Coefficient	Standard Error
Last Trial Sentence on Appeal	0.001	0.001*	**0.001**	**0.001****	0.001	0.001	**−0.001**	**0.001****
Percentage Big Fish	−0.273	0.416	0.100	0.375	−0.009	0.340	−0.535	0.334
OTP Fair to Me	0.150	0.434	0.831	0.604	0.468	0.552	0.422	0.387
Defense Fair to Me	0.117	0.280	0.089	0.284	0.077	0.260	**0.783**	**0.246*****
ICTY Fair toward Witnesses	0.223	0.165	0.276	0.158	**0.393**	**0.165****	0.209	0.146
ICTY Fair toward Defendants	**0.491**	**0.182*****	**0.514**	**0.174*****	0.171	0.152	0.175	0.152
Experiences	0.028	0.025	0.020	0.024	0.016	0.023	0.000	0.020
Contributed to Truth	**1.040**	**0.365*****	**0.990**	**0.417****	0.042	0.416	0.345	0.319
Contributed to Justice	0.451	0.334	**0.901**	**0.368****	**1.520**	**0.506*****	0.230	0.320
Female	−0.330	0.350	−0.139	0.359	0.325	0.334	−0.096	0.300
Education	−0.087	0.082	−0.001	0.082	−0.047	0.076	**−0.188**	**0.069*****
Age	−0.002	0.012	−0.009	0.013	0.009	0.012	0.006	0.011
Constant	−1.412	1.073	−3.002	1.224	−3.366	1.223	−0.153	0.948

Note: $N = 169$. Statistically significant coefficients are bold.
* p < ..1, ** p < .05 one-tailed test *** p < .01.

cally insignificant across seven of the eight models (the four measures of ICTY performance for each of the two categories of witness types). The only exception was the fit of the model for defense witnesses on the truth measure, where the likelihood ratio indicated that the multilevel model was to be preferred to a standard probit model. We do find, however, that the average sentence given on appeal for the last trial in which prosecution witnesses testified is related to their opinions of the ICTY determination of responsibility (table 5.9). The coefficient for this variable is statistically significant and positive, which indicates that witnesses are more likely to approve of the ICTY's performance in this area as the average sentence length increases. In the truth model for prosecution witnesses (table 5.9), the coefficient for sentence length was positive but missed conventional levels of statistical significance. Our results also show that sentence length is negatively related to satisfaction with the ICTY's performance in deterring future war crimes, which contradicts our expectations for the prosecution witnesses. The overall lack of statistical significance and the diverse results cast doubt on the impact of sentence length, as measured in these analyses, as an important determinant of witness opinions.

TABLE 5.10. Multilevel Model of Support for ICTY Goals for Defense Witnesses

	Truth		Responsibility		Punishment		Deterrence	
	Coefficient	Standard Error	Coefficient	Standard Error	Coefficient	Standard Error	Coefficient	Standard Error
Last Trial Sentence on Appeal	−0.002	0.002	−0.004	0.003	0.000	0.002	0.000	0.001
Percentage Big Fish	−0.759	0.596	−1.401	0.926	0.169	0.509	0.353	0.377
OTP Fair to Me	−0.500	0.395	0.522	0.655	−0.310	0.384	0.366	0.289
Defense Fair to Me	0.220	0.668	−1.470	0.932	0.579	0.688	0.697	0.497
ICTY Fair toward Witnesses	0.207	0.213	0.556	0.295	0.382	0.233	**0.404**	**0.170****
ICTY Fair toward Defendants	0.234	0.259	**0.733**	**0.285*****	**0.557**	**0.242****	−0.106	0.221**
Experiences	−0.008	0.036	−0.097	0.059	0.018	0.034	−0.011	0.025
Contributed to Truth	0.581	0.458	0.813	0.612	−0.008	0.461	0.006	0.340
Contributed to Justice	0.028	0.461	0.743	0.646	0.821	0.486	0.501	0.340
Female	0.065	0.749	n/a		−0.068	0.683	0.854	0.539
Education	−0.081	0.122	n/a		**−0.432**	**0.158*****	−0.145	0.103
Age	−0.009	0.020	n/a		0.019	0.020	0.015	0.015
Constant	1.525	1.653	0.179	1.252	−1.494	1.511	−1.762	1.179

Note: $N = 113$. Statistically significant coefficients are bold. Where "n/a" occurs, variables were dropped as the model estimates failed to converge.

* $p < ..1$, ** $p < .05$ one-tailed test *** $p < .01$.

We explored a variety of model specifications to assess the impact of case outcomes, dropping variables whose coefficients were generally statistically insignificant and using different measures of sentencing outcomes, to determine if sentence length played any role in witness evaluations. We still found no solid evidence of statistically significant relationships. Regardless of whether we considered the average sentence in the first trial in which the witness testified, the average sentence of the first trial after appeal, the average sentence in the last trial in which the witness appeared, or the final average sentence on appeal from that last trial, the coefficients were consistently statistically insignificant (results not shown). Furthermore, we examined whether there were differences depending on the number of acquittals there were in trials in which the witnesses testified, but these outcomes also did not influence opinions of the ICTY's performance across its four mandate goals. We must conclude that, at least insofar as we have measured trial outcomes, they do not appear to be as meaningful in witness evaluations of the ICTY as other factors.

Lastly, we undertook one final set of model estimations, in which we utilized a variant of the dependent variable. Thus far, we have measured our dependent variables as dichotomous measures of support for the ICTY that do not distinguish based on intensity of support, grouping those who expressed disapproval with those who offered no opinion or indicated that they did not know. We chose to combine these various groups into our zero value, as we reasoned that there was a clear difference between, on the one hand, those who indicated they supported the work of the tribunal and, on the other, everyone else, but it is also important to examine other possible ways of measuring the dependent variable. In the last tables in this chapter, we provide the estimates we obtain when we employ an ordinal probit model where the dependent variable is coded 1 for "strongly disagree" (with the questions, provided earlier, that asked respondents to evaluate the ICTY's performance across the four measures of success), 2 for "disagree," 3 for "agree," and 4 for "strongly agree." All other responses are coded as missing. We also included a variable measuring whether the witness testified for the prosecution, in order to control for the impact of the calling party on our measure of sentence length, as we did not separate out all of these analyses for the prosecution and defense witnesses. The results are in tables 5.11–5.14.

Most of the findings from our previous model estimations hold up here. The coefficients for the variables by ethnic group mostly do not attain statistical significance, although Serb witnesses are statistically more likely to disapprove of the ICTY's efforts at determining truth and responsibil-

TABLE 5.11. Ordered Probit Estimates of Witness Evaluations of the ICTY Truth Mission

	Coefficient	Standard Error	Z Score	P Value
Bosniak	–0.164	0.338	–0.490	0.627
Serb	–1.281	0.353	-3.630	0.000***
Croat	–0.257	0.340	–0.760	0.450
Kosovar Albanian	–0.191	0.428	–0.450	0.655
Last Trial Sentence on Appeal	0.000	0.001	0.320	0.751
Percentage Big Fish	0.257	0.242	1.060	0.288
Experiences	0.039	0.018	2.220	0.026**
OTP Fair to Me	0.289	0.245	1.180	0.239
Defense Fair to Me	0.326	0.226	1.440	0.150
ICTY Fair toward Witnesses	0.553	0.126	4.400	0.000***
ICTY Fair toward Defendants	0.167	0.134	1.250	0.211
Contributed to Truth	0.631	0.278	2.270	0.023**
Contributed to Justice	0.162	0.279	0.580	0.561
Female	–0.263	0.269	–0.980	0.329
Education	–0.058	0.062	–0.940	0.350
Age	–0.005	0.010	–0.470	0.641
OTP Witness	0.230	0.242	0.950	0.341

Note: $N = 174$.
* $p < ..1$, ** $p < .05$ one-tailed test *** $p < .01$.

TABLE 5.12. Ordered Probit Estimates of Witness Evaluations of the ICTY Responsibility Mission

	Coefficient	Standard Error	Z Score	P Value
Bosniak	–0.037	0.375	–0.100	0.921
Serb	–0.954	0.416	–2.290	0.022**
Croat	–0.708	0.408	–1.740	0.082*
Kosovar Albanian	–0.502	0.490	–1.020	0.306
Last Trial Sentence on Appeal	0.000	0.001	–0.040	0.970
Percentage Big Fish	0.008	0.264	0.030	0.977
Experiences	0.018	0.017	1.030	0.304
OTP Fair to Me	0.580	0.265	2.190	0.028**
Defense Fair to Me	0.241	0.230	1.040	0.296
ICTY Fair toward Witnesses	0.387	0.126	3.070	0.002***
ICTY Fair toward Defendants	0.333	0.135	2.460	0.014***
Contributed to Truth	0.079	0.278	0.280	0.776
Contributed to Justice	0.963	0.280	3.430	0.001***
Female	–0.321	0.275	–1.170	0.244
Education	0.002	0.061	0.030	0.979
Age	–0.016	0.010	–1.620	0.106*
OTP Witness	0.563	0.263	2.140	0.032**

Note: $N = 163$.
* $p < ..1$, ** $p < .05$ one-tailed test *** $p < .01$.

TABLE 5.13. Ordered Probit Estimates of Witness Evaluations of the ICTY Punishment Mission

	Coefficient	Standard Error	*Z* Score	*P* Value
Bosniak	−0.009	0.362	−0.030	0.979
Serb	−0.245	0.396	−0.620	0.536
Croat	−0.014	0.382	−0.040	0.971
Kosovar Albanian	0.464	0.491	0.950	0.344
Last Trial Sentence on Appeal	0.001	0.001	1.310	0.191
Percentage Big Fish	−0.174	0.246	−0.710	0.480
Experiences	0.005	0.018	0.250	0.801
OTP Fair to Me	0.121	0.250	0.480	0.629
Defense Fair to Me	0.521	0.223	2.340	0.019**
ICTY Fair toward Witnesses	0.222	0.119	1.860	0.062**
ICTY Fair toward Defendants	0.399	0.126	3.180	0.001***
Contributed to Truth	0.005	0.277	0.020	0.987
Contributed to Justice	0.969	0.275	3.520	0.000***
Female	0.036	0.280	0.130	0.898
Education	−0.043	0.064	−0.670	0.501
Age	−0.007	0.010	−0.720	0.468
OTP Witness	0.229	0.244	0.940	0.348

Note: $N = 159$.

* $p < ..1$, ** $p < .05$ one-tailed test *** $p < .01$.

TABLE 5.14. Ordered Probit Estimates of Witness Evaluations of the ICTY Deterrence Mission

	Coefficient	Standard Error	*Z* Score	*P* Value
Bosniak	−0.246	0.341	−0.720	0.471
Serb	−0.347	0.337	−1.030	0.303
Croat	−0.391	0.331	−1.180	0.237
Kosovar Albanian	−0.627	0.452	−1.390	0.165
Last Trial Sentence on Appeal	0.001	0.001	1.250	0.210
Percentage Big Fish	−0.143	0.250	−0.570	0.565
Experiences	0.001	0.016	0.030	0.975
OTP Fair to Me	0.624	0.251	2.490	0.013**
Defense Fair to Me	0.281	0.237	1.190	0.236
ICTY Fair toward Witnesses	0.349	0.122	2.860	0.004***
ICTY Fair toward Defendants	0.067	0.133	0.510	0.612
Contributed to Truth	0.148	0.267	0.550	0.580
Contributed to Justice	0.497	0.268	1.860	0.064*
Female	−0.193	0.247	−0.780	0.435
Education	−0.151	0.060	−2.530	0.011**
Age	0.003	0.009	0.340	0.733
OTP Witness	0.110	0.237	0.470	0.642

Note: $N = 172$.

* $p < ..1$, ** $p < .05$ one-tailed test *** $p < .01$.

ity as we have seen before. We see the influence of witness evaluations of ICTY fairness positively related to approval of the ICTY's performance. Individuals who are more likely to believe that the ICTY treated other witnesses fairly are more likely to approve of the ICTY's effectiveness in advancing truth, responsibility, punishment, and deterrence. The corresponding measure of ICTY treatment of defendants is positive and statistically significant in the responsibility and punishment models (tables 5.12 and 5.13). Those who believe that they contributed to the provision of justice are still more likely to support the tribunal and express satisfaction with its efforts to establish responsibility (table 5.12), deliver punishment (table 5.13). and advance deterrence (table 5.14). Among the other diverse results we see, witnesses who experienced greater levels of harm during the Balkan wars are more likely to approve of the ICTY's efforts at establishing the truth (table 5.11), and prosecution witnesses are more likely to approve of the tribunal's efforts at establishing responsibility. Finally, once again, our measure of sentence length does not appear to be an important determinant of witness attitudes, as the coefficient for this variable never attains statistical significance.

Conclusions

We keep our conclusions brief here, as we use the final chapter of this book to summarize our final findings as well as the rest of the evidence we have gathered in the previous chapters. One set of our hypotheses introduced in this chapter proved to be quite influential in our statistical models, while one factor does not appear to be related to witness evaluations. Witnesses' sense of their own personal efficacy and the impact of their testimony on truth and justice appear to be the critical set of factors. Either or both variables were statistically significant in almost every type of model estimation we attempted. Individuals who believe that their testimony contributed to truth and justice are more likely to support the ICTY. Their positive attitudes are clearly reflected in the following words of a Croatian witness:

> I was fortunate to survive and had the opportunity to describe what happened for the sake of truth and nothing but the truth, and give my contribution to justice. I was happy to be given the opportunity to contribute to international justice with my testimony, so that those responsible, the perpetrators or those who brought about that situation, that massacre, receive the punishment they deserve by law and God.

In this book's conclusion, we comment further on the meaning of this finding. Clearly, it will be critical that future research accounts not just for individual identity and perceptions of fairness but also for witnesses' own expectations regarding their testimony and what they feel they have gained from it.

The factor that did not prove to be important, insofar as we make such determinations based on the statistical significance of the variable coefficients in our models, was the variable of traumatic wartime experiences. We tested to determine whether the quantity or type of such traumas made a difference in witness evaluations, but we found little evidence of such linear relationships in these data. Our hypothesized relationships are based on research showing that individuals who have lived through significant levels of violence are more apt to develop prosocial attitudes. It is possible that these prosocial attitudes do not extend beyond their communities, to encompass the international context and the work of international justice. The witnesses in our sample who experienced substantial levels of violence may still evidence prosocial attitudes, but these attitudes may exercise an impact on other aspects of the witnesses' relationships with the tribunal, such as their level of motivation to testify (King and Meernik 2017). In this book's conclusion, we suggest other methods by which future research might explore these emerging findings to determine the extent to which they are applicable to international versus domestic institutions and behaviors.

SIX

Conclusion

> I am aware that the truth is not one and is not borne by one man, and that is why I think that the people who know something about this, especially this that was going on here among us, should testify, and there should have been quite a number of witnesses, so that as much light as possible would be shed onto the truth.
>
> ICTY Witness

Our survey of three hundred witnesses from the International Criminal Tribunal for the Former Yugoslavia is the first systematic survey of those who testified at the tribunal and is perhaps the most comprehensive scientific survey undertaken of any witnesses who have taken part in international criminal justice. Its data supply an incredibly rich source of information on multiple subjects beyond the issues of the witnesses' evaluations of international justice, such as the impact of testifying on witness security and on witnesses' physical and psychological health, witness motivations for testifying, and the witnesses' open-ended observations on the work of the tribunal and their advice to other witnesses at international courts. The question of justice is perhaps the most fundamental of all, for the very purpose of the ICTY, as well as the other ad hoc tribunals and the permanent International Criminal Court, is to provide truth, justice, retribution, and, hopefully, a more peaceful world. If this justice has been delivered in a manner that speaks to the needs of these witnesses and the other victims of the Balkan wars, the legacy of the ICTY and of long-lasting, expensive and extraordinary international courts can be a positive one that helps build the foundation for the increased reliance on international law and for greater peace and security in the region. If truth and justice are flawed in some critical or fundamental way, the prospects for ensuring the tribunal's lasting legacy and its ability to foster peace and security in the affected lands is diminished.

Because of the deep and wide level of information the survey provides, we were able to rigorously test our comprehensive IFE (identity, fairness, and experience) theory of witness evaluations of justice. Our theory rests, furthermore, on two critical observations of the nature of justice at the international level. First, while there are similarities in the general missions of domestic and international courts to prosecute cases of wrongdoing and to help deter future criminal activities, we must remain cognizant of critical differences as we develop a theory of witness attitudes toward international justice. The events at issue at the international level concern society-wide power disputes involving systemic violence that will affect nearly everyone in some manner. They concern battles over the very future of the societies and nations involved. The amount and severity of the violence dwarfs what we find in ordinary domestic trials. Hence, the consequences of the judges' decisions at the international tribunals are hugely significant and will shape developments in the affected countries for years to come. Getting justice right in this international setting is critical for the witnesses, the victims, and the world. Second, the witnesses are among the most critical stakeholders (if not the most critical one) in international justice, for without the witnesses, there is no justice. They are unique in that they both experienced the violations of international law and publicly testified about them. They sit at the crossroads of conflict and courts. Any rigorous analysis of a theory of public opinion of international justice should be tested against data on their experiences and perceptions.

Our research has shown that witness evaluations of international justice are a complex amalgam of the background and experiences they bring to their moment on the witness stand, as well as their own fundamental values about justice and the nature of their contributions to this strange and complicated enterprise that is the modern international criminal tribunal. Our aim was not to develop a theory of witness attitudes toward justice that stressed the importance of a single, powerful predictor. Nor was it to assess the utility of a lengthy list of potentially important decision cues. Rather, our IFE model identifies three core areas of witness evaluations, and our analytical chapters derive the essential hypotheses that we contend are the most critical variables shaping witness opinions. We learned that while each of the three core areas of identity, fairness, and experience make specific and vital contributions to our understanding of what justice means for the witnesses, these elements also interact with one another and must be viewed in their entirety and in context, if we are to properly assess just how witnesses develop their perceptions of international justice.

In this concluding chapter, we review our major findings from our witness research. We begin by discussing the implications regarding our hypotheses that were confirmed. We review the evidence regarding the impact of identity, fairness, and witness efficacy on evaluations of the ICTY. These were the three factors on which we found the most consistent and supportive evidence, although the identity variables did not always make their impact felt directly. We review both our theoretical expectations and the more specific findings on which we can build in future research. As we review these confirmatory findings, we suggest avenues for further research to build on this work and extend it into other national and international settings. We then assess those factors that did not prove to be useful predictors of attitudes—namely, the witnesses' wartime experiences and the outcomes of the trials in which they testified. We discuss the reasons why these hypotheses may not have been supported and what future research might study to (dis)confirm these findings. In the penultimate section of the conclusion, we discuss how our enhanced understanding of the witness experience may affect the future administration of international justice and the role of international courts in world politics. We conclude with a small set of suggestions for future research on public opinion and international justice, to transcend our focus on the witnesses at this one particular international tribunal.

Identity and Ethnicity

We began the development of that part of our theory pertaining to identity by emphasizing how the nature of the cases before the ICTY, as well as most other domestic and international transitional justice mechanisms, is intimately bound up with issues of identity. Not every conflict situation that is the subject of a domestic truth commission or that comes before an international tribunal, such as the International Criminal Court, will find identity issues woven so deeply into the patterns of violence. Yet, understanding how the messy political, historical, and emotional complexities of conflict situations can be filtered into and processed out of black-and-white law and judicial processes is essential for explaining how those affected by these conflicts come to understand the meaning and purpose of justice.

While individual cases at the international tribunals may resemble those at the domestic level in that they turn on questions of who did what to whom, the relevant parties in the international disputes are not just the specific witnesses and accused perpetrators but include groups of thousands and often millions of people, divided by ethnicity, religion, social status, or political party. The implications of the outcomes of these trials extend far beyond the immediate participants, to encompass entire countries and regions of the world.

We found evidence of the role played by ethnicity in the ICTY witnesses' opinions of international justice. While the findings were not always as substantively and statistically significant as others have reported using bivariate analyses, we do find modest support for the importance of ethnicity in evaluations of justice. We demonstrated that the Serbian witness population was generally disapproving of the ICTY's performance across our four measures of delivering truth, determining responsibility, providing punishment, and advancing deterrence of future criminal violations of international law. In our final set of estimates, however, Serbian witnesses were statistically more likely to disapprove of the ICTY's performance on just the measures pertaining to truth and responsibility. Croatians were also often more likely to be negatively inclined against the tribunal, although the evidence for this was markedly weaker than the results pertaining to the Serbian witness population. Some evidence in some model specifications and on some measures of ICTY success suggests that Bosniaks and Kosovar Albanians were more disposed to give the ICTY good marks in its mission goals. Even these findings, however, were either too weak or too inconsistent across the multivariate estimates for us to conclude that witnesses from these groups were generally more likely to be supportive of the ICTY.

Previous research, which often lacked access to a wide variety of information on a broad cross section of the former Yugoslavia, has generally found that some ethnic groups are typically more critical of the ICTY than others—namely, that Serbians and Croatians are more critical than Bosniaks and Kosovar Albanians (Arzt 2006; Clark 2009c; Ford 2012; Hagan and Ivković 2006b; Klarin 2009; Meernik 2015a; Nettelfield 2010; Orentlicher 2008; Subotić 2009). We have shown that ethnic identity must be viewed in the context of other factors, especially those relevant in the individual experience prior to and during the testimonial process. While individuals arrive in The Hague with significant predispositions regarding past and present history in the Balkans, the novelty and high-stakes drama of testifying before the world can also exercise a powerful role in shaping individual evaluations. Such singular experiences may even overwhelm preexisting identity filters, especially for those who find the ICTY a more welcoming environment than they supposed. Future research ought to focus on the extent to which opinions about international justice may change after testimony, to ascertain whether these institutions can alter witnesses' perceptions of justice, especially among those inclined to distrust such institutions.

While consistent findings of support or opposition from the four ethnic groups that were the subject of nearly all of the ICTY cases would have allowed us to tell a more uniform story of support for justice, our findings reveal a great deal that will better help advance our theories of individual attitudes toward international justice. In fact, we suggest that because ethnic identity structures and influences a great deal of the other key components of the witness experience, we must be alert to other pathways through which identity affects opinions. For example, the violence of the wars in the former Yugoslavia was not evenly distributed throughout the region but tended to occur in areas in which there were prominent ethnic fault lines, such as in the eastern border of Bosnia, alongside Serbia, and in the Krajina border region between Croatia and Serbia. The following quotation from a witness who experienced the conflict in Kosovo illustrates how giving a testimony affected those who felt compelled to describe the events that happened to their people:

> Further, this opportunity of testifying for the first time gave me mixed feelings, satisfaction on one hand that I would unfold and make public what I had kept inside myself, would make it known not only to the Albanian community, but also international community, all the hardships and ordeal my people had gone through. On the other hand, I was a bit insecure whether I was the right person to recount all the sufferings and experiences, all the destruction that I had witnessed in Kosovo, that's why I had mixed feelings.

We know that Bosniaks tended to experience the greatest amount and greatest variety of traumatic wartime experiences, while Serbians tended to experience less trauma (see Borger 2016, xxii). Identity also tends to be strongly related to witness type, as Bosniaks and Kosovar Albanians are typically called as witnesses for the prosecution rather than the defense, while Serbians are primarily called by the defense. Hence, regarding support for the ICTY across the four major ethnic groups, the stark differences we saw in our initial, bivariate analyses were generally not so prominent once we began controlling for other factors, many of which are also bound up in ethnic identity distinctions. Therefore, we do not see our results as directly challenging those who have found stark differences in support for the ICTY across ethnic divides (Arzt 2006; Clark 2009c; Ford 2012; Hagan and Ivković 2006b; Ivković and Hagan 2016; Klarin 2009; Meernik 2015a; Nettelfield 2010; Orentlicher 2008; Subotić 2009; UNDP 2005). Rather, we see our research as pointing toward productive refinements of our expectations regarding the impact of ethnicity on opinions of international justice. For example, future research might focus on the development of models for particular ethnic groups based on regional or conflict specific attributes—whether in the former Yugoslavia or in a different conflict zone.

In considering the impact of identity on attitudes about international justice, we must be acutely aware of the critical differences of opinion that emerge about the ICTY depending on the type of question being asked. While ethnic identity can help us explain support for each of the four measures of ICTY success, this concept was particularly potent in accounting for what are perhaps the tribunal's most relevant goals, providing truth and determining responsibility. We do not wish to downplay the importance of punishment and deterrence in the international justice enterprise, but the notions of truth and responsibility are at the core of the battle over competing narratives in the courtroom. They are also central elements of any judicial system. Perhaps the ICTY's most consequential decisions are its affirmation of one group's claims of political and ethnically motivated violence, on the one hand, and the tribunal's dismissal of another group's claims that such violence was defensive and not as serious as other groups contend, on the other hand. When the tribunal accepts a group narrative in a particular case, it has vindicated that group's version of history and affirmed the veracity of the victims' accounts. Furthermore, such judgments represent the international community's verdict in the ethnic competition that is played out in politics, on the battlefield, and eventually in court. For the group whose narrative has been given the tribunal's seal of approval, all good things flow from such determinations, and support for the ICTY's efforts to establish truth and responsibility increases.

Attitudes regarding punishment and deterrence are also critical for witnesses, but they may lack the immediacy and emotional resonance of opinions about issues that are at the core of ethnic identity. While truth, responsibility, and punishment all pertain to what we might consider as normal and appropriate court functions and, thus, as more relevant to the witnesses' encounters with the ICTY, the deterrence mission is quite different. The evidence regarding the effects of the tribunal's deterrence mission is found not necessarily in verdicts and court administration but in the politics and events in the former conflict zones. Hence, the degree to which witnesses associate the ICTY with the presence or absence of violence in their homeland is likely to be more tenuous and contingent on other factors than their expectation that the ICTY properly performs its judicial functions. The results here show that we need a better understanding of whether such institutions deter future violence because evidence is mixed—identity matters, but fair treatment across groups matters for believing that institutions can violent conflict. Therefore, we suggest that future research make similar, discriminating efforts to measure attitudes about and support for international justice, considering how identity issues may assume greater or lesser relevance depending on which aspect of the tribunal's efforts is being evaluated.

Regarding support for transitional justice, we need to develop a set of both general and more specific questions that allow us not only to distinguish support across the various missions of these institutions but also to make meaningful comparisons of support by the type of mechanism (e.g., criminal trial, truth commission, memorialization), the level of effort (international, domestic), and the duration of the efforts. We also suspect that identity issues will play a key role in public support for other elements of peace processes, such as elections, governance, and economic reconstruction.

Identity issues should be explored whenever transitional justice and conflict resolution are being debated and evaluated. We urge researchers to focus on whatever aspect of identity is most relevant in a given conflict—ethnicity, religion, language, politics, or whatever ways in which people are grouping themselves and distinguishing their group from "the other." These issues tend to act as a powerful, preliminary filter that helps guide opinions, and they may also be related to other relevant factors, such as the level of trauma suffered. By determining how perceptions of conflict are structured, we can establish baseline indicators (albeit somewhat subjective ones) of the extent to which members of a particular group may be more or less apt to support international justice.

We would also like to better understand how long identity affects attitudes about international justice specifically and transitional justice more generally. Does the impact of identity lessen over time, as the issues over which groups contested fade in importance and as the conflict provocateurs die out or become discredited? Or does the nature of the political settlement preserve such divisions and even harden them, as the Dayton

Accords did by freezing in place the ethnic divisions at the end of the Bosnian War? Furthermore, we would like to know what sorts of differences of opinion over transitional justice may emerge when we differentiate in our survey research between those who played an active role in the proceedings and those who did not take part in transitional justice. Are the victim witnesses a tougher audience to convince of the benefits of international justice, because they personally have so much at stake in these trials? Or do the witnesses enjoy the benefit of having been forced to think through their traumas and see how their accounts have been interpreted by the judges, giving witnesses a more realistic view of what international justice can provide? We see identity issues both as among the most important for scholars and practitioners to grapple with in their efforts to understand perceptions of international justice and as the factor that will demand the most creativity and ingenuity in ferreting out its effects on individuals and societies.

Fairness

One concept that has its origins in the study of domestic courts proved to be generalizable to the international level and particularly powerful in accounting for opinions about the ICTY. The notion of fairness has long been held to be a core component of individuals' views of judicial systems and their personnel (Tyler 1990). Individuals expect courts and the police to be motivated by concern for justice, to operate with good motives, and to treat people with respect, politeness, neutrality, and honesty. Individuals especially want courts to give them the opportunity to tell their story. While fairness has been studied principally in the context of the American court system, we believe that this concept holds great promise at the international level as well.

For the witnesses in our sample, the notion of fairness is multifaceted. Fairness was a concept we asked witnesses to apply in evaluating how they were treated personally by the principal actors of the ICTY—the Trial Chamber, the Victims and Witnesses Section, and especially the Office of the Prosecutor and the defense. The witnesses were also surveyed on whether they believed that the tribunal had given fair treatment to the defendants and other witnesses. The witnesses in our sample overwhelmingly believed that they themselves were treated fairly by the judges and the VWS. Strong majorities believed that they were treated fairly by the OTP and defense, although witnesses were more likely to believe that whichever party called them to testify treated them more fairly than did the counsel for the opposing side. The statistical findings, however, show an inconsistent impact of witness perceptions of the fairness with which they were treated by the OTP and defense. While some evidence in our most comprehensive multivariate analysis indicated that those believing they were treated fairly by these two actors were more likely to approve of the tribunal's performance in deterring future war crimes, we did not find evidence that personal treatment of the witnesses was influential in shaping their views across the multiple dimensions of ICTY effectiveness in our multivariate estimates. Given that all witnesses gave all the principal actors with whom they interacted generally high marks for fairness, this concept may have lost some of its potency in helping us to differentiate among those more or less likely to approve of the ICTY's performance of its core missions.

Our findings related to personal fairness are quite remarkable. There is certainly ample opportunity for the witnesses to have negative experiences with the ICTY given the powerful emotions involved in testifying and the high stakes of the identity conflicts. The length of time over which witnesses interact with the tribunal (some witnesses may have been contacted and given statements years before their actual testimony) and the numerous points of contact and interactions with ICTY personnel must address everything from logistics and security, to emotional well-being and substantive testimony. That witnesses came away from these experiences with positive impressions of their fair treatment is extraordinary, especially when viewed in light of the negative press that the tribunal often receives in the region. While our data do not tell us precisely why witnesses have such opinions, the potential reasons for their positive assessments could range from a deference to authority (as a result of years of living under a communist regime) to a sense of satisfaction with their own testimony. Of course, their views also may be the result of the professional demeanor of and their treatment by tribunal personnel.

Although witnesses' evaluations of the tribunal's fair treatment of others certainly matters, the substantive and statistical insignificance of the personal treatment variables should give rise to caution in the manner in which we conceptualize the role of fairness in opinions about justice. Research by most scholars (Moorhead, Sefton, and Scanlan 2007, Tyler 1990, 2001; Tyler and Huo 2002; Wood et al. 2015) concerns this micro-level fairness. We suggest that personal treatment is not nearly so important at the international level, for several reasons that suggest, further, why international justice may not be so distinct from its domestic counterparts.

First, there may be a special level of professionalism in the treatment of witnesses to these horrific crimes (as distinct from domestic treatment of individuals in more mundane situations, such as a traffic stop or the report of a crime), given the awareness of the traumas these individuals have suffered and because of the staffing of victim support offices with social workers and others who are very cognizant of witness fragility. Simply put, international courts may just do a better job at providing witness support than does the typical domestic criminal justice system. While there are still opportunities for witnesses to perceive that they have been treated unfairly (especially when they undergo vigorous cross-examination), personal treatment seems to matter less in evaluations at the international level, perhaps because it is generally so good.

Second, as we discussed when viewing the role of ethnicity in justice evaluations, it may be that, for many individuals, this wholly new and emotionally overpowering process of testifying at an international tribunal overwhelms many of the predispositions individuals bring to this encounter. Indeed, in this setting where so many individuals have labored to create an environment in which individuals can relate their stories effectively (in comparison to their wartime and postconflict experiences, where their circumstances were often difficult and dangerous), individuals may well feel a deep gratitude toward ICTY personnel who have looked after them. As one witness from Kosovo stated, "Yes, it has certainly been something special testifying during those three times because I was given the opportunity to disclose all what was locked inside my mind and my soul for years." For these reasons, we believe that our research sheds new light on the role of fairness in how individuals perceive justice. We should not reflexively assume that personal experience matters most, especially in situations where such treatment is generally quite good and stands in stark comparison to witnesses' past experiences. Instead, these results suggest that our theories and models of fairness should make more comparative assessments of justice, to identify those structural features across institutions, whether domestic or international, that indicate which judicial systems have developed better witness support structures and which are lacking such support and thus lead to more variable assessments of justice. We would like to know, for example, whether witnesses at the International Criminal Tribunal for Rwanda would give similarly high marks to their treatment and whether these assessments affect their evaluations of the work of that tribunal.

In contrast to many studies of fairness that focus on the individual experience, we found that witnesses' perceptions of how the ICTY treated others matter more. Witnesses were more apt to approve of the tribunal's performance across the truth, responsibility, punishment, and deterrence missions when they believed that the tribunal had treated other witnesses fairly (both those of their ethnicity and those from other ethnic groups). They were also more likely to express approval of the ICTY when they believed that the tribunal was fairly treating defendants—again, both those of their ethnicity and those from other ethnic backgrounds. In fact, unlike our measure of personal fairness, where respondents overwhelmingly indicated belief that they were treated fairly, there is significantly more variation in the witnesses' assessments of how the tribunal has treated others. Even while the witnesses were less likely to believe that they themselves were treated fairly by the prosecution (79 percent) and the defense (71 percent) in comparison to their views of fair treatment by the judges and the VWS (more than 90 percent in each case), their positive impressions in these cases far outstrip their assessments of how fair the ICTY has been toward other witnesses. For example, 63 percent believed that the ICTY was fair to witnesses of their ethnicity, and 48 percent believed that the tribunal was fair toward witnesses from other ethnic backgrounds. They were even less likely to believe that the ICTY was fair to the defendants. Only one-third believed that the tribunal was fair to defendants of their ethnicity, while just 26 percent believed that the ICTY treated defendants from other ethnic groups fairly. Opinions are much more divided on the issues of fairness toward individuals other than the witnesses themselves. The impact of attitudes regarding ICTY fairness toward other witnesses and the defendants was also substantial. In fact, the marginal impact coefficients for these variables generally showed that as witnesses' attitudes regarding fairness toward each of these groups increased, they became, on average, approximately 12 percent more likely to approve of the ICTY's performance across the various measures.

Our composite measures of fairness proved to be among the most consistently powerful predictors of witness attitudes toward the ICTY and deserve greater theoretical scrutiny and empirical testing. Interestingly, research on public opinion regarding domestic justice systems often does not address issues involving fairness toward others, although one strand of research on race and fairness is relevant here and supports our contention. Some scholars have found African American populations to have more negative views of the fairness of criminal justice systems (e.g., Hurwitz and Pefley 2005; Tyler 1988, 2006a, 2006b). Where identity carries political meaning and consequences, it may influence the attitudes of those who are members of the group. The relevance of how courts treat people as groups demonstrates, again, that identity issues are critical for understanding perceptions of fairness. We have shown that when courts are perceived as arbiters in disputes that have a strong (if not dominant) identity component, their work will be judged not just on the basis of treatment toward the individual but on that individual's perception of how the court views the group to which they belong. For African Americans, identity issues pertaining to perceptions of the police as unfairly targeting young males in their population may lead to a more negative assessment of the justice system. For the Bosniaks, Serbians, and Croatians in our witness population, identity issues also pertain to perceptions of unfair targeting, as well as to opposition to the judges' verdicts on their group's narratives.

In previous research on fairness in the US court system, Tyler (1990) and his coauthors (see, especially, Tyler and Huo 2002) argued and found that individuals are concerned more with fairness than with outcomes. Those findings were corroborated here. Despite the fact that our initial analyses seemed to suggest that outcomes—measured as sentence length—did matter (the longer the average sentence of the last trial in which an individual testified was, the more likely prosecution witnesses were to support the ICTY, while defense witnesses were less likely to indicate approval of the tribunal), our final, multivariate analyses showed that in the presence of other variables, outcomes did not seem linked to witness evaluations. While our confirmation of the critical role played by fairness fits comfortably with other analyses, we are still somewhat perplexed as to why outcomes do not matter as much. Especially given that group narratives regarding who was to blame for the atrocities occupy such a prominent place in the opinions of so many in the former Yugoslavia, we would expect that severe punishment for the guilty and acquittal of the innocent would be more important than fairness in evaluating the ICTY. We return to the discussion of outcomes later in this chapter, to puzzle through these findings.

We believe that the consistency and impact of these findings should be a tremendous spur to the further refinement of our model of individual evaluations of international justice. It would be especially useful to couple additional studies at the international level (especially of the International Criminal Court) with research on those societies in which both international and domestic trials in transitional justice have been utilized. For example, Bosnia-Herzegovina and Kosovo have dealt with many lower-ranking individuals accused of war crimes and other violations of international law in their domestic courts. In fact, a new international entity headquartered in The Hague, the Kosovo Specialist Chambers & Specialist Prosecutor's Office, will focus on trying citizens of Kosovo who are alleged to have committed crimes against ethnic minorities. More in-depth studies of public opinion regarding the need for and efficacy of these different types of justice would be particularly useful. Future research might explore public opinion across Bosnia-Herzegovina and Kosovo, to develop robust samples that will allow researchers to explore the meaning and role of fairness in how individuals perceive domestic and international justice. It will be critical to utilize larger samples than ours, because of the need to ensure sufficiently large subsamples of the key ethnic groups. Such analyses would allow researchers to better determine how identity affects evaluations of international and domestic justice, as well as other relevant aspects of the witness experience.

Research should also focus on the meaning of fairness in complex conflict situations with competing identity groups. Our study used some fairly basic questions to probe witness attitudes toward fairness, but we suggest that future research provide individuals with a much wider variety of questions that focus on various aspects of fairness. For example, one of our findings that we have struggled to understand is how individuals come to believe that the ICTY has been less fair to other ethnic groups and *more* fair to their own, when the dominant sociocultural narratives typically focus on the grievances of one's own group. We speculated that perhaps many individuals look at fairness in a much more relativist and expansive dimension, in which there is unfairness related to negative treatment (how we are accustomed to understanding a lack of fairness, in which individuals receive less respect, honesty, and neutrality than they believe they deserve) and unfairness related to perceived excessively positive treatment of others. We suspect, albeit without much evidence (except the impressions of the VWS personnel who administered our survey), that some individuals may regard the ICTY as too lenient on some individuals and groups. This leniency or perception of "inappropriate" favorable treatment is defined as *too much* fairness, which may then be perceived as unfair treatment or, more precisely, favoritism. Hence, fairness is not just an absolute standard on which individuals may possess differing opinions; it is contextually based, as it seems to depend, to some extent, on identity. A witness might perceive unfairness as occurring both when individuals from the witness's group are denied due process or treated disrespectfully and when individuals from other groups are accorded benefits (e.g., lighter sentences, leaves of absence from the ICTY detention unit) that may have been unavailable to members of the witness's group. Perceptions of fairness may also be more outcome-based at the international level, if individuals define fairness based on whether the verdicts of international tribunals support or disconfirm their predominant conflict narrative. There is still much we do not know about this puzzle of fairness.

We suggest that future research on witness views of international justice, such as research on the International Criminal Court, focus on asking more in-depth questions about fairness. For example, witnesses might be asked questions about fairness in specific trials or toward particular defendants, as well as given the opportunity to offer their own definitions. The general type indicators we used in our survey project provide us with a solid and fairly objective measure of witnesses' views of fairness and its importance in evaluations of international justice, but there is sometimes no substitute for asking witnesses directly.

Much more detailed analysis of fairness at the international level is needed to determine how individuals define and measure this concept. We should also seek to better understand how types of venue and of transitional justice mechanism influence perceptions of fairness and justice. For example, do individuals report higher or lower levels of fairness in criminal trials versus more restorative forms of transitional justice, such as truth commissions or within local war crimes courts. The best place to begin future study on these issues may well be with a more focused, qualitative analysis of the views of witnesses and others affected by identity conflicts.

Contributing to Truth and Justice

The third element of our IFE theory of public opinion and international justice is premised on the wartime experiences that individuals have undergone and on their own experience on the witness stand. The final multivariate analyses revealed that the witnesses' views of the work of the ICTY are, in part, a product of their evaluations of their own performance. Those witnesses who believe that their testimony helped contribute to the provision of justice and the discovery of the truth are more likely to express positive opinions of the tribunal's efforts to provide truth, determine responsibility, allocate punishment, and help prevent war crimes from occurring again in the former Yugoslavia. To put it even more succinctly, witnesses tend to equate their success with the success of the tribunal. A sense of personal efficacy is critical not just for the individual witness but for the tribunal more generally. The following words of a witness from Bosnia-Herzegovina are especially apt in this context:

> I looked the criminals in the eye. I had absolutely no reason to look either straight in front of me or sideways. Simply put, that was my way of saying that I was speaking the truth, perhaps of bringing them to a catharsis, making them understand that their actions had brought ill and injustice to people who were absolutely innocent. . . . When I finished my testimony, I felt a great, great, great relief, because I knew that the Tribunal would be fair and that it would reach such decisions as those against whom I had testified probably deserved.

We have argued that witnesses' cognitive decision-making processes would lead them to make this connection between their sense of personal efficacy and their evaluations of the ICTY. Because these witnesses suffered to an extraordinary degree during the Balkan wars, lived to tell their stories, and made the difficult journey to The Hague to relate their experiences, we argued that there would be significant psychological needs to justify these costs. The following words of a witness from Kosovo demonstrate the profound impact that the events of the war and giving testimony have on individuals:

> Giving testimony has had a very important and positive impact on my being, because through testifying, my ego, my soul was . . . was purified, relieved of certain things that worried me; and after my testimony, I felt a bit relieved, believing that with my testimony, I significantly contributed to making these events heard and that they serve as an example for the future generations so that they are not repeated, and in particular for potential future dictators, so that they fear the truth and stop such massacres in the future.

We suggest that most individuals confronted with undertaking a high-risk, high-cost endeavor would feel a strong need to justify the psychological costs of the behavior by believing that their actions were worth the price. Although we cannot look into the minds of our survey witnesses to identify the nature of this linkage between beliefs about their personal success and beliefs about the ICTY's success (or lack thereof), the statistical significance of the coefficients for the personal efficacy variables attest to their powerful impact in the model. We also justified the inclusion of the efficacy variables for a somewhat more pedantic reason: we suggested that individuals who believe that they were successful in contributing to truth and justice might conclude, from their own success, that the tribunal was doing well in general. Regardless of the methods by which individuals equate their success with that of the tribunal's, personal efficacy is one of the three most critical components of evaluations of the ICTY.

While we have been emphasizing the psychological explanations for the effect of personal efficacy, this concept has long been employed in studies of public opinion and, in particular, political participation. In research dating back to such political science luminaries as David Easton (Easton and Dennis 1967) and in more recent attempts to employ efficacy to explain decision-making (Morrell 2005) and to measure the concept itself (Niemi, Craig, and Mattei 1991), "researchers have identified a strong connection between an individual's sense that they can make a difference—their sense of efficacy—and their level of civic participation" (Kahne and Westheimer 2006, 289). Efficacy has been linked to political engagement and political beliefs. While some research has discussed the role of external political efficacy in evaluations of government—the belief that governments are responsive to the needs of the people (Ostrom and Simon 1985)—we are not aware of studies that find a link between personal political efficacy and evaluations of institutions. Our study is one of the first to demonstrate this linkage. Nonetheless, we believe that this concept holds great promise to help explain how individuals evaluate institutions of transitional justice, such as the ICTY.

For all postconflict states, the stakes are enormous for society in general and especially for the individuals who suffered during the violence and must now repair themselves and their communities in its aftermath. When these nations embark on whatever form of transitional justice they choose or is imposed on them (like the ICTY), it is critical that these processes help people confront the past and build a productive future, so that more witnesses will share the sentiments of the following statement from one of the witnesses in our survey:

> I feel fulfilled even after so many years, when it happened, perhaps nearly twenty years ago, and that feeling of satisfaction and pride because I was a part of this has not, has not diminished at all.

Transitional justice, if it is to mean anything at all, must abide by the dictate of physicians, "First, do no harm." Transitional justice should not exacerbate identity divisions or undermine stability. Thus, to the extent that the institutions of transitional justice can work effectively with witnesses to ensure that they provide their testimony in a safe and secure environment and that the leaders of these institutions respect and value the contributions of witnesses, their support can aid both these witnesses and the larger society. Institutions that are fair and that facilitate such feelings of personal empowerment would be more likely to be accepted and to realize their aims. The stakes are huge for all citizens in a society and especially for those who are part of transitional justice processes, for they are the ones speaking truth to power. They are the ones at most risk in transitional justice. If transitional justice is ill-equipped to function in this manner, the consequences for all are likely to be quite detrimental. Ensuring witnesses believe that their testimony and the burdens they have borne are appreciated and respected is crucial to the more general effectiveness of transitional justice. One witness stated,

> I went there to testify of my own free will, and especially since I am a woman witness, which meant a lot to me. I wanted to testify, of my own free will, so that people should know what happened in the part of the world where I lived and what I have survived and how, otherwise, if we don't testify and if we don't speak about what happened so that it is recorded, then it hasn't happened at all.

Future research on efficacy should begin by exploring in depth what individuals and especially witnesses are thinking about when they evaluate their own contributions to transitional justice. Do they have in mind a particular, tangible piece of evidence they testified about at the tribunal? Are they thinking more in terms of their general contribution to the larger enterprise of justice? Perhaps they are assessing their contribution in terms of their ability to relate their personal story to the tribunal. Many of these issues are closely related to the discussion of fairness, as the witnesses indicated that some part of their evaluations of the fairness with which they were treated by the tribunal was tied to their ability to relate their personal narrative, which is their contribution to truth and justice. Hence, further research on the meaning and role of personal efficacy must be part of a larger exploration of how institutions of transitional justice treat witnesses.

In addition to analyzing what witnesses are thinking of when they consider personal efficacy, scholars should develop surveys of witness perceptions and opinions that can be administered contemporaneously (Cody et al. 2014, 2015). Such surveys would provide greater insight into what types of issues might be foremost in witnesses' minds shortly after their testimony, which might prove to be more reliable than surveys taken after a considerable passage of time. We might better understand how the general treatment of the witnesses by the court (or whatever transitional justice mechanism is being utilized) intersects with more basic concerns—such as the length of testimony, translation, and security—to affect witness perceptions. Cross-national and cross-institutional research would help us better understand whether some types of transitional justice are better suited to protecting and advancing the interests of victims and witnesses, as some believe truth commissions are, or whether the attitudes and behavior of transitional justice personnel are most responsible for how witnesses develop opinions of their own performance and the performance of the institution.

Witness Evaluations of International Justice: The Hypotheses That Were Not Confirmed

We hesitate to argue that the variables measuring concepts from some of our hypotheses that did not prove to be statistically significant simply do not matter. We are not yet convinced that two of these factors—witness experience during the war and the sentences handed down to the guilty—do not play some role in witness evaluations of international justice. It is not our intention to blame the concepts or the statistical techniques for these findings. Rather, we would put the onus on the manner in which we utilized these concepts, as we believe that more sophisticated theoretical and statistical approaches might yield different results. Thus, our aim is to suggest what such approaches might entail.

Perhaps the most important issue we must consider in new and improved approaches for understanding the roles of experience and outcomes is their close connection to ethnicity. We know that Bosniaks and Kosovar Albanians experienced the most significant levels of wartime trauma and that ethnicity is related, in both direct and indirect pathways, to evaluations of international justice. Clearly, a larger sample of all the ethnic subgroups would be optimal, allowing separate testing to determine the extent to which these concepts matter in the opinions of the specific groups with which individuals identify. If exposure to wartime violence leads to more prosocial attitudes (obviously, such attitudes do not imply that individuals will be more pro-tribunal in their opinions), we should find its impact manifest across all ethnic groups. Larger samples would allow us to evaluate this potential relationship in a more rigorous fashion. We would like to assess whether the hypothesized prosocial attitudes of those who have experienced significant wartime violence are relevant regardless of ethnicity or if there is a different route by which experience influences opinions. A larger sample would also allow us to determine if any selection effects are present; that is, are individuals who agree to testify before an international tribunal or domestic court more resilient already than others who are unable or unwilling to undertake such a difficult responsibility? The witnesses in our sample may already be exceptional in this regard and may hence exhibit less variation in their exposure to violence and opinions about international justice than would be exhibited by wider populations of the various ethnic groups.

Future research that follows a more explicitly psychological perspective, rather than a political science one, might also investigate whether specific experiences, thresholds of experience, and coping mechanisms for dealing with these experiences influence witness attitudes. For example, some wartime experiences, such as sexual assault, undoubtedly leave more severe psychological scars that substantially interfere with victims' recovery and, hence, their ability to speak openly about what happened. Other individuals may have been exposed to continual wartime suffering, such as the ever-present shelling and sniping in Sarajevo that led some to have greater resolve to speak their truth. Others might endure similar suffering but reach a breaking point when such suffering takes a more personal turn—for example, if a family member is killed. Research that probes such issues regarding timing, duration, and the differential impact of different types of experiences would assist in testing ideas about their influence on witness attitudes. In addition, more objective measures of the impact of traumatic experience, measures based on the observations of trained professionals, would be exceptionally useful. Such third-party evaluations would provide for more robust testing of these hypotheses.

We should also consider how effectively witnesses are coping with these traumas. Our previous research revealed that many (if not most) witnesses relied on their own internal coping mechanisms and were either unable or unwilling to utilize professional help (King and Meernik 2017). Whatever coping mechanisms individuals employ, those people who are better able to address these past traumas in a psychologically healthy manner may be the more resilient and prosocial among the larger population of witnesses as well as among the citizens of the former Yugoslavia. The interaction of trauma and coping mechanisms creates an additional layer of complexity that should be investigated to better understand the impact of wartime trauma on perceptions and opinions of international justice.

We also recommend that scholars undertake a deeper dive into the role of outcomes in evaluations of international justice. While our initial findings using a bivariate model of witness evaluations indicated that outcomes, as measured by the average sentence of the last case in which an individual testified, did seem to make a difference (especially for prosecution witnesses), these findings did not hold up when we estimated our final set of complete statistical models. We are not yet convinced that the sentences do not matter. Individuals in the former Yugoslavia are certainly aware of and have strong opinions about the ICTY, its verdicts, and its punishments (Clark 2009a, 2009b; Ford 2012; Hagan and Ivković 2006b; Saxon 2005; Subotić 2009). One witness goes straight to the point: "I have the impression that they have not been adequately severely punished. I believe the Court does not impose proper, appropriate punishments." Indeed, the verdicts and sentences are probably the most visible of all the events associated with the international tribunals, with the possible exception of the apprehension of high-ranking officials. It makes sense, then, that opinions about the ICTY's punishments would matter in evaluations. Why do our results seem to indicate otherwise?

It may be that our survey witnesses, who possess greater familiarity with the tribunal because of their personal experience in testifying, have developed different or more complex decision-making processes for assessing its work. For example, we know that the witnesses' opinions of their own contributions to truth and justice matter a great deal. Such direct personal decision-making inputs may dominate attitude formation, while other factors, especially ones measured at the level of aggregation of our sentencing variables, may be less influential. Therefore, future research might make more focused inquiries regarding which verdicts and sentences are most familiar to individuals, to determine if these specific outcomes matter where the aggregated outcomes we have utilized do not. As we alluded to in chapter 3, the witnesses and perhaps the general population of the former Yugoslavia might be more attuned to the sentence in a particular case whose outcome is a more easily accessible decision cue than the more complex average of sentences we utilized. More focused questions on trial outcomes (as in Hagan and Ivković 2016) and individual opinions on them would be useful. Additional data on public opinion in the former Yugoslavia and especially in other countries that have been the subject of international tribunals more generally would be useful in testing these ideas, especially in assessing whether outcomes matter in other contexts, such as in countries that have not been engulfed by conflict like Bosnia, or where criminal justice processes were used to prosecute government leaders for their repression of human rights in countries without civil war (e.g., Argentina and Chile). Perhaps the volume of cases at the ICTY (the largest of any tribunal) makes the identification of relationships between outcomes and opinions more difficult than in situations where trials focused on just a handful of visible and high-ranking leaders. We believe that there is much to be learned from further refinement of these hypotheses and from the expansion of data into additional cases of transitional justice.

Final Thoughts

We are gaining a better understanding of the experiences, perceptions, and opinions of individuals who have lived through severe violence and who subsequently choose to speak about these events in institutions of transitional justice. As more societies become involved in transitional justice, we see three particularly compelling needs for both scholars and researchers. The academic community and the communities of those who manage these institutions would best be served by research that expands our understanding across time, across countries, and across different types of transitional justice mechanisms.

By researching across time, especially within nations and ideally with panel studies, we begin to understand how opinions about international justice may change for the better or the worse and, in particular, which factors are affecting attitudinal change. We would suspect that critical events in the history of the transitional justice institutions—such as delivery of highly visible outcomes, the apprehension of suspects, government reactions, and media coverage—will shift opinions, especially if those events tend to redound to the advantage of one group over another. What impact might these factors have in the context of societies where information may be scarce, delivered and manipulated by government, or perceived through the lens of identity groups? The snapshot research that most scholars and practitioners have utilized (including the present study) can help us understand what constellation of variables are related at a given point in time, but it does not really help us to understand how these opinions are formed and evolve. While it is doubtful that frequent and regular surveys might be conducted in most of these nations, which are often poor and have challenging infrastructure, even a small number of surveys that ask the same questions over time would prove extraordinarily useful. Institutions of international justice are dynamic institutions whose priorities and procedures, to say nothing of their watershed events and milestones, may change over time. Our models of public opinion should take these changes into account.

Survey research on public opinion regarding transitional justice mechanisms should also involve cross-national research. A more complete analysis and understanding of public opinion regarding these institutions would be helped tremendously by data from a variety of states in terms of their geography, their political and conflict history, and the diversity of identity groups and other such factors that will vary across nations utilizing transitional justice. As these are all important precursors to the types of conflicts and human rights atrocities that nations experience and for how these events are perceived, it is critical that key distinguishing cross-national characteristics be factored into our understanding of public attitudes. For example, the period before the outbreak of wars in the former Yugoslavia was marked by governance under a more benign type of dictatorship, while the genocide in Rwanda was preceded by decades of ethnic tension and violence. Some countries may make the transition from repression to peace without widespread and organized violence, as has South Africa for the most part, while the transition process may be much more violent for other states, as in East Timor. Indeed, there is an enormous diversity of national and individual experiences before, during, and after conflict and in the transitional justice period. Our understanding of transitional justice ultimately requires that we take this diversity into account in our theories and our analyses. Doing so will better enable us to determine if more retributive forms of justice lead to higher levels of satisfaction than those that focus on truth telling or on more restorative judicial remedies.

Data across time and space are quite rare, and public opinion survey research administered across multiple transitional justice mechanisms using the same questions and methodologies is almost nonexistent. The Red Cross did undertake a series of surveys in a number of postconflict states, but very few of the questions focused on transitional justice (see Meernik and King 2013). One of the most fascinating elements of transitional justice is the variety of mechanisms used. While criminal trials and truth commissions have been among the most prevalent (Olson, Payne, and Reiter 2010), states also utilize amnesties (one of the most popular), memorialization, reparations, and other more local forms of restorative justice. Indeed, even among such mechanisms as truth commissions and courts, there are many types. Truth commissions can be created with more or less power to offer amnesty to perpetrators in exchange for testimony, to name names, and to issue recommendations among many other elements of their mandates. Trials may be domestic or international, courts may be limited in their decisions and punishments or given full judicial independence, and trials may be conducted either shortly after the end of conflict or the downfall of a repressive regime or many years later, after new regimes have cemented their power. Some individuals find greater satisfaction with models of transitional justice that are more restorative in nature, while others may demand nothing less than the severest of punishments for the guilty. Understanding of which types of institutions are most preferred by the public can best be gained by cross-national research. While it is possible to examine how the presence or absence of the various types of transitional justice efforts can affect the likelihood of future violence, if we do not understand why these institutions did or did not gain popular legitimacy, we cannot completely understand why they may contribute to other outcomes. Thus, we urge scholars to develop standard survey measures that might be utilized in discrete single-country studies or larger, multinational survey research, to allow us to gain traction on these critical questions of the legitimacy and impact of transitional justice.

It is all well and good to earnestly make such suggestions in the hopes that other researchers or the workers involved in transitional justice figure out how such complex, time-consuming, and expensive research can be conducted. Our next step before embarking on contributing to this larger enterprise of data collection, however, is to focus more closely on what the ICTY witnesses think about transitional justice. At the conclusion of our survey of the witnesses, we asked for their thoughts and opinions on three issues, with the following questions:

Could you describe what the experience of testifying for you personally, in your life, means or has meant to you?
What advice would you give to help future witnesses at war crimes trials prepare for and cope with the process of testifying?
What would you change about the proceedings or the process of testifying?

Some interviewees spoke for just a few minutes, while others spoke for lengthy periods of time. Every word they uttered was recorded and transcribed. Their responses to these open-ended questions provide a rich repository of the mostly unfiltered thoughts and feelings of the witnesses, which will enable us to develop a nuanced understanding of what the witnesses think about issues like fairness, punishment, justice, the importance of testifying in their lives, and what they think is important about international justice. Not only can analyses of these issues provide us with a more developed appreciation for and understanding of what it means to bear witness, but the insights gained from such analyses can also be used to develop future survey questions.

Finally, we would be remiss if we did not comment on the future of transitional justice in general and, especially, of international criminal tribunals in particular. Almost all of the ad hoc tribunals have completed their business. The International Criminal Tribunal for Rwanda and the Special Court for Sierra Leone are finished, while the ICTY has finally closed its doors. The Extraordinary Chambers in the Courts of Cambodia and the Special Tribunal for Lebanon limp along, but their lack of defendants has made their prominence and impact marginal at best. That leaves the International Criminal Court as the principal international tribunal. The future of the ICC, however, is uncertain. It has completed only a small number of trials, has been unable to obtain custody of some of its most prominent suspects in countries like The Sudan and Libya, and has been forced to shut down some of its cases, as in the Kenyan situation. Given this track record, we must wonder what the future of international justice looks like. More to the point, if there is a decreasing willingness to use such institutions or a diminished effectiveness of their judicial processes, opinions about the efficacy of international justice will likely suffer.

The current decline in international support for international institutions, evident in the cases mentioned above, may presage a movement toward greater use of domestic institutions of transitional justice. Some nations are already beginning to resist ICC involvement and pursue their own forms of justice; such as Colombia, which recently ended decades of violence with the largest of its rebel groups. As we develop a greater understanding of the impact of all of these institutions of transitional justice on victims and others affected by severe violence, scholars and practitioners can use this knowledge to help develop more appropriate and effective mechanisms of transitional justice. To the extent that institutions of transitional justice—whether national or international—can be designed to best address the needs of the people in a society, we would presume that those institutions would operate more effectively, develop more legitimacy, and ultimately help break the cycles of violence that plague so many countries. The only way to understand what works is to ask the very people whom transitional justice is designed to help.

For international tribunals, especially the ICC, to succeed, we contend that they will need to gain, at a minimum, the level of trust the ICTY has earned from witnesses. Individuals who testified at the ICTY gave all the major actors, especially the judges and VWS personnel, very high marks for their fair treatment, as reflected in the following effusive praise from a witness from Serbia:

> I really have no words, I cannot praise it enough, and perhaps I can express my thanks in this way to the Victims and Witnesses Unit which really worked exceptionally, exceptionally, as far as I am concerned, and I only have words of praise for don't know, but if there is some sort of highest grade, and what I wrote to you, it's all the best, best, best, in any event, best!

Sizable majorities of these witnesses also indicated belief that their testimony had contributed to truth and justice, as illustrated by the following remarks from a Serbian witness:

> And there were a number of people who told me: "Are you crazy, why are you going to testify, what do you need that for, they are going to set you up too, they'll create problems for you here and there, they can even arrest you, they can even bring you in!" I was aware of all of that but, but I think that every witness still has to be conscious about the fact that the truth is the most important. And even at the cost of that risk, the risk that something might happen, if it's going to happen, then you let it happen.

Taken together, this type of support would seem to be critical—perhaps a necessary but not sufficient condition—for ultimately earning legitimacy in the eyes of stakeholders. While many in the former Yugoslavia still perceive the ICTY as unfair and illegitimate (Clark 2014), those who have a greater level of interaction with the tribunal appear to come away with positive impressions of its personal treatment toward them.

Witness perceptions of fairness and efficacy can help erode many of the negative perceptions of international justice as remote and alien from ordinary people's lives. Public support and legitimacy will be critical if institutions are to be perceived as legitimate in the eyes of the affected populations. As deGuzman (2012, 268) writes, "The globalization of communications increasingly means that an institution's legitimacy depends on the opinions of ordinary citizens around the world." One witness from Kosovo provided the following especially eloquent depiction of the importance of testimony and, implicitly, the need for international tribunals to encourage such attitudes:

> In the course of my work I meet on a daily basis with potential witnesses, both before national courts and the Tribunal and, I've always

> had one bit, one bit of advice for them: "Many people will urge you to forgive and forget. I ask you one thing, on behalf of my people who have survived nine genocides, if they forgive, that's a matter of the individual, forgetting is a collective matter. If you find it in your heart to forgive, do, always do forgive, that's human, humane, ecumenical, but you must never forget, no one must. Never and no one." And, *vis-à-vis* of that, I always tell the witnesses: "It is your duty, if not for your own sake then for the sake of the future, for the sake of the truth and the legal system, both ours and international, to testify, not to refuse, to go and present that truth, so it could be recorded. For, what is not recorded — never happened. Unfortunately, we've paid the price, exactly for that reason."

As the ICC struggles to remain relevant in the world, it would do well to engender these sorts of positive impressions from its stakeholders.

International justice must also find a way to confront the propaganda of states and other actors that are hostile to its mission, especially those who use such disinformation to bolster their own claims of innocence, such as the Sudanese government under President Omar al-Bashir and the Kenyan government of President Uhuru Kenyatta. The ICTY has grappled with the suspicions and biases raised by state-controlled media in Croatia and Serbia over the years and has never really succeeded in effectively confronting the negative stereotypes produced by state propaganda. While few institutions could successfully defend themselves against the continual onslaught of negative press coverage in repressive states, it is nonetheless critical for international courts to find a way to erode the biases that such propaganda produces in their witnesses. Earning trust and legitimacy from the witnesses is an uphill battle in this context.

This is an issue of critical importance not just for international justice but for the world. The very same nationalism that inspired and fanned the flames of the Balkan conflicts and other states often endures and keeps open the wounds and divisions that may well lead to renewed outbreaks of violence. Hence, state supporters of international justice and those engaged in peacebuilding might consider taking a more assertive stand against this propaganda. Institutions of international justice should undertake extensive public outreach campaigns to provide a more accurate and comprehensive perception of international justice, like the campaigns of the Special Court for Sierra Leone, which has generally earned praise for its efforts (Kelsall 2010). The ICC has undertaken more systematic efforts to incorporate the views and needs of victims in its deliberations, but more initiatives that engage local audiences, such as holding some portions of trials in the affected states, seem necessary for institutions to earn the respect of witnesses and legitimacy in the eyes of the rest of the population and to help institutions counter the negative propaganda.

At the same time, scholars, advocates, and those who authorize the establishment of international tribunals should temper expectations for international justice. These institutions have extensive missions. In addition to providing justice, international courts are expected to further deterrence, foster reconciliation, and contribute to peace and security. When we oversell the promise of international justice, we risk exacerbating the suspicion and cynicism that exists in many conflict states whose peoples may have already been led to believe that the international cavalry was going to ride in and save them (e.g., Bosnia-Herzegovina, Rwanda). Hence, some part of engagement with witnesses and stakeholders should be oriented toward advancing a realistic assessment of what tribunals can and cannot do. Indeed, many of the witnesses are aware of such shortcomings. One explains,

> The purpose of it all is to establish the truth. However, it is definitely not the absolute truth, which is being established at the Court. Absolute truth is very different from the narrative truth. The truth is being established only with regards to the matters included in the indictment.

While developing such holistic and nuanced attitudes toward international justice is not easy, institutions can undertake certain steps to help educate people. For example, our analysis of the views of witnesses at the ICTY (King and Meernik 2017), as well as research on the Special Court for Sierra Leone (Stepakoff et al. 2014), demonstrates that witnesses want to learn more about the workings of these courts, especially important developments. Organizing regular and comprehensive public awareness campaigns about what international justice is doing and what it can do, released as investigations are launched and at other key moments, seems to be an essential step in educating populations about what to expect. Again, outreach to witnesses and other stakeholders is critical in helping local populations develop realistic appraisals of what international justice can provide.

The meaning of justice and the quest to obtain justice for those affected by human rights abuses is as powerful as it is complex. Justice is personal, social, and international. It is personal in that each witness and each victim must determine what sort of resolution to their loss and pain will sufficiently right their scales of justice. While no verdict or sentence may ever alleviate the suffering that so many individuals experience in the course of these conflicts, healthy individuals and peaceful societies would seem to need, at a minimum, some type of "good-enough justice" that moves them forward instead of leaving them mired in the past. Individuals may need to confront a defendant, tell their stories, or see perpetrators and ringleaders behind bars. One witness remarked, "I felt it—not as an obligation, but as my duty as a human being before all the people who had lost their lives, who are not with us any more to testify themselves, so in the name of my friends, relatives and acquaintances who lost their lives it was my moral duty." Another stated, "I felt that if I were to fail to take part in it, it would weight heavily on my mind for the rest of my life, that I would be lumbered by the fact that I had the opportunity to speak, to accuse, rather than just indulge in idle chat about it." Whatever form this "personal justice" takes, it is a powerful force that, if acknowledged and appropriately channeled by the institutions of international justice through fair treatment and care of victims and witnesses, can help these individuals attain the satisfaction they seek. Ignored or mismanaged, these individual needs can undermine the foundations of international justice, if victims and witnesses perceive international justice as one more challenge in life to be overcome.

As we scale up to the level of society, the complexities and obstacles involved in providing a justice that meets the needs of all citizens become ever more problematic. Our discussion and analysis of the divisions in the former Yugoslavia could certainly lead one to believe that no form of justice will ever work for everyone. Research (Mason and Meernik 2006) has shown, however, that once a nation experiences one civil war, there is a 50 percent probability that it will suffer through another one. Justice must provide a reckoning that will decrease those odds, not increase them. Whether in the form of a tribunal, a truth commission, or some other mechanism, justice must provide ways for diverse narratives to be acknowledged and addressed in some manner, even if such remedies cannot meet the demand of every group in society. For example, the South African Truth and Reconciliation Commission did much great work and was lauded by many, but it was also controversial and unpopular with many others, on all sides of the racial divides (Gibson 2007). It was not perfect. Nonetheless, South Africa did not lapse into civil war. Constructing this type of satisficing justice may take enlightened leadership, a forceful international community, or some other actor that can bring all sides together. Somehow, these societal needs must be divined, and a societal justice that can address the root and proximate causes of violence must be established. That is a tall order. Perhaps one place to begin this process is to listen to those individuals who were most affected by the violence. These witnesses have much to teach us, and by understanding the opinions of victims and witnesses, we can develop an international justice that does more good than harm. One witness stated,

> The mere existence of this court has done much contribution to the strengthening of lawfulness and order. Because in this area, the area of the Balkans, the war conflicts and the war crimes are constantly repeated. And that goes from generation to generation.

One might think that justice on the international plane would be the most complicated and thorny aspiration of all, yet we argue that it is not. Those accused of violating international laws must be charged and brought to trial if these laws are to mean anything and if there is to be hope of deterring future violence. Those are the most fundamental and universal goals of these institutions. The conduct of fair trials and the determination of appropriate punishments are the indispensable elements of international justice. The administration of justice is fairly straightforward, but the interpretations and evaluations of this justice by individuals and by societies is not nearly so clear and direct. A fair and good process does not guarantee acceptance of outcomes.

The remove of the international tribunals from the conflicts over which they adjudicate is both a blessing and a curse in their efforts to define and deliver justice. It is a blessing precisely for those reasons that make justice so difficult at the individual and society levels. The international community writ large does not generally have near the level of passion and engagement in these conflicts as the actual participants. The Hague is the quintessential location for change of venue for those cases in which local actors are either unable or unwilling to hold a fair trial domestically. As such, dispassionate international justice is achievable with proper support and can provide evidence-based legal and historical truths that can enlighten the world and the affected societies.

The objectivity of international justice is often accompanied, however, by international indifference. Those states that have the power to help guide and support international justice and tribunals in productive directions that ameliorate the potential for future violence must be convinced of the necessity of these efforts. In recent years, we have seen a waning of support for the ICC, for example, among many states, which calls into question whether international justice will grow increasingly imperfect. The meaning of justice for the world is becoming increasingly cloudy. If there is support for this international justice from all states, especially the major powers, international courts can contribute to justice for the affected peoples. Absent such support, there are diminishing prospects for international justice to realize its broadest aims and to become legitimate in the eyes of its stakeholders.

We conclude this study by suggesting that a return to first principles is in order for international justice to work. Those who advocate for this justice and those who administer it would be well advised to understand the opinions of the victims and witnesses and to build justice from the best of those perspectives. The witnesses in our sample provide a rich trove of information that can advance this knowledge base and help design right-sized justice for those nations whose conflicts become the caseload for a future international justice. We close with the following words from a witness:

> Let it just never happen again to anyone and let those who really deserve it get their just desserts and go down as they are judged, both in this world and in the one beyond, let them be held accountable for their crimes, because nobody should be able to commit crimes and not to answer for them.

Notes

CHAPTER 1

1. Witness from the Echoes of Testimonies study (2016). Throughout the course of this book we rely on quotes from interviews provided by the witnesses during the open-ended portion of the survey. These interviews were audio-taped and transcribed by ICTY staff according to translation protocols developed by the ICTY. Because these are the witnesses words as they have been translated and checked for accuracy, we have not altered the grammar of the witnesses because this is "in their own words."

2. Herein, we often use the terms *court* and *tribunal* interchangeably when talking generically about international courts, and we use proper names when discussing a specific institution, such as the ICTY.

3. "Robert H. Jackson: Opening Statement Nuremberg Trials, 1945," http://www.pbs.org/wnet/supremecourt/personality/sources_document12.html

4. UN Security Council Resolution 827, May 25, 1993, available at http://www.icty.org/x/file/Legal%20Library/Statute/statute_827_1993_en.pdf

5. Information on the numbers of witnesses is available on the ICTY website, at http://www.icty.org/en/about/registry/witnesses/statistics

6. The Memorandum of Understanding between the University of North Texas and the ICTY specified that no witness could be surveyed that appeared in any current and ongoing trials (such as Mladic). In both cases of excluding witnesses, both of them had testified in other trials. They did the survey and then after that, they were called again by the ICTY to testify in Mladic. As per the MOU their surveys were excluded.

7. The percentages are available at http://www.icty.org/en/about/registry/witnesses/statistics

8. Sometimes there are slightly smaller numbers of witnesses from ethnic groups from the various nations when compared to the number of people who

claim a particular ethnicity, because some individuals do not reside in either of the nations with which they are usually associated, such as Bosnia or Serbia for the Serb witnesses (who may reside in Croatia or some other nation).

9. Indeed, 4 percent of the witnesses that were reached for recruitment calls had passed away, while one witness passed after the recruitment call and before the scheduled interview.

10. Because witnesses can testify multiple times for different sides (OTP, defense, or Trial Chamber) or can testify on the same side in the same case more than one time, the separate numbers for witness, OTP, and defense appearances do not add up to the total number of respondents.

11. The statistics are available at http://www.icty.org/en/about/registry/witnesses/statistics

CHAPTER 2

1. ICTY Statute, Article 5 (e). Other tribunals have a somewhat different definition of persecution as a crime against humanity. The ICTR, for example, defines such crimes as targeting "any civilian population on national, political, ethnic, racial or religious grounds" (ICTR Statute, Article 3).

2. Some ethnic groups were dominated by the Austro-Hungarian Empire, while, during some periods, others were ruled over by the Ottoman Empire and other powerful states in southeastern Europe. Indeed, the different regions had diverse experiences during World War II, depending on whether they were conquered by the Germans, Italians, Bulgarians, or Hungarians.

CHAPTER 3

1. The UNDP findings are available at http://www.ks.undp.org/content/dam/kosovo/docs/TJ/English-Web_965257.pdf

2. *Overview of Federal Criminal Cases, Fiscal Year 2013* (Washington, DC: United States Sentencing Commission, 2014), 5, available at http://www.ussc.gov/sites/default/files/pdf/research-and-publications/research-publications/2014/FY13_Overview_Federal_Criminal_Cases.pdf

3. Life sentences are set at the highest nonlife sentence issued by any of the international tribunals (the ICTY, ICTR, ICC, and Special Court for Sierra Leone), which is fifty-two years, or 624 months. The longest sentence issued at trial at the ICTY was for Radislav Krstic, who was sentenced to 552 months in prison, although his sentence was later reduced on appeal. There is actually no good way of comparing life sentences to sentences of finite terms, as the two concepts are dissimilar. We must especially keep this in mind as we consider the views of the witnesses, many of whom expect to see life sentences for the top leaders and for those who committed the most heinous acts.

4. For the seventy-five ICTY defendants in our sentencing database (Meernik 2011) who appealed their sentences, the ICTY Appeals Chamber upheld the defendant's sentence thirty-eight times, decreased the sentence thirty-two times, and increased the sentence five times.

CHAPTER 5

1. To identify the most appropriate questions to ask these individuals, we utilized a modified version of the Harvard Trauma Questionnaire, which lists events or activities common in times of conflict (Palić et al. 2105). For more information on the Harvard questionnaire, see http://bit.ly/2grLHTQ

References

Akhavan, Payam. "Are International Criminal Tribunals a Disincentive to Peace? Reconciling Judicial Romanticism with Political Realism." *Human Rights Quarterly* 31.3 (2009): 624–54.

Allwood, Carl Martin, Karl Ask, and Pär Anders Granhag. "The Cognitive Interview: Effects on the Realism in Witnesses' Confidence in Their Free Recall." *Psychology, Crime & Law* 11.2 (2005): 183–98.

Anderson, Christopher J., and Matthew M. Singer. "The Sensitive Left and the Impervious Right: Multilevel Models and the Politics of Inequality, Ideology, and Legitimacy in Europe." *Comparative Political Studies* 41.4–5 (2008): 564–99.

Arzheimer, Kai. "Contextual Factors and the Extreme Right Vote in Western Europe, 1980–2002." *American Journal of Political Science* 53.2 (2009): 259–75.

Arzheimer, Kai, and Elisabeth Carter. "Christian Religiosity and Voting for West European Radical Right Parties." *West European Politics* 32.5 (2009): 985–1011.

Arzt, Donna E. "Views on the Ground: The Local Perception of International Criminal Tribunals in the Former Yugoslavia and Sierra Leone." *Annals of the American Academy of Political and Social Science* 603.1 (2006): 226–39.

Ask, Karl, and Pär Anders Granhag. "Motivational Sources of Confirmation Bias in Criminal Investigations: The Need for Cognitive Closure." *Journal of Investigative Psychology and Offender Profiling* 2.1 (2005): 43–63.

""Backer, David. "Watching a Bargain Unravel? A Panel Study of Victims' Attitudes about Transitional Justice in Cape Town, South Africa." *International Journal of Transitional Justice* 4.3 (2010): 443–56.

Bandes, Susan. "Victims, Closure, and the Sociology of Emotion." *Journal of Law and Contemporary Problems* 72.2 (2009): 1–26.

Barria, Lilian A., and Steven D. Roper. "How Effective Are International Criminal Tribunals? An Analysis of the ICTY and the ICTR." *International Journal of Human Rights* 9.3 (2005): 349–68.

Bartels, Brandon L., and Christopher D, Johnston. "On the Ideological Foundations of Supreme Court Legitimacy in the American Public." *American Journal of Political Science* 57.1 (2013): 184–99.

Bauer, Michael, Christopher Blattman, Julie Chytilová, Joseph Henrich, and Tamar Mitts. "Can War Foster Cooperation?" *Journal of Economic Perspectives* 30.3 (2016): 249–74.

Becchetti, Leonardo, Pierluigi Conzo, and Alessandro Romeo. "Violence, Trust, and Trustworthiness: Evidence from a Nairobi Slum." *Oxford Economic Papers* 66.1 (2014): 283–305.

Bellah, Robert N., Richard Madsen, William M. Sullivan, Ann Swidler, and Steven M. Tipton. *Habits of the Heart.* Berkeley: University of California Press, 1985.

Benesh, Sara C. "Understanding Public Confidence in American Courts." *Journal of Politics* 68.3 (2006): 697–707.

Borger, Julian. *The Butcher's Trail.* New York: Other Press, 2016.

Bourbeau, Philippe. "Resilience and International Politics: Premises, Debates, Agenda." *International Studies Review* 17.3 (2015): 1468–2486

Brounéus, Karen. "The Trauma of Truth Telling: Effects of Witnessing in the Rwandan Gacaca Courts on Psychological Health." *Journal of Conflict Resolution* 54.3 (2010): 408–37.

Byrne, Catherine C. "Benefit or Burden: Victims' Reflections on TRC Participation." *Peace and Conflict: Journal of Peace Psychology* 10.3 (2004): 237–56.

Caldeira, Gregory A., and James L. Gibson. "The Legitimacy of the Court of Justice in the European Union: Models of Institutional Support." *American Political Science Review* 89.2 (1995): 356–76.

Casper, Jonathan D., Tom Tyler, and Bonnie Fisher. "Procedural Justice in Felony Cases." *Law & Society Review* 22.3 (1988): 483–507.

Cassar, Alessandra, Andrew Healy, and Carl Von Kessler. "Trust, Risk, and Time Preferences after a Natural Disaster: Experimental Evidence from Thailand." *World Development* 94 (2017): 90–105.

Cibelli, Kristen, and Tamy Guberek. *Justice Unknown, Justice Unsatisfied? Bosnian NGOs Speak Out about the International Criminal Tribunal for the Former Yugoslavia*. Education and Public Inquiry and International Citizenship at Tufts University (EPIIC), 2000.

Clark, Janine Natalya. "From Negative to Positive Peace: The Case of Bosnia and Hercegovina." *Journal of Human Rights* 8 (2009a): 360–84.

Clark, Janine Natalya. "Judging the ICTY: Has It Achieved Its Objectives?" *Southeast European and Black Sea Studies* 9.1–2 (2009b): 123–42.

Clark, Janine Natalya. "The Limits of Retributive Justice: Findings of an Empirical Study in Bosnia and Hercegovina." *Journal of International Criminal Justice* 7.3 (2009c): 463–87.

Clark, Janine Natalya. "Plea Bargaining at the ICTY: Plea Agreements and Reconciliation." *European Journal of International Law* 20.2 (2009d): 415–36.

Clark, Janine Natalya. *International Trials and Reconciliation: Assessing the Impact of the International Criminal Tribunal for the Former Yugoslavia*. New York: Routledge, 2014.

Cody, Stephen Smith, Alexa Koenig, Robin Mejia, and Eric Stover. *Bearing Witness at the International Criminal Court: An Interview Survey of 109 Witnesses*. Berkeley: Human Rights Center, University of California, Berkeley, 2014.

Cody, Stephen Smith, Eric Stover, Mychelle Balthazard, and Alexa Koenig. "*The Victims' Court? A Study of 622 Victim Participants at the International Criminal Court.*" Berkeley: Human Rights Center, University of California, Berkeley, 2015.

Collier, Paul, and Ian Bannon, eds. *Natural Resources and Violent Conflict: Options and Actions*. Washington, DC: World Bank, 2003.

Collier, Paul, V. L. Elliott, Håvard Hegre, Anke Hoeffler, Marta Reynal-Querol, and Nicholas Sambanis. *Breaking the Conflict Trap: Civil War and Development Policy*. Washington, DC: World Bank, 2003.

Cryer, Robert. "Witness Tampering and International Criminal Tribunals." *Leiden Journal of International Law* 27.1 (2014): 191–203.

Cryer, Robert, Håkan Friman, Darryl Robinson, and Elizabeth Wilmshurst. *An Introduction to International Criminal Law and Procedure*. Cambridge: Cambridge University Press, 2007.

Davies, Arwel. "State Liability for Judicial Decisions in European Union and International Law." *International and Comparative Law Quarterly* 61.3 (2012): 585–611.

deGuzman, Margaret. "Choosing to Prosecute: Expressive Selection at the International Criminal Court." *Michigan Journal of International Law* 33 (2012): 265–320.

Dembour, Marie-Bénédicte, and Emily Haslam. "Silencing Hearings? Victim-Witnesses at War Crimes Trials." *European Journal of International Law* 15.1 (2004): 151–77.

Denny, Elaine K., and Barbara F. Walter. "Ethnicity and Civil War." *Journal of Peace Research* 51.2 (2014): 199–212.

Doak, Jonathan. "Honing the Stone: Refining Restorative Justice as a Vehicle for Emotional Redress." *Contemporary Justice Review* 14.4 (2011): 439–56.

Doak, Jonathan. "Enriching Trial Justice for Crime Victims in Common Law Systems: Lessons from Transitional Environments." *International Review of Victimology* 21.2 (2015): 139–60.

Drumbl, Mark A. *Atrocity, Punishment, and International Law*. Cambridge: Cambridge University Press, 2007.

Easton, David, and Jack Dennis. "The Child's Acquisition of Regime Norms: Political Efficacy." *American Political Science Review* 61.1 (1967): 25–38.

Elcheroth, Guy. "Individual-Level and Community-Level Effects of War Trauma on Social Representations Related to Humanitarian Law." *European Journal of Social Psychology* 36.6 (2006): 907–30.

Elcheroth, Guy, and Dario Spini. "Public Support for Prosecution of Human Rights Violations in the Former Yugoslavia." *Peace and Conflict: Journal of Peace Psychology* 15.2 (2009): 189–214.

Findlay, Mark, and Ralph J. Henham. *Transforming International Criminal Justice: Retributive and Restorative Justice in the Trial Process*. Cullompton, UK: Willan, 2005.

Findlay, Mark, and Ralph J. Henham. *Beyond Punishment: Achieving International Criminal Justice*. Basingstoke: Palgrave Macmillan, 2010.

Findlay, Mark, and Sylvia Ngane. "Sham of the Moral Court? Testimony Sold as the Spoils of War." *Global Journal of Comparative Law* 1.13 (2012): 73–101.

Fjelde, Hanne, and Lisa Hultman. "Weakening the Enemy: A Disaggregated Study of Violence against Civilians in Africa." *Journal of Conflict Resolution* 58.7 (2014): 1230–57.

Ford, Stuart K. "A Social Psychology Model of the Perceived Legitimacy of International Criminal Courts: Implications for the Success of Transitional Justice Systems." *Vanderbilt Journal of Transnational Law* 45.2 (2012): 405–76.

Garland, Howard, and Stephanie Newport. "Effects of Absolute and Relative Sunk Costs on the Decision to Persist with a Course of Action." *Organizational Behavior and Human Decision Processes* 48.1 (1991): 55–69.

Gibson, James L. "Understandings of Justice: Institutional Legitimacy, Procedural Justice, and Political Tolerance." *Law & Society Review* 23.3 (1989): 469–96.

Gibson, James L. "The Legitimacy of the U.S. Supreme Court in a Polarized Polity." *Journal of Empirical Legal Studies* 3 (2007): 507–38.

Gibson, James L., and Gregory A. Caldeira. "Blacks and the United States Supreme Court: Models of Diffuse Support." *Journal of Politics* 54.4 (1992): 1120–45.

Gibson, James L., and Gregory A. Caldeira. "The Legitimacy of Transnational Legal Institutions: Compliance, Support, and the European Court of Justice." *American Journal of Political Science* 39.2 (1995): 459–89.

Gibson, James L., Milton Lodge, and Benjamin Woodson. "Losing, but Accepting: Legitimacy, Positivity Theory, and the Symbols of Judicial Authority.. *Law & Society Review* 48.4 (2014): 837–66.

Gilligan, Michael J. "Is Enforcement Necessary for Effectiveness? A Model of the International Criminal Regime." *International Organization* 60.4 (2006): 935–67.

Goldstein, Joshua S. *Winning the War on War: The Decline of Armed Conflict*. London: Penguin, 2012.

Gosling, R. *Survey of Litigants' Experiences and Satisfaction with the Small Claims Process*. DCA Research Series 9/06. London: Department for Constitutional Affairs, 2006.

Graven, Jean. *Les crimes contre l'humanité*. 1950.

Greig, J. Michael, and James David Meernik. "To Prosecute or Not to Prosecute: Civil War Mediation and International Criminal Justice." *International Negotiation* 19.2 (2014): 257–84.

Hagan, John, and Sanja Kutnjak Ivković. Review of *Overcoming Apartheid: Can Truth Reconcile a Divided Nation?*, by James L. Gibson. *Law & Society Review* 40.3 (2006a): 731–33.

Hagan, John, and Sanja Kutnjak Ivković. "War Crimes, Democracy, and the Rule of Law in Belgrade, the Former Yugoslavia, and Beyond." *Annuals of the American Academy* 605.1 (2006b): 129–51.

Hamber, Brandon. *Transforming Societies after Political Violence: Truth, Reconciliation, and Mental Health*. New York: Springer, 2009.

Hamber, Brandon, Dineo Nageng, and Gabriel O'Malley. "'Telling It Like It Is . . .': Understanding the Truth and Reconciliation Commission from the Perspective of Survivors." *Psychology in Society* 26 (2000): 18–42.

Harmon, Mark B., and Fergal Gaynor. "Ordinary Sentences for Extraordinary Crimes." *Journal of International Criminal Justice* 5.3 (2007): 683–712.

Hatay, Ann-Sofi Jakobsson. "The Paradox of Peace: Leaders, Decisions, and Conflict Resolution." *Journal of Peace Research* 44.1 (2007): 128–29.

Hayashi, Nobuo, and Cecilia M. Bailliet, eds. *The Legitimacy of International Criminal Tribunals*. Cambridge, UK: Cambridge University Press, 2017.

Henham, Ralph. "The Philosophical Foundations of International Sentencing." *Journal of International Criminal Justice* 1.1 (2003): 64–85.

Henham, Ralph. "Developing Contextualized Rationales for Sentencing in International Criminal Trials: A Plea for Empirical Research." *Journal of International Criminal Justice* 5.3 (2007a): 757–78.

Henham, Ralph. "International Sentencing in the Context of Collective Violence." *International Criminal Law Review* 7.2 (2007b): 449–68.

Henham, Ralph. "Some Reflections on the Legitimacy of International Trial Justice." *International Journal of the Sociology of Law* 35.2 (2007c): 75–95.

Henham, Ralph, and Paul Behrens, eds. ""*The Criminal Law of Genocide: International, Comparative and Contextual Aspects* London: Routledge, 2007.

Hobfall, Stevan E., Anthony D. Mancini, Brian J. Hall, Daphna Canetti, and George

A. Bonanno. "The Limits of Resilience: Distress Following Chronic Political Violence among Palestinians." *Social Science & Medicine* 72.8 (2011): 1400–1408.

Hodžić, Refik. "Living the Legacy of Mass Atrocities Victims' Perspectives on War Crimes Trials." *Journal of International Criminal Justice* 8.1 (2010): 113–36.

Holá, Barbora, Catrien Bijleveld, and Alette Smeulers. "Punishment for Genocide: Exploratory Analysis of ICTR Sentencing." *International Criminal Law Review* 11.4 (2011): 745–73.

Holá, Barbora, Catrien Bijleveld, and Alette Smeulers. "Consistency of International Sentencing: ICTY and ICTR Case Study." *European Journal of Criminology* 9.5 (2012): 539–52.

Holá, Barbora, Alette Smeulers, and Catrien Bijleveld. Corrigendum to "Is ICTY Sentencing Predictable? An Empirical Analysis of ICTY Sentencing Practice." *Leiden Journal of International Law* 22.2 (2009): 411.

Holá, Barbora, Alette Smeulers, and Catrien Bijleveld. "International Sentencing Facts and Figures: Sentencing Practice at the ICTY and ICTR." *Journal of International Criminal Justice* 9.2 (2011): 411–39.

Horn, Rebecca, Simon Charters, and Saleem Vahidy. "Testifying in an International War Crimes Tribunal: The Experience of Witnesses in the Special Court for Sierra Leone." *International Journal of Transitional Justice* 3.1 (2009): 135–49.

Human Rights Watch. *Justice for Atrocity Crimes: Lessons of International Support for Trials before the State Court of Bosnia and Herzegovina*. 2012. https://www.hrw.org/sites/default/files/reports/bosnia0312_0.pdf

Hurwitz, Jon, and Peffley, Mark. "Explaining the Great Racial Divide: Perceptions of Fairness in the U.S. Criminal Justice System." *Journal of Politics* 67.3 (2005): 762–83.

Isen, Alice M. "The Influence of Positive and Negative Affect on Cognitive Organization: Some Implications for Development." In *Psychological and Biological Approaches to Emotion*, edited by Nancy L. Stein, Bennett Leventhal, and Tom Trabasso, 75–94. Hillsdale, NJ: Lawrence ErlbaumAssociates, Publishers, 1990.

Ivković, Sanja Kutnjak. "Justice by the International Criminal Tribunal for the Former Yugoslavia." *Stanford Journal of International Law* 37.2 (2001): 255.

Ivković, Sanja Kutnjak, and John Hagan. "The Politics of Punishment and the Siege of Sarajevo: Toward a Conflict Theory of Perceived International (In) Justice." *Law & Society Review* 40.2 (2006): 369–410.

Ivković, Sanja Kutnjak, and John Hagan. *Reclaiming Justice: The International Tribunal for the Former Yugoslavia and Local Courts*.Oxford, UK: Oxford University Press, 2011.

Ivković, Sanja Kutnjak, and John Hagan. "Images of International Criminal Justice in the Former Yugoslavia." *Transitional Justice: Images and Memories*, edited by Christine Bell, 181–204. London: Routledge Press, 2016a.

Ivković, Sanja, and John Hagan. "Pursuit of Justice and the Victims of War in Bosnia and Herzegovina: An Exploratory Study." *Crime, Law and Social Change* 65.1–2 (2016b): 1–27.

Jackson, Cecile. "Speech, Gender and Power: Beyond Testimony." *Development and Change* 43.5 (2012): 999–1023.

Jackson, J., B. Bradford, Mike Hough, A. Myhill, P. Quinton, and T. R. Tyler. "Why Do People Comply with the Law? Legitimacy and the Influence of Legal Institutions." *British Journal of Criminology* 52.6 (2012): 1051–71.

Jo, Hyeran, and Beth A. Simmons. "Can the International Criminal Court Deter Atrocity?" *International Organization* 70.3 (2016): 443–75.

Kahne, Joseph, and Joel Westheimer. "The Limits of Political Efficacy: Educating Citizens for a Democratic Society." *PS: Political Science & Politics* 39.2 (2006): 289–96.

Kalyvas, Stathis N. "The Ontology of 'Political Violence': Action and Identity in Civil Wars." *Perspectives on Politics* 1.3 (2003a): 475–94.

Kalyvas, Stathis N. "The Sociology of Civil Wars: Warfare and Armed Groups." Unpublished manuscript, 2003b. http://www.armedgroups.org/index.php

Kalyvas, Stathis N. "Unsecular Politics and Religious Mobilization." In *European Christian Democracy: Historical Legacies and Comparative Perspectives*, edited by Thomas Kselman and Joseph A. Buttigieg, 293–320. Notre Dame: University of Notre Dame Press, 2003c.

Kelly, J. Patrick. "The International Court of Justice: Crisis and Reformation." *Yale Journal of International Law* 12.2 (1987): 342.

Kelsall, Tim. *Culture under Cross-Examination: International Justice and the Special Court for Sierra Leone*. Cambridge: Cambridge University Press, 2009.

Kim, Hunjoon, and Kathryn Sikkink. "Explaining the Deterrence Effect of Human Rights Prosecutions for Transitional Countries." *International Studies Quarterly* 54.4 (2010): 939–63.

King, Kimi Lynn, and Megan Greening. "Gender Justice or Just Gender? The Role of Gender in Sexual Assault Decisions at the International Criminal Tribunal for the Former Yugoslavia." *Social Science Quarterly* 88.5 (2007): 1049–71.

King, Kimi Lynn, and James David Meernik. "A Distant Court: Assessing the Impact of the International Criminal Tribunal for the Former Yugoslavia: Balancing International and Local Interests While Doing Justice." In *The Legacy of the International Criminal Tribunal for the Former Yugoslavia*, edited by Goran Sluiter, Bert Swart, and Alexander Zahar, 7–54. Oxford: Oxford University Press, 2011.

King, Kimi Lynn, and James David Meernik. *The Witness Experience: Testimony at the ICTY and Its Impact*. New York: Cambridge University Press, 2017.

Klarin, Mirko. "The Impact of the ICTY Trials on Public Opinion in the Former Yugoslavia." *Journal of International Criminal Justice* 7.1 (2009): 89–96.

Kunda, Ziva. "Motivated Inference: Self-Serving Generation and Evaluation of Causal Theories." *Journal of Personality and Social Psychology* 53.4 (1987): 636.

Kunda, Ziva. "The Case for Motivated Reasoning." *Psychological Bulletin* 108.3 (1990): 480–98.

Levanthal, Gerald. S. "What Should Be Done with Equity Theory?" In *Social Exchange: Advances in Theory and Research*, edited by K. J. Gergen, M. S. Greenberg, and R. H. Weiss, 27–55. New York: Plenum, 1980.

Lyubomirsky, Sonja, Laura King, and Ed Diener. "The Benefits of Frequent Positive Affect: Does Happiness Lead to Success?" *Psychological Bulletin* 131.6 (2005): 803–55.

McAdam, Jacqueline. "Coping and Adaptation: A Narrative Analysis of Children and Youth from Zones of Conflict in Africa." In *Handbook of Resilience in Children at War*, edited by Chandi Fernando and Michael Ferrari, 163–77. New York: Springer, 2013.

McAllister, Jacqueline. "On the Brink: Understanding When Armed Groups Might Be More Susceptible to International Criminal Tribunals' Influence." Paper presented at the Annual Meeting of the American Political Science Association, Washington D.C., 2014.

Meernik, James David. "Equality of Arms? The Individual vs. the International Community in War Crimes Tribunals." *Judicature* 86.6 (2003): 312–19.

Meernik, James David. "Justice and Peace? How the International Criminal Tribunal Affects Societal Peace in Bosnia." *Journal of Peace Research* 42.3 (2005): 271–89.

Meernik, James David. "Sentencing Rationales and Judicial Decision-Making at the International Criminal Tribunals." *Social Science Quarterly* 92.3 (2011): 588–608.

Meernik, James David. "What Kind of Bargain Is a Plea?" *International Criminal Law Review* 14.1 (2014): 200–217.

Meernik, James David. "Explaining Public Opinion on International Criminal Justice." *European Political Science Review* 7.4 (2015a): 567–91.

Meernik, James David. "The International Criminal Court and the Deterrence of Human Rights Atrocities." *Civil Wars* 17.3 (2015b): 318–39.

Meernik, James David. *International Tribunals and Human Security*. Lanham, MD: Rowman and Littlefield, 2016.

Meernik, James David, and Jose Raul Guerrero. "Can International Criminal Justice Advance Ethnic Reconciliation? The ICTY and Ethnic Relations in Bosnia-Herzegovina." *Southeast European and Black Sea Studies* 14.3 (2014): 383–407.

Meernik, James David, and Kimi Lynn King. "The Sentencing Determinants of the International Criminal Tribunal for the Former Yugoslavia: An Empirical and Doctrinal Analysis." *Leiden Journal of International Law* 16.4 (2003): 717–50.

Meernik, James David, and Kimi Lynn King. "A Psychological Jurisprudence Model of Public Opinion and International Prosecution." *International Area Studies Review* 17 (2013): 3–20.

Meernik, James David, Kimi Lynn King, and Geoffrey Dancy. "Judicial Decision Making and International Tribunals: Assessing the Impact of Individual, National, and International Factors." *Social Science Quarterly* 86.3 (2005): 683–703.

Mendeloff, David. "Truth-Seeking, Truth-Telling, and Postconflict Peacebuilding: Curb the Enthusiasm?" *International Studies Review* 6.3 (2004): 355–80.

Mendeloff, David. "Trauma and Vengeance: Assessing the Psychological and Emotional Effects of Post-conflict Justice." *Human Rights Quarterly* 31.3 (2009): 592–93.

Mladjenovic, Lepa. "The ICTY: The Validation of the Experiences of Survivors." In *International War Crimes Trials: Making a Difference*. Proceedings of an interdisciplinary conference at the University of Texas School of Law, Austin, Texas, November 6–7, 2003.

Moghalu, K. Chiedu. "Reconciling Fractured Societies: An African Perspective on the Role of Judicial Prosecutions." In *From Sovereign Impunity to International Accountability: The Search for Justice in a World of States*, edited by R. Thakur and P. Malcontent, 197–223. Tokyo: United Nations University, 2004.

Moore, Bert S., and Alice M. Isen. *Affect and Social Behavior*. Cambridge: Cambridge University Press, 1990.

Moorhead, Richard, Mark Sefton, and Lesley Scanlan. ""*Just Satisfaction? What Drives Public and Participant Satisfaction with Courts and Tribunals*. London: Ministry of Justice, 2007.

Morrell, Robert. "Youth, Fathers and Masculinity in South Africa Today." *Agenda* 30.8 (2005): 84–87.

Muggah, Robert, ed. *No Refuge: The Crisis of Refugee Militarization in Africa*. Zed Books, London, UK: 2013.

Nadler, Ruby T., Rahel Rabi, and John Paul Minda. "Better Mood and Better Performance: Learning Rule-Described Categories Is Enhanced by Positive Mood." *Psychological Science* 21.12 (2010): 1770–76.

Nettelfield, Lara. *Courting Democracy in Bosnia and Herzegovina*. Cambridge: Cambridge University Press, 2010.

Nickerson, Raymond S. "Confirmation Bias: A Ubiquitous Phenomenon in Many Guises." *Review of General Psychology* 2.2 (1998): 175.

Niemi, Richard G., Stephen C. Craig, and Franco Mattei. "Measuring Internal Political Efficacy in the 1988 National Election Study." *American Political Science Review* 85.4 (1991): 1407–13.

Nussbaum, Felicity A. *The Brink of All We Hate: English Satires on Women, 1660–1750*. Lexington: University Press of Kentucky, 2015.

Olsen, Tricia D., Leigh A. Payne, and Andrew G. Reiter. "The Justice Balance: When Transitional Justice Improves Human Rights and Democracy." *Human Rights Quarterly* 32.4 (2010): 980–1007.

Olusanya, Olaoluwa. *Sentencing War Crimes and Crimes against Humanity under the International Criminal Tribunal for the Former Yugoslavia*. Europa Law, Amsterdam, Netherlands: 2005.

Orentlicher. Diane F. *Shrinking the Space for Denial: The Impact of the ICTY in Serbia.* New York: Open Society Justice Initiative, 2008.

OSCE (Organization for Security and Cooperation in Europe). *Witness Protection and Support in BiH Domestic War Crimes Trials: Obstacles and Recommendations a Year after Adoption of the National Strategy for War Crimes Processing*. 2010. http://www.osce.org/bih/69314

Ostrom, Charles W., and Dennis M. Simon. "Promise and Performance: A Dynamic Model of Presidential Popularity." *American Political Science Review* 79.2 (1985): 334–58.

Palic, Sabina, Jessica Carlsson, Cherie Armour, and Ask Elklit. "Assessment of Dissociation in Bosnian Treatment-Seeking Refugees in Denmark." *Nordic Journal of Psychiatry* 69.4 (2015): 307–14.

Peffley, Mark, and Jon Hurwitz. *America: The Separate Realities of Blacks and Whites.* Cambridge: Cambridge University Press, 2010.

Peskin, Victor. "Beyond Victor's Justice? The Challenge of Prosecuting the Winners at the International Criminal Tribunals for the Former Yugoslavia and Rwanda." *Journal of Human Rights* 4.2 (2005): 213–31.

Peskin, Victor. *International Justice in Rwanda and the Balkans: Virtual Trials and the Struggle for State Cooperation*. Cambridge: Cambridge University Press, 2008.

Rawls, John. *A Theory of Justice*. 1971.Cambridge MA: Harvard University Press

Research and Documentation Center Sarajevo. 2008. Human Losses in Bosnia and Herzegovina 91–95. Sarajevo: Research and Documentation Center.

Salzman, Ryan, and Adam Ramsey. Judging the Judiciary: Understanding Public Confidence in Latin American Courts. *Latin American Politics and Society* 55 (2013): 73–95.

Saxon, Dan. "Exporting Justice: Perceptions of the ICTY among the Serbian, Croatian, and Muslim Communities in the Former Yugoslavia." *Journal of Human Rights* 4.4 (2005): 559–72.

Scheffer, David. "Tribunal Influence in Recent US Jurisprudence on Corporate Liability for Atrocity Crimes." *Student Transnational Legal Policy* 44 (2012): 47.

Schwartz, Bernard. "Administrative Law in the Next Century." *Ohio State Law Journal* 39 (1978): 805.

Schwartz, Bryan. "Woodward's Estate: A Case of Nonconstitutional Law." *Queen's Law Journal* 4 (1978): 124.

Schwartz, Murray L. "The Professionalism and Accountability of Lawyers." *California Law Review* 66.4 (1978): 669–97.

Schwartz, Richard D. Moral Order and Sociology of Law. *Annual Review of Sociology* 4 (1978): 577–601

Sears, David O., John J. Hetts, Jim Sidanius, and Lawrence Bobo. "Race in American Politics: Framing the Debates." In *Racialized Politics: The Debate about Racism in America*, edited by David Sears, Jim Sidanius, and Lawrence Bobo, 1–43. Chicago: University of Chicago Press, 2000

Sen, Amartya. *The Idea of Justice*. Cambridge, MA: Harvard University Press, 2011.

Seymour, Lee J. M., Kristin M. Bakke, and Kathleen Gallagher Cunningham. "E Pluribus Unum, ex Uno Plures: Competition, Violence, and Fragmentation in Ethnopolitical Movements." *Journal of Peace Research* 53.1 (2016): 3–18.

Simmons, Beth, and Allison Danner. "Credible Commitments and the International Criminal Court." *International Organization* 64.2 (2010): 225–56.

Sloane, Robert D. "Sentencing for the 'Crime of Crimes': The Evolving Common Law of Sentencing of the International Criminal Tribunal for Rwanda." *Journal of International Criminal Justice* 5.3 (2007): 713–34.

Spini, Dario, Guy Elcheroth, and Rachel Fasel. "The Impact of Group Norms and Generalization of Risks across Groups on Judgments of War Behavior." *Political Psychology* 29.6 (2008): 919–41.

Staub, Ervin. "Reconciliation after Genocide, Mass Killing, or Intractable Conflict: Understanding the Roots of Violence, Psychological Recovery, and Steps toward a General Theory." *Political Psychology* 27.6 (2006): 867–94.

Staub, Ervin. "Building a Peaceful Society: Origins, Prevention, and Reconciliation after Genocide and Other Group Violence." *American Psychologist* 7 (2013): 576–89.

Stepakoff, Shanee, G. Shawn Reynolds, Simon Charters, and Nicola Henry. "Why Testify? Witnesses' Motivations for Giving Evidence in a War Crimes Tribunal in Sierra." *International Journal of Transitional Justice* 8.3 (2014): 426–51.

Stepakoff, Shanee, G. Shawn Reynolds, Simon Charters, and Nicola Henry. "Self-Reported Psychosocial Consequences of Testifying in a War Crimes Tribunal in Sierra Leone." *International Perspectives in Psychology: Research, Practice, Consultation* 4.3 (2015): 161–81.

Stover, Eric. *The Witness: War Crimes and the Promise of Justice in The Hague*. Philadelphia: University of Pennsylvania Press, 2005.

Stover, Eric. *Bearing Witness at the International Criminal Court: An Interview Survey of 109 Witnesses.* Berkeley: Human Rights Center, University of California, Berkeley, 2014.

Subotić, Jelena. *Hijacked Justice: Dealing with the Past in the Balkans.* Ithaca: Cornell University Press, 2009.

Taber, Charles S., and Milton Lodge. "The Automaticity of Affect for Political Leaders, Groups, and Issues: An Experimental Test of the Hot Cognition Hypothesis." *Political Psychology* 26.3 (2005): 455–82.

Taber, Charles S., and Milton Lodge. "Motivated Skepticism in the Evaluation of Political Beliefs." *American Journal of Political Science* 50.3 (2006): 755–69.

Themnér, Lotta, and Peter Wallensteen. "Armed Conflicts, 1946–2011." *Journal of Peace Research* 49.4 (2012): 565–75.

Thibaut, John, and Laurens Walker. *Procedural Justice: A Psychological Analysis*. Hillsdale, NJ: Erlbaum, 1975.

Tyler, Tom R. "The Role of Perceived Injustice in Defendants' Evaluations of Their Courtroom Experience." *Law & Society Review* 18.1 (1984): 51–74.

Tyler, Tom R. "What Is Procedural Justice? Criteria Used by Citizens to Assess the Fairness of Legal Procedures." *Law & Society Review* 22.1 (1988): 103–36.

Tyler, Tom R. *Why People Obey the Law*. New Haven, CT: Yale University Press, 1990.

Tyler, Tom R. "Public Trust and Confidence in Legal Authorities: What Do Majority and Minority Group Members Want from the Law and Legal Institutions?" *Behavioral Sciences & the Law* 19.2 (2001): 215–35.

Tyler, Tom R. "Procedural Justice, Legitimacy, and the Effective Rule of Law." *Crime and Justice* 30 (2003): 283–357.

Tyler, Tom R. "Psychological Perspectives on Legitimacy and Legitimation." *Annual Review of Psychology* 57 (2006a): 375–400.

Tyler, Tom R. *Why People Obey the Law*. Princeton, NJ: Princeton University Press, 2006b.

Tyler, Tom R., and Fay L. Cook. "The Mass Media and Judgments of Risk: Distinguishing Impact on Personal and Societal Level Judgments." *Journal of Personality and Social Psychology* 47.4 (1984): 693.

Tyler, Tom R., and John Darley. "Building a Law-Abiding Society: Taking Public Views about Morality and the Legitimacy of Legal Authorities into Account When Formulating Substantive Law." *Hofstra Law Review* 28.3 (2000): 707–39.

Tyler, Tom R., and E. Allan Lind. "A Relational Model of Authority in Groups." *Advances in Experimental Social Psychology* 25 (1992): 115–91.

Tyler, Tom R., and Yuen Huo. *Trust in the Law: Encouraging Public Cooperation with the Police and Courts*. New York: Russell Sage Foundation, 2002.

UNDP (United Nations Development Programme). *Human Development Report 1994*. New York: Oxford University Press, 1994. http://hdr.undp.org/sites/default/files/reports/255/hdr_1994_en_complete_nostats.pdf

Unnever, J. D. "Race, Crime, and Public Opinion." In *The Oxford Handbook of Ethnicity, Crime, and Immigration*, edited by Sandra Bucerius and Michael Tonry, 70–106. Oxford, UK: Oxford University Press, 2014.

Ura, Joseph Daniel. "Backlash and Legitimation: Macro Political Responses to Supreme Court Decisions." *American Journal of Political Science* 58.1 (2014): 110–26.

Valentino, Benjamin, Paul Huth, and Sarah Croco. "Covenants without the Sword: International Law and the Protection of Civilians in Times of War." *World Politics* 58.3 (2006): 339–77.

van der Meer, Tom W. G., Jan W. van Deth, and Peer L. H. Scheepers. "The Politicized Participant Ideology and Political Action in 20 Democracies." *Comparative Political Studies* 42.11 (2009): 1426–57.

Voeten, Erik. "Public Opinion and the Legitimacy of International Courts." *Theoretical Inquiries in Law* 14.2 (2013): 411–36.

Wald, Patricia M. "Dealing with Witnesses in War Crime Trials: Lessons from the Yugoslav Tribunal." *Yale Human Rights & Development Law Journal* 5 (2002): 1–21.

Weldon, Steven A. "The Institutional Context of Tolerance for Ethnic Minorities: A Comparative, Multilevel Analysis of Western Europe." *American Journal of Political Science* 50.2 (2006): 331–49.

Weldon, S. Laurel. "The Structure of Intersectionality: A Comparative Politics of Gender." *Politics & Gender* 2.2 (2006): 235–48.

Wood, Lesley J., and Charles Tilley. *Social Movements, 1768–2012*. London: Routledge, 2015.

Wood, Martin, Katriina Lepanjuuri, and Caroline Paskell (NatCen Social Research) Jane Thompson, Lorna Adams and Sarah Coburn (IFF Research). 2015. Victim and Witness Satisfaction Survey. London: Crown Prosecution Service.

Index

Note: Page numbers in italics refer to illustrations and tables.